FAKE SCIENCE 101

adamsmedia
Avon, Massachusetts

FAKE SCIENCE 101

ASTRONOMY

▲ The sun during its lesser known "blue period."

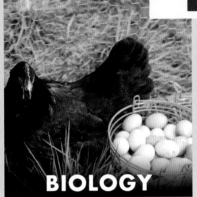

BIOLOGY

▲ Biology answers big questions. The chicken or the egg: which tastes better?

CHEMISTRY

▲ This beautiful Styrofoam box didn't grow naturally. It was made through chemistry.

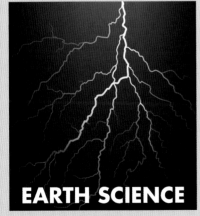

EARTH SCIENCE

▲ Lightning provides the electric power for thunder to play so loudly.

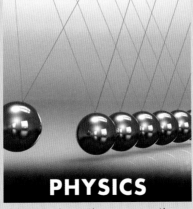

PHYSICS

▲ Learn about the conservation of energy, one of science's strongest arguments for napping.

A LESS-THAN-FACTUAL

GUIDE TO OUR AMAZING WORLD

PHIL EDWARDS

*To my parents, who have always allowed me to
remain untethered from reality.*

Published by Adams Media,
a division of F+W Media, Inc.
57 Littlefield Street, Avon, MA 02322. U.S.A.
www.adamsmedia.com

ISBN 10: 1-4405-2701-6
ISBN 13: 978-1-4405-2701-2
eISBN 10: 1-4405-3013-0
eISBN 13: 978-1-4405-3013-5

Printed in China.

10 9 8 7 6 5 4 3 2 1

If you find a copy of this book without the cover, it
may be stolen. Or the cover was ripped off by your
little brother. He gets away with everything. But not
this time. *Not this time.* Let's just say that this book
includes a very useful section on arsenic that will
affect your little brother's future dramatically, though
it should be clear that *Fake Science 101* does not con-
done or encourage fratricide. Then again, can you really
be blamed if he keeps destroying everything you own
and blames it on the fact that he's "eight"? Seriously,
when you were eight, weren't you a more mature and
responsible person than that little dork? Of course you
were, but guess who gets spoiled rotten because he's the
"baby" of the family? It's time that the Golden Child
faced consequences for his actions, and if that means
losing his life, then at least you'll gain a little peace.

Illuminated Bible, Leonardo da Vinci sketches, Join
or Die poster, Nobel coin, and Copernicus images are
Public Domain.

All or part of space images on pages 48, 51, 53, 54,
55, 62, 67, 70, 71, 73, 75, 76, 77, 80, 81, 82, 85, 86
Courtesy NASA. Image on page 57 Courtesy NASA/
JPL-Caltech.

All other photos © iStockphoto.com.

*This book is available at quantity discounts for
bulk purchases.
For information, please call 1-800-289-0963.*

FOR WHEN THE FACTS ARE TOO CONFUSING

Fake Science 101

A LESS-THAN-FACTUAL GUIDE TO OUR AMAZING WORLD

BOX NO. ______

NAME ______

SUBJECT ______

WHO YOU COPIED FROM ______

BRIBE ______

FAVORITE TEACHER ______

NUMBER OF PAGES YOU'LL LEAVE BLANK ___

By Phil Edwards

Einstein= invented the perm
Hawking= robot disguised as man
Watson and Crick: folk music duo
that sang about DNA

Reference Table

Conversion

ENGLISH	METRIC
Inches	Centimeters
Miles	Kilometers
Showers	More Cologne
Hard Work	Socialism
Apple Pie	Baguettes?

States of Matter

Solid, Liquid, Gas, A Bit Gassy, Not Really Sure, Kansas

Aardvark or Chester A. Arthur?

Aardvark

Chester A. Arthur?

Aardvark

Arthur

Solar Calendar

DATE	SIGNIFICANCE
March 20	Vernal equinox, when both day and night are exactly equal length at the equator, which is great for equator people, whoever they are.
June 21	Summer solstice and the longest day of the year, excluding Thanksgiving at your aunt's house.
Sept. 22	Autumnal equinox, as it's called by people who are too fancy to just say "Fall."
Dec. 21	Winter solstice. If you have a Wiccan girlfriend, you'll be in BIG trouble if you forget about it.

Life on Earth

PERIOD	LIFE
Cambrian (488–542 Million Years Ago)	A few fishlike things, the first examples of "boring" animals.
Devonian (359–416 Million Years Ago)	More fish, though no one is around to fry them or put them in aquariums.
Cambrian II (251–299 Million Years Ago)	Strapped for ideas, nature just reruns the Cambrian period. Still boring.
Jurassic (146–200 Million Years Ago)	Dinosaurs begin a 200-million-year campaign to win the hearts of 6-year-old boys.
Paleogene (23–65.5 Million Years Ago)	Grass appears, so early mammals have something to watch grow.
Quaternary (1 Million Years Ago to Present Day)	Woolly mammoths, unicorns, and humans develop. Only one survives.

You Know, What's That Thing That the Plants Do to Get, Like, Food and Stuff, but They Aren't Eating Food, They're Using the Sun?

Photosynthesis.

Periodic Table

π

3.14159265358979323846264334 83279502884197169399375105820 974944592307816406286208998 628034825342117067982148 086513282306647093844609 Really? You're still reading? Who are you trying to impress?

Contents[1]

---

[1] Many scientific books also include an "index" of the information covered in their pages. However, *Fake Science 101* has learned that indices require a lot of tedious work and an advanced knowledge of the alphabet. Pending further review, the index has been omitted from this edition.

WARNING It is advised that you not read the entire book in one sitting. The rapid influx of knowledge into your brain may cause your cerebral cortex to explode.

INTRODUCTION
So, You Want to Be a Scientist

The world is full of questions, and science provides every answer.[1] Once you learn these answers, you're guaranteed to half-remember them for the rest of your life. Don't wander around the world without a clue about how things work when, instead, you can have a vague impression about how things work. If you're uncertain about anything, science is the answer. Maybe.

Science is all around us, waiting to be discovered by somebody like you. And while some people will insist that you need years of training, intellectual rigor, and medium to high intelligence, those people probably haven't heard of this book. Please don't tell them about it, either. They're the type of people who know lawyers.

Who are scientists? Scientists are people who invent amazing things and then, a few years later, invent new things to save us from their earlier inventions.[2] Scientists are people who shout the truth to the world through dense articles in scientific journals that circulate to eight, or even twelve, people. Scientists bunk and then debunk our continually amazing world.

Derived from the word *scio*, which means "hard" in Latin, science has guided our culture for thousands—if not billions—of years. There's a good chance you've already encountered science in your living room, unless that was your television, not science. Still, the lesson stands. Also, you should really upgrade to HDTV—the picture quality is amazing!

By reading *Fake Science 101*, you'll finally be able to answer all of life's unanswerable questions. Some of your answers may even be correct. But no matter what, they'll all be answers. As long as you speak in a loud, clear voice and look the other person in the eye, they probably won't even notice that you just said "physics" is spelled with an *x*.

So read on. We'll cover biology, geology, and all the other top -ologies. If we remember chemistry and physix, we'll talk about them too. Once you're done, you can share the world's secrets with your family and friends. If you don't have family and friends, strangers will suffice.

When should you use Fake Science? Only use it when the facts are too confusing. So, in simpler terms, you should use it all the time.

> » SCIENTIFIC FACT
>
> "Introductions" are useful tools to make textbook authors believe that someone actually cares what they think.

---

[1] Question: Will you go out with me? Answer: Evolution and Sally McNerney both say "No."

[2] Scientists will be critical in the future, when the giant refrigerator they build to counteract global warming gives all the polar bears Freon poisoning.

Introductory Quiz

Multiple Choice

1. **What does science provide the answer to?**
    a. Everything
    b. Naughty questions
    c. Man's existential void
    d. This quiz

2. **Where does the word *science* come from?**
    a. No one knows
    b. Inside a volcano
    c. Scientists invented it
    d. A mixture of benzene and butterfly kisses

3. **Why should you pursue science as a career?**
    a. A chance to confuse your friends
    b. An opportunity to have journalists misinterpret your theories
    c. It's cooler than math
    d. Tap dancing doesn't pay like it used to

Short Answer

1. **Is it possible to have too short a chapter for a chapter quiz? If so, why are you so lazy?**

    _____
    _____
    _____
    _____
    _____

2. **Scientists around the world work hard every day. Whose work do you want to coast off of? How will you pay for the inevitable lawsuits?**

    _____
    _____
    _____
    _____
    _____

Essay Questions

1. **Write your own 3,000-word introduction to *Fake Science 101* and craft a short note giving the rights for Fake Science to use it in a future edition of this book. Please send it to the Fake Science labs as soon as possible, preferably typed. But really, anything will be accepted. These deadlines are brutal.**

    _____
    _____
    _____
    _____
    _____
    _____
    _____
    _____

2. **Science and the arts occasionally have a strained relationship. Still, it's important to learn about the arts. Write a short essay about what you would do if you met a poet, a musician, and an artist. Then describe how you would use science to cure them so they could do something useful with their lives.**

    _____
    _____
    _____
    _____
    _____
    _____
    _____
    _____

WHAT IS SCIENCE?

LET US KNOW IF YOU FIND OUT

Before You Start This Chapter . . .

- Try to find a wealthy uncle who can name a species of plant after you.
- It's time to set childish things aside, burn them, and then write a brief paper about the chemical reaction.
- Science requires discipline, so before you start reading, destroy all the baked goods and poetry books in your home.
- Skim this textbook at least once so you can become acclimated to the smell.
- Say goodbye to your loved ones and pets.
- Purchase a second copy of this textbook so you can frame each page of your first copy.
- Take down any shelves and paintings in your bedroom to make space for "Silly Einstein" posters.
- Jump in the air while your mind is still empty.
- Practice turning pages so you can read with maximum efficiency.

What You'll Be Devoting Your Life To

To become a scientist, you must first understand what science is. If that's not an option, you should at least pretend you understand it.[1]

If you haven't read this textbook already, the only excuse is that you're a toddler and are just learning how to read. You've made the right choice for your first book, since most published text is downhill from here. That's because the subject matter of this textbook is of the utmost importance. If you don't know what the word "utmost" means, just move on and start memorizing chemical formulae, because ammonium nitrate doesn't care about your vocabulary.

Science is one of man's highest pursuits, when there's time for it. Whether it's sending billionaires into space or finding new ways to wax body hair, science helps mankind achieve its greatest goals. If you've ever gawked at the amazing inventions on late-night television or enjoyed a luxurious tanning salon, they exist because the inventor once talked to, met, or saw a scientist.[2]

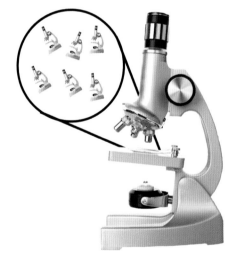

It's not just about inventions, though. It's about discovering our amazing world. For example, did you know that the average rainforest has 6,212 endangered species?[3] Or that the laws of physics govern the entire universe?[4] Scientists discovered those facts after years of research and a lot of drinking.

Let's learn how every day of your life is touched by science.

◀ The discovery of microscopes aided science significantly.

---

[1] One easy way to indicate your knowledge is to ask small children questions and then laugh at their responses. Apparently, Lucy Childress down the street thinks that we're all stork babies.

[2] The Combo Cucumber Slicer/Back Massager 5000 didn't invent itself. And for four monthly payments of $49.99, you can't afford to pass it up!

[3] It's now down to 6,194.

[4] Including no shirt, no shoes, no service.

Your Incredibly Scientific Day

It Watches You While You Sleep, My Precious

It's easy to think that science isn't important for you. "Me?" you might say. "But I'm just a little old medical doctor." But even you are affected by science. Let's look at an average day. It starts before you even wake up.

Science is around when you sleep. The REM cycle creates your dreams, while the ERM cycle is what your loved ones say when you bore them by talking about your dreams. The ERM cycle is usually caused by rambling paragraphs about how "we were in this house that was like our childhood house, but with a fire pole and a bunch of talking dogs."

In the morning, you finally wake up and wipe the sleep out of your eyes. What is the "sleep" you find at night? There's not a complete consensus. Some scientists say it's a crust of mucus that forms to protect your eyes. Other sources say it's fairy dust. Until the scientific community agrees on this issue, little boys and girls still have a chance to fly.

> **» SCIENTIFIC FACT**
>
> Snooze buttons existed before alarm clocks, when primitive humans hit roosters with their clubs.

Why Do You Yawn in the Morning?

When you wake up, your body is depleted of energy by your dreams.

By yawning, you create a space for flying Twinkies, insects, and other food to enter into your mouth.

Don't cover your mouth the next time you yawn—your life may depend on it.

The Smell of Science in the Morning

Once you wake up, you have breakfast and begin a tiny science lesson.[1]

Many scientists recommend you have coffee with your breakfast.[2] Coffee is the unique interaction of biology, chemistry, and crippling addiction. You can choose between caffeinated coffee, which is made from coffee beans, and decaffeinated coffee, which is made from dirt. Coffee with caffeine will make you smarter, more focused, and faster with your trigger finger. Don't have time to brew a fresh cup? You can always eat coffee grounds and digest the caffeine directly. That way, you won't waste any water diluting coffee's powers.

[1]So please wear lab goggles at all times.

[2]Especially if you are going to see, meet, or think about other human beings.

How to Make Small Talk More Scientific

As you've seen in this section, science pops up everywhere. Yet, too much of our small talk at work centers around sports, gossip, and other inconsequential topics. Here are a few icebreakers to help you steer the small talk to science:

- When discussing the weather, try to address the way axial tilt changes temperatures.
- If a coworker shows you baby pictures, mention that their pride in their offspring is an impressive example of evolutionary kinship theory.
- If you're invited to an office party, ask if it's acceptable for you to bring a portable rock-polishing kit instead of alcohol. It will be more fun and more geological.
- Energy efficiency is crucial, especially in a competitive work environment. By placing a small generator on your office chair, you can save time and calories.
- The next time your boss asks for a PowerPoint presentation, include a few additional slides about the reproductive habits of fruit flies.
- Update your résumé to include all of the elements of the periodic table. Employers will be impressed by your knowledge of nature's building blocks.

Commuting Is Like an Experiment Gone Wrong

When breakfast is done, you begin your commute to work or school. Science joins you for the extremely long ride.[1]

Every step of your commute is touched by science. If you listen to your car's sound system, radio waves are used to transmit some of the most innovative sound effects in the nation.[2] If you have your window open, you give yourself an opportunity to breathe a wide range of exciting chemicals. Many of these chemicals will give you a chance to visit hospitals in the future.

In fact, some scientists are working to address the problem of traffic jams.[3] Although the research is still in the hypothesis stage, in ten to twenty years scientists will have established whether traffic is good or bad. At that time, they can begin to search for a solution.

▲ Traffic jams are related to science, since they give you time to perform complex equations and question your existence.

Work Tests Your Endurance

Once you reach your destination, science unbuckles its seatbelt right next to you. Have you ever used an automatic door at your place of work? They require you to wave your hands so you can get a morning workout. In addition, they fail to open one out of every three times, which may cause you to slam straight into the glass. That sharpens your predatory instincts, assuming you don't suffer a concussion.

Eventually, you'll reach your desk and grab for that second pot of coffee. If that doesn't wake you up, your polyester-filled, highly electronic office should generate an energizing static shock. What causes that electric jolt in the morning? Usually, it's the result of rubbing your feet on carpet. This is the main reason people don't urinate on the floor—the static electric current could cause instant electrocution.

---

[1] And spends the entire time shouting, "Are we there yet?"

[2] Morning DJs are credited with significantly advancing research into sonic flatulence.

[3] Although more resources are allocated toward strawberry jams.

Your Social Life Is a Petri Dish

When you leave work, you probably head straight to the library to see if the newest edition of *Fungi Quarterly* is out yet. But even if you don't spend your nights in study, science is still a part of your life.[1]

In fact, even a fun date can be a highly scientific exercise. When you go out to that hot new club, bar, or scientific-supplies store, you're exhibiting some of the evolutionary traits Darwin first theorized about. In fact, Darwin invented evolution for this very reason, since he needed a more intelligent-sounding way to ask women to breed with him.

> **» SCIENTIFIC FACT**
>
> Strong teeth are a sign of strength. When on a date, pry open your lips and bare your teeth as soon as possible.

Good Chemistry Requires Chemistry

Alcohol utilizes many scientific principles. If you've enjoyed wine, you've benefitted from a process called "fermentation," which makes old grapes expensive. Beer is made using wheat, barley, and hops, which are crucial for people who like to demonstrate their superior knowledge by constantly noting that a beer is "hoppy."[2] Since plants are involved, both drinks are healthy.

When people drink alcohol, their evolutionary instincts are elevated. Modern society has created concepts like prudence, frugality, and self-respect. By eliminating these, alcohol allows us to make the mistakes that keep humanity going. It's estimated that human breeding would cease entirely without the assistance of fermented grains.

▲ Not all drinks are understood. As with cold fusion, the "missing link," and the origin of the cosmos, scientists remain baffled by the appletini.

---

[1] But seriously, you should be spending your nights in study. Who knows what friends you'll make amid the dusty library stacks?

[2] Example: "I love how hoppy this beer is; should we combine our genetic material and let it ferment?"

Science Is a Dish Best Served Reheated

But if you don't care to throw back a drink, science is still part of your life. Have you made yourself a delicious meal? Chances are you've used science. Frozen dinners were developed using principles of cryogenics. Salisbury steaks wanted an opportunity to be revived at a future date when they could be cured of their bad taste. Though that date has not yet arrived, we still benefit from the convenience.

If you're a gourmand, you've probably sampled organic food, which is food made of organs like calf's livers, chicken kidneys, and monkey brains. After dinner, you'll probably have another pot of coffee to ease into your bedtime routine. An after-dinner drink can cleanse the palate.[1] It also ensures you wake up in the middle of the night to check on the status of your bathroom.

▲ Salisbury steaks like this one chose to be frozen for years in the hopes of seeing flying cars, a cure for cancer, and the first teleporter.

Going to Bed with Science

Science doesn't go away when it's time to go to bed; in fact, it's only just beginning.[2]

First, you brush your teeth using toothpaste. Then you pretend to floss. Before you go to sleep, you'll probably want to open your journal and/or spreadsheet and document all the science in your day. As you drift into slumber, your body will fall into a state of comfortable paralysis, which is the only time you'll be able to focus enough to think about string theory.

It's hard to believe that one day could include so much science. Now you know that nobody can hide from science.[3] Let's learn about the history and practice of this inescapable discipline.

---

[1] Palate is a technical term for "taste on your tongue."

[2] If your dreams don't involve balancing chemical equations, you're doing something wrong. Consider an extra dose of Ritalin before bed.

[3] Outlaws Clyde Barrow and Bonnie Parker were famously gunned down by Enrico Fermi.

A History of Science

They Lived in Caves, What Did You Expect?

Though it's impossible to know exactly when science began, it's worth making a wild guess.

Science began millions of years ago when the first cave men developed language.[1] With a new ability to convey information, they were able to share experiences and observe their world.[2] They spent most of their time complaining about the weather and wishing they weren't so dumb. During idle moments, however, they began to ponder the mysteries of earth.[3]

Many problems cave men had could be solved with science. The discovery of fire can be attributed to an early version of science.[4] As cave culture developed, so did early forms of scientific inquiry. Most cave experiments involved hitting people on the head with clubs. Every scientist has to start somewhere.

Once cave scientists made definitive conclusions about hitting people on the head, they began using science to improve their world. One of the first innovations was dividing each tribe into hunters and gatherers. Hunters were strong, courageous men who tracked down prey and provided food for the tribe. Gatherers were the leftovers, and they soon became scientists. It would be centuries until a third group, Butlers, developed the perfect behavior to serve gentlemen of means.

Though science was in its infancy, these gatherers quickly sought a new solution to their problem: Walking around all day gathering berries was very dull. In addition, about half of the berries were poisonous, which was bad for morale. Thus, the quest for advancement began.

>**SCIENTIFIC FACT**

Early mix-ups occurred when hunters hunted gatherers. Most gatherers were too shy to correct the error.

▲ The discovery of fire was quickly followed by the discovery of insurance fraud.

---

[1] Anthropologists believe that most of the words contained the syllable "Ugh."

[2] This included warnings to run from lions, run from mastodons, and to gossip about Grak's new hairdo.

[3] As you would expect, the answer to most of the mysteries was some variation of "Ugh."

[4] However, it is believed that before the discovery of fire, cave men tried and failed to invent hovercrafts and microwaves.

Early Steps Toward Scientific Inquiry. And Lots of Grunting.

Science sprung from early man's desire to transcend his animal origins and serve basic needs.[1] As hunting and gathering improved man's life, he began to understand the value of study and inquiry into the world. It was a common occurrence to find a cave man looking at the stars and scratching his head, though that may have been due to lice.

The boredom of berry gathering and the difficulty of hunting were the impetus for early scientific development. The gatherers developed agricultural practices and learned how plants worked, from the types of soil they needed to grow to the best times to harvest these plants. Meanwhile, the hunters made sharp things.[2]

As both sides developed their techniques, both hunters and gatherers began to exceed simple survival and to strive for greater things in life.[3] They wanted to live in a world where their goal was not simply survival but understanding. In addition, most of them wanted to try living beyond the age of twenty-five.

▲ Cave drawings helped cave men to express themselves in many different ways. This drawing is believed to depict the first cave talk show.

From these humble origins, science was born. Documentation was sparse because of the absence of typewriters in cave times. However, in the artifacts of ancient man, we can observe the development of science from guesswork into a discipline. Eventually, one cave man finally invented the razor and shaved his beard.

Science was truly born, now that it looked respectable.

[1] Fire, water, decent opera.

[2] It should be noted, however, there are some records of farmers using a bow and arrow to harvest plants.

[3] So began the multimillennial quest for a truly universal remote control.

Great Scientists

History's Most Memorable Forgotten Names

Name: Grog
Scientific Field: N/A
Greatest Strength: Almost able to count
Greatest Weakness: Easily beat up
Greatest Discovery: Almost discovered something, really

Born in a small cave in an up-and-coming tribe, Grog knew from early life on that he was interested in the way the world worked.

However, his relatively high intelligence left him subject to the mockery of his fellow tribe members. Hunters like Mog, Logor, and Durg all frequently beat him up and smashed his primitive glasses, which he had fashioned from his collection of rocks.

Despite his persecution, Grog pursued fields of scientific inquiry. But being one of the first scientists left him without many scientific precedents on which to base his work. In between gathering berries, he tried to develop theories about the world and create new inventions.

Impotent and blinded, he spent years wandering the desert while claiming he was "surveying it." This led to a bourgeoning career in archaeology, in which he found the oldest record of man's existence: his grandfather. However, his family was not pleased when Grog returned home and immediately showed them Forg's skull and bones.

Invention was always Grog's true calling, however. Sadly, most of his ideas failed. His theory about the stars being tiny white birds proved wrong in the long run, despite the fact that people believed almost anything was a bird back then. Even worse, Grog's persistence furthered his reputation as one of the first "nerds" in the world. Mog, Logor, and Durg continued to attack him, and they were joined by Sorg, Trag, and the other Durg.

Despite the adversity, Grog developed some innovations in gathering, including the idea to hold the berries in a container and avoid feeding the berries to bears. Though his scientific work is not used today, he is widely recognized for putting in a good effort.

Grog's life ended peacefully at the old age of twenty-seven, whereby he left behind two children and his wife, Felicity. She quickly married the other Durg.

You Have to Invent the Wheel Before You Reinvent It

With science officially begun, cave men approached their world. For reasons unknown to modern scientists, cave men didn't make moving out of the cave their first priority.[1] Many cave people were satisfied with hanging beside the same stalagmites their entire lives. Even though they smelled like "cave" all the time, these scientists still had musty ambition.

The first objective was to invent an easy way to transport goods: the wheel. It would be much easier than rolling things over children who were lying down. However, the round shape of the wheel always gave the cave men difficulty. Their engineering was undercut by the absence of circular objects and the inability to remember exactly what a circle was. This stalled development of both transportation and the coaster.[2]

---

[1] In the cave man's defense, many of the caves were tastefully decorated with cave drawings. In addition, many cave landlords had required a two-year lease, which was longer than most cave men would live.

[2] Archaeologists have found countless stains on ancient cave coffee tables.

"The round shape of the wheel always gave the cave man difficulty."

The Greeks: Smart and Usually Naked

The former cave men settled in Greece, a beautiful island chain known for its bountiful supply of feta.[1] Fueled by cheese and olives, they turned to science.

Philosophers: The Original Imagineers

Some of the most famous Greek thinkers were actually philosophers.[2] These early scientists were able to pontificate on the world without the burden of knowing anything.

There were many philosophers. Plato spent all his time talking about "the cave" in a desperate attempt to recapture cave man glory. Meanwhile, Socrates developed "the Socratic method," a teaching technique that helps teachers hide the fact that they don't know anything.

> » **SCIENTIFIC FACT**
>
> Aristotle was one of the first scientists to develop his theories by taping ideas to a dartboard.

The philosophers were led by Aristotle, who was wrong about almost everything. For over a thousand years, Aristotle helped scientific progress. If a scientist had a theory, he could see if Aristotle agreed with him. If he did, then the scientist knew that the theory was wrong.

Aristotle divided his time between many incorrect theories. He categorized the world into five elements: fire, earth, air, water, and tzatziki sauce, which goes great with pita bread. He also categorized all the animals on a scale of perfection.[3] Like most scientists, Aristotle spent the rest of his time writing plays.[4]

Eventually, other scientists emerged and advanced science further by performing actual experiments and knowing basic math.

▲ Supposedly, science also occurred in India and China. But the Greeks spent the most time making sculptures of their heads.

---

[1] Greece is also known for the half bull, half man beast called the Minotaur. But it's better to focus on the feta.

[2] The word *philosopher* means "love of sitting around chatting."

[3] Aristotle placed himself at the top of the list, which was great to pick up women.

[4] While Aristotle's philosophic plays are widely read, Eugene O'Neill's treatises on solar flares remain obscure.

It's Greek to Me!

Greece's Greatest Scientists and Their Achievements

Scientist	Achievement
Anaxagoras	Developed theories about eclipses, meteors, and rainbows, which he described as "really, really pretty."
Archimedes	A well-known mathemetician, he shouted "Eureka!" when he entered a bathtub and water spilled out. Shortly thereafter, he invented the shower.
Aristarchus	The first scientist to put the sun at the center of the solar system, he was rebuked by the scientific community and his own mother, who asked why he couldn't be more like that "nice geocentric boy, Aristotle."
Eratosthenes	The first to use the term *geography*, he calculated the circumference of the earth and made a map of the world, which is, of course, hilarious.
Heraclitus	Known as the "weeping philosopher," he usually sat by himself at lunchtime. He is renown for saying that one cannot step into the same river twice, especially if the water is too cold.
Hippocrates	The father of medicine, Hippocrates created the "Hippocratic Oath," in which doctors swear to always take Wednesdays off for golf.
Pythagoras	Mathematician and philosopher, he developed the Pythagorean theorem, $a^2+b^2=c^2$. Sadly, no one ever learned what a, b, or c meant. Probably the size of squares, or something like that.

Roman Science: How to Kill Things Better

In Their Words

"Seriously, there's only one way to know who would win in a battle between a lion and a man."

—COMMODUS, ROMAN EMPEROR, SCIENTIST

Roman emperors conducted many experiments, most of which required a lot of cleanup afterwards.

While the Greeks were idealists in their scientific pursuits, the Romans who followed them were realists. They were most interested in science for its practical applications, like helping them kill people, though they enjoyed maiming people as well.

These martial innovations were technologically robust but not intellectually stimulating. While the Greeks spent their day in circles, conversing about great truths in the world, Romans spent their days in bigger circles, watching people kill other people. Most of their experiments were of the combative nature.[1]

Aqueducts: Scientific Alternative to Rain Dancing

▲ Historians believed the Romans could have saved time and money by buying bottled water instead of building the aqueducts.

Perhaps the greatest feats of Roman science were the aqueducts.[2] These large-scale engineering projects carried water from one province to another.[3] Though we are familiar with above-ground aqueducts, many of them were built underground in order to keep pranksters from putting bubble bath in the water supply. Disease was also a concern with aqueduct water, so most Romans boiled the water, let it evaporate, and then waited for it to rain down again until they drank it.

The previous method had slaves cup their hands, fill them with water, and run as quickly as possible.

---

[1] Although Romans spent much of their time conquering the world, they no doubt talked about science in passing, right before chopping off somebody's head.

[2] The aqueducts worked because of the gentle slope in the structures, which let water flow freely. Though this principle was employed unsuccessfully in the Leaning Tower of Pisa, it was also the forerunner to the modern water slide.

[3] The previous method had slaves cup their hands, fill them with water, and run as quickly as possible.

Emperors of Rome: Pioneers in Clinical Psychology

Rome was ruled by emperors for most of its existence. Though these emperors did not actively pursue science, they did help man understand the difference between sanity and insanity. The product of inbreeding, coddling, and frequent grape-feedings, these emperors devoted most of their time to putting their own heads on coins and sculptures.

However, some emperors took an interest in science. Hadrian built a large wall that surrounded the Roman Empire, though he died before he could build the ceiling. Nero studied music so seriously that he even played violin when he was in great personal danger. Marcus Aurelius pursued philosophy and promoted stoicism, which eschewed emotion for reason. For this reason, he's believed to have been one of the first geeks. Gordian III was a later emperor, but his invention of Roman numerals was crucial, since it allowed him to be able to count himself.

Though the emperors had few major scientific achievements, they did keep people entertained.

Caligula's Passion: Equestrian Science

One Roman emperor actually took a tireless interest in the pursuit of truth: Caligula.

From a young age, Caligula could be found in the horse's stables at all times, carefully studying and analyzing his favorite horse from all angles. As Caligula matured, his scientific pursuits matured as well. In adulthood, he became obsessed with trying to crossbreed a man and a horse, and he pursued it with numerous personal attempts. These experiments often lasted late into the night. Due to his studies, we now know that horses respond well to romantic candlelit dinners and a really nice bottle of wine.

Though Caligula ultimately failed, this early genetic experiment paved the way for equestrian science. To commemorate it, Caligula made sure his work was worth something by putting his horse on the most valuable Roman coins.

Mayans: So Great That They Disappeared

▲ Some Mayan ruins. Apparently, some people are impressed by miserable failure.

After the ancient Greeks, scientific progress stalled. Progress traveled across the ocean to the land we today call South America. It wasn't until the Mayans that scientific progress truly continued.

According to many experts, the Mayans were the most amazing thing ever, if you don't take into account the fact that they basically disappeared off the face of the earth. Great work, guys. Really amazing civilization you built there, before you failed at existing anymore. It's highly unlikely that their original intention was to be world leaders in "ruin tourism."

The Great Mystery of the Mayan Calendar

One of the greatest Mayan accomplishments was their calendar, which extends from the sixth century B.C. until December 21, 2012. Many speculate that the world will end on that day, so if you owe money, try to put off paying it until the 22nd. That said, the Mayan calendar carries many more great secrets.

- The work week is not actually five days but only three. So, according to the Mayans, you may be owed a few years in vacation time. It's advised that you take it immediately.

- Though a blue moon is traditionally defined as the second full moon in one month, the Mayans defined it as "whatever floats your boat."

- The special "Hottest Mayan Firefighters" edition of the calendar was by far the most popular.

◀ This is actually an Aztec calendar. If you're a Mayan and upset about it, just raise your hand. Nobody? Nobody? That's what we thought.

Despite their disappearance, the Mayans did have a notable scientific record. Most notable is their calendar, which included both a "word of the day" and cute pictures of kittens. In addition to their notable calendar, Mayans are believed to have invented the number zero, which is highly useful when you are counting nothing. In addition to this, they were able to count very high. Needless to say, Mayans should have spent less time counting and a little more time avoiding extinction. Thanks to the Mayans, it's easy to count how many Mayans are left: zero.

We may never know the full extent of Mayan scientific development due to the civilization's collapse. Many theories abound as to why the Mayans disappeared. Some blame drought. Others believe that they migrated to a cooler climate with better skiing.[1] A few even speculate that the Mayans were abducted by aliens. When you resort to aliens as an excuse, it's usually a sign that things are pretty bad.

---

[1] Many Swedes enjoy counting. Coincidence? Unlikely.

- All Mayans were required to be married on the same day. Originally, it was believed to be for religious reasons, but scholars now agree that it was so no Mayan men would ever forget their wedding anniversaries.

- February was still the shortest month, since it lasted only 4.5 days.

- Due to the absence of Presidents' Day from the Mayan culture, historians believe mattress sales were held at random.

- The Mayans stopped making calendars because a 2,500-year calendar meant sales fizzled out once households had bought their copy.

- It's worth mentioning that according to some versions of the calendar, you have a dental appointment Thursday. You should start flossing now.

▲ Why is Canada Day nowhere to be found on any Mayan calendar? Does this ancient Mayan prophecy doom Canada?

The Dark Ages: The Cave Men Would Feel Right at Home

▲ Dark Ages scientists used leeches to suck blood, because patients felt less pain once the leech killed them.

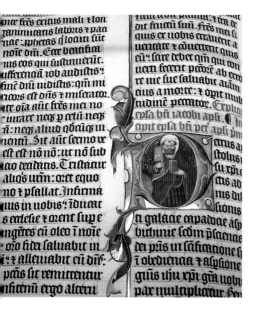

▲ Medieval monks spent much of their time working on elaborate books, even though only three people knew how to read.

In Europe, science had stalled since the downfall of the Greeks. Instead of following the enlightened principles of that age, Europeans spent most of their time using science to kill people more efficiently. They made molten liquid traps for attackers and long-range bows and arrows.[1] The English invented their unique cuisine, which served as both food and blunt weapon against their enemies. What they couldn't invent, like gunpowder, they imported from the more able Chinese.[2] At some point, they also figured out how to make bread, though raisin toast was still a few centuries away.

The famous philosopher Petrarch referred to these times as "the Dark Ages," and most of his friends thought it was a little rude when he mentioned it at parties. Most agreed with him, however, especially since most intellectuals could only obtain work as swine herders.

That said, the Dark Ages weren't a total loss. They included the development of the compass, although for the first century of its use, everyone held it upside down. In addition, architecture of the era was notable for its use of math in building complex buildings, though almost all of them still lacked central air conditioning. Some modern scholars have even reconsidered renaming the era the "Just a Little More Light and They Would Have Been Okay" Ages.

What caused the Dark Ages? Some blame the natural drought of lab coats. Others believe there was an eclipse that lasted five hundred years. There's no way to know for sure, so just be glad you weren't around.

The Dark Ages did not last forever. One day, people grew tired of eating gruel, catching deadly plagues every month or so, and dying in childbirth. Science began anew.[3]

---

[1] These weapons were also used to develop the modern food fight.

[2] However, Europeans condemned the use of Chinese infant labor, since in their own society you had to be at least eight years old to get a factory job.

[3] Though most people still had terrible, difficult lives.

Dumping of Slop

This scene from the famous Bayeux Tapestry depicts the Dark Ages dumping of slop. It was, admittedly, more sanitary than keeping it around.

The Renaissance: Science Becomes the New Black

Emerging from the Dark Ages was the period called the Renaissance. Finally, man returned to the ideals of the Greeks, instead of focusing on making cannon balls that really, really hurt. The flourishing scientific culture yielded many discoveries, chief among them the realization that Aristotle was completely insane and should be ignored at all costs.[1]

▲ In this famous painting, Michelangelo depicted what happens when two people rub their feet on the carpet and then touch fingers.

Scientists during the Renaissance used empirical study to prove their points. Empirical study means that instead of making up science off the top of their heads, they attempted to actually prove what they thought. They did this through experiments, data, and furious stroking of their long beards.

Empirical study was a wildly radical idea at the time, and the scientists were promptly persecuted by the government, the Church, and the Society for the Earth Being in the Center of the Universe.[2] Despite these obstacles, science was finally back and bigger than ever. There were even rumors that they were going to make a movie about it, once movies were invented.

---

[1] This included Aristotle's theories that cats were simply dogs in masks, and ocean waves were controlled by the bowel movements of a whale.

[2] Many celebrities of the era were members of this influential organization.

The Scientific Revolution: Much More Important Than the Scientific Suggestion

This period of rebirth during the Renaissance was known as "the Scientific Revolution." Instead of relying on superstition and religion, scientists began to rely on test tubes and things written in Latin.[1]

The revolution was not without obstacles. Precedent declared that science had already explained everything perfectly, or at least well enough to satisfy inquisitive children. The Church declared that science was evil, since there was almost no time for prayer while dissecting a frog. Even peasants did not believe the scientists, though peasants weren't necessarily the best source, since they spent most of their time running into walls and drooling.

However, artists led the charge. Leaders like Leonardo da Vinci tricked people into learning by mixing science with pretty pictures.[2]

> **» SCIENTIFIC FACT**
>
> Before the Scientific Revolution, governments frequently tried to ban gravity.

---

[1] It's believed that the genitive case in Latin is responsible for ending the Black Plague.

[2] A technique still used in textbooks today.

The Scientific Revolution's Greatest Changes

- Placement of the sun in the center of the solar system, even though nobody knew what the "solar system" was.
- Agreement that "because" was no longer a valid scientific explanation.
- Adoption of new rules against dissecting peasants. Instead, only slaves and immigrants could hit the cutting board.
- Establishment of a system of measurement other than bigger or smaller than a bread box.
- Sorcerers relegated to high-concept theme parks and kings' deathbeds.
- Significantly less reliance on newt, toad, and frog warts.
- Banning of alchemy, unless you really needed the money.
- Scientists began wearing lab coats in the lab instead of short shorts.
- Men of science became slightly more important than the court jester, though not as important as the lute player.
- Development of non-leech medicine.
- Slop-dumping limited to only twice a day.
- Started saying the word *science* without fear of being drawn and quartered.

The Mysteries of
DA VINCI

Leonardo da Vinci was a legendary artist and scientist. But if you look closer, you can find even greater secrets in his work.

The Name	The Work	Look Closer
Helicopter		Da Vinci's helicopter never flew, but by flapping his lips, da Vinci could make a noise that sounded just like one.
Giant Crossbow		Though da Vinci's giant crossbow was never used in practice, it was a forerunner to the T-shirt cannon.
Graduation of Shadows on Spheres		Da Vinci studied how shadows covered a sphere, which came in handy when he drew the first basketball.
Flying Machine		This prototype was not actually able to fly, but the kitchen would have made some of the best in-flight food ever.

Da Vinci's "Vitruvian Man"

His drawing was considered a landmark study in anatomy, until people realized Vitruvian Man had too many arms and was shy about nudity.

The New Bad Boys of Science

▲ Galileo Galilei: One of science's most difficult names to spell.

There was no single scientist that made the Scientific Revolution occur. Galileo Galilei, Nicolaus Copernicus,[1] Tyco Brahe, Sir Francis Bacon,[2] Johannes Kepler, René Descartes, and Sir Isaac Newton are just a few of the famous names of the era.[3]

They all suffered for their cause. Galileo was forced to undergo a trial due to his heliocentric theory. The pope accused him of heresy for his claims about the sun and Galileo's failure to mention the papal hat in any of his work.

Galileo and other scientists had new tools and methods to discover the universe. The telescope helped them see the stars, and the turkey thermometer helped them be certain that their poultry was fully cooked. They also collaborated to help each other solve the most difficult scientific problems and crossword puzzles.

---

[1] Persecuted for his science and the way he spelled "Nicholas."

[2] Incidentally, Bacon was a vegetarian.

[3] At the height of the Scientific Revolution, their joint lectures attracted thousands of viewers, though ticket scalping and counterfeit merchandise was a significant problem.

Newton's Apple

Born in the 1600s, Sir Isaac Newton was a renowned physicist.

One day, he was sitting under a tree when a round object fell on his head. Like any great scientist, Newton did not run away. Instead, he sampled the round object. It had a red hue and brown stem. He bit into it and was pleasantly surprised. He had just discovered the apple.

After his discovery of the apple, Newton became obsessed with the strange new fruit. Apple juice, apple strudel, and apple pie (pictured at left) are all due to his discovery.

The Enlightenment (Candlelight Only)

The Scientific Revolution culminated in the Age of Enlightenment in the 1600s and 1700s, during which thinkers and scientists realized they could be far more productive if they turned on the lights.

Once they did, they came up with a new driving force: reason.[1] They decided to abandon the irrational motives of the past, cast aside their preconceptions about the world, and even start washing their hands.[2]

The political climate of the Enlightenment era matched the scientific climate. Across the world, people began discussing things other than plagues. The legal system advanced, as craftsmen learned to make more comfortable wigs for judges to wear. Academic institutions formed, and the intellectual community flocked to high-minded discussions and frequent keg parties. Scientists and statesmen like Ben Franklin invented amazing things and slept with beautiful French women.[3] A new era had truly begun.

In Their Words

"Honey, where did I put my keys? What? They're on the kite? Oh crap."

—BENJAMIN FRANKLIN, SCIENTIST AND STATESMAN

Benjamin Franklin discovered electricity during an experiment when he put a key on a kite.

▲ This early American poster demonstrates an Enlightenment era scientific discovery: a chopped-up snake usually dies.

The End of History

Though the specifics of science have changed over the years, the principles have stayed the same. Man reached out of the darkness and, after hitting his toe on the bedpost, discovered science as we know it today.

Now it's time to learn what that means.

---

[1] For a brief period, raisins were also considered.

[2] However, it would be another hundred years or so until they started washing their hands with soap.

[3] Beautiful by his standards.

Doing Science Good

Types of Science: Natural Science and Science for People Who Are Bad at Math

Modern science is categorized into two main types: natural science and social science. Natural science studies the way the world actually works, from the nuts and bolts of biological life[1] to the truth about the cosmos. Social science is for people who found high-school algebra difficult.

Social sciences include psychology, sociology, anthropology, talking about your feelings, history, classic cartoons, and freakonomics. Social scientists claim they are scientists because they act off of empirical data. That is like a six-year-old claiming he's a superhero because he's wearing a cape: it's endearing, but it's also completely incorrect.

If you aren't sure whether you're a social scientist or a natural scientist, there are a few tests you can perform. Look at your feet. Are you wearing shoes? If you are, you are a scientist. Now look at your surroundings. Are you in a clean, well-lit lab, ready to do important experiments? If so, you are a scientist. Is it difficult to see because of all the smoke in the room? You are probably a social scientist. That siren is the police coming to break up the party.

▲ Many social scientists show up late to the classes they teach, usually because they forgot what room they were in.

The real sciences are to be revered at all times. They are the disciplines that rescued man from chaos and gave life meaning.[2] They are also much easier to get a patent on, which is crucial when you need money to fund the University Student Center's new rock-climbing wall.

When you're choosing which science to pursue, consider a few key questions. For example, which do you think is more important: the creation of the universe or the government of Lichtenstein? Is it better to understand how gravity works, or why apples are different prices at different groceries? Once you make that choice, you'll be a real scientist, assuming you know how to make good decisions.

---

[1] Remember, most animals are not actually made of nuts and bolts.

[2] And also gave man plastic, seedless watermelons, and cryogenics.

How Social Scientists and Natural Scientists Solve the Same Problems

Problem	Natural Scientists	Social Scientists
	Lock down the biohazard area. After making sure it is impossible for contaminants to spread, diagnose the threat, search for a cure, and try to help the victims.	Do a quick re-read of Albert Camus's *The Plague*, since it's especially resonant during a time of existential crisis. Write a forty-page treatment on how to reform city government to deal with plagues, using an approach that mirrors the medieval Swedish government. Finally, flee the area if still alive.
	Using past weather patterns, accurately predict where the tornado will appear. Use meteorological devices to track the location of the tornado and predict the future path of the storm.	Have twenty students receive extra credit for filling out a three-hour survey about how tornados make them feel. Learn that tornados make them sad. Have students notify you whenever they feel sad and assume that means a tornado is in the immediate vicinity.
	Locate a proper replacement battery, remove the dead battery, and insert the new battery.	Survey the history of past battery replacements and create a scatter plot of the data. Cross-reference that data with price fluctuations in batteries while controlling for inflation. Conclude that, despite the absence of power, the battery should actually still be functional and therefore does not need to be replaced.

The Scientific Method

Real scientists use the scientific method in order to make and classify their discoveries. Carefully refined, the scientific method has contributed knowledge and inspired other work.[1]

The scientific method consists of a question, research, a hypothesis, experimentation, analysis, and a conclusion.[2] When you're finished, you'll have the answer to any question, or an unmitigated disaster.

---

[1] Method acting, the rhythm method, etc.

[2] If necessary, you should rinse and repeat, similar to shampoo.

Discarded Alternatives to the Scientific Method

Method	The Scientific Coin Flip	Sciencey! (See Local Listing)	Polly Bensen
Description	The strategic use of heads or tails to answer all scientific questions. Used to classify plants into vegetables or fruits.	This short-lived game show was used to solve every problem from the speed of light to the division of cells.	This eight-year-old prodigy answered the most perplexing questions with grace and consistency.
Greatest Strength	Right half of the time.	More clapping and cheering than modern science.	Astonishingly correct about everything.
Greatest Weakness	Requires a coin.	Major discoveries bet away in hopes of winning a trip to Costa Rica.	Took too many naps.

The Scientific Method Through History: The Method That Keeps on Giving

You might wonder why you should use the scientific method. "Why bother?" you might say. "I developed my own method using a pot-bellied pig and series of hoof taps."[1]

In fact, the scientific method has proven useful throughout the history of science. Many times, scientists would have stumbled if it weren't for the method's strong guiding hand, frequently placed on their lower back.[2]

- **The Question:** Did you know that Al Einstein originally spent more time cloud gazing than studying science? One day, he formed a question. He began with "Does that cloud look more like a bunny or a muffin?" After careful revision, he ended up with a Nobel Prize and started making people call him "Albert."
- **Research:** Before Jonas Salk tackled polio, he was fascinated with the shape of the earth. However, the research stage showed him that somebody had already discovered that the planet was round. The rest is history.
- **The Hypothesis:** When developing the nuclear bomb, J. Robert Oppenheimer developed the hypothesis that it might blow things up. As a result, he stayed clear of the blast.

- **Experiment:** For years, Socrates assumed that drinking hemlock was good for you. However, when he conducted his final experiment, he learned the truth about the plant.
- **Analysis:** At first the data was confusing and difficult to understand, but after years of analysis, Crick and Watson were able to conclude that people preferred calling them Watson and Crick.
- **Conclusion:** Alfred Nobel didn't know what to think of his invention of dynamite. But once he proceeded through the entirety of the scientific method, the conclusion was clear: Dynamite blows things up good.

Now that you've seen how important the scientific method has been in history, you can learn to use it yourself. Remember to pore over every step carefully—one misstep could turn your science into science fiction.

» SCIENTIFIC FACT

If you develop a hypothesis after drinking too much coffee, it's called a hyperthesis.

---

[1] Pot-bellied pigs are great pets, but in most situations they are not acceptable coworkers.

[2] The scientific method loves you too much to let you go.

The Scientific

QUESTION

KEY STEP IN WHICH YOU REVEAL HOW LITTLE YOU KNOW. ALSO KNOWN AS "PROBLEM," BECAUSE HAVING TO ANSWER IT IS DEFINITELY A PROBLEM.

RESEARCH

USE THIS TIME TO DOODLE IN THE MARGINS OF BOOKS. HEY, THAT LITTLE MAN YOU DREW AT THE BOTTOM IS GREAT! HAVE YOU EVER CONSIDERED BECOMING A FULL-TIME CARTOONIST?

HYPOTHESIS

COME UP WITH A HALF-BAKED PREDICTION, EVEN THOUGH THE REASON YOU'RE DOING THE EXPERIMENT IS BECAUSE YOU DON'T KNOW WHAT WILL HAPPEN.

Method

EXPERIMENT

WASH YOUR HANDS AT LEAST ONCE AND SIGN A WAIVER PROMISING YOU WON'T SUE. LIGHT THE MATCH AND CLOSE YOUR EYES. IT'S ALL GOING TO BE OKAY.

ANALYSIS

RECOVER FROM YOUR INJURIES AND LOOK AT YOUR "DATA," WHICH IS IMPOSSIBLE TO READ AND HIGHLY DISORGANIZED. MAKE SOME PIE CHARTS AND BAR GRAPHS.

CONCLUSION

NOTIFY THE NOBEL COMMITTEE.

Scientific Theories: The Easiest Way to Never Be Wrong

It's important to note that all the history, hard work, and collaboration that go into science don't create absolute certainty about anything. That would be too easy. Science explains the way the world works, but that isn't any reason to stop feeling lost and confused.

That's because scientific work results in theories, not laws. Any theory can be proven or disproven by a future scientist looking to make another theory, which will later also be disproven. Theories are crucial to furthering scientific progress, and they limit legal liability.

That said, it's important that you protect your theory if you have one. Theories are named after the scientists who created them and can result in academic acclaim, employment, and having sandwiches at delis named after you. No matter how wrong it may be, defend your theory until your opponents agree to give up or credit you as a co-debunker. That way you have a chance at keeping your reputation in tact until you're dead.

» **SCIENTIFIC FACT**

Nikola Tesla and Thomas Edison frequently challenged the other's theory about who was "awesomer."

Words You Can Use to Explain Flaws in Your Theories

co·in·ci·dence
"The fact that those mice died after injection of the drug is just a coincidence. I'll be fired if we don't continue with production."

a·nom·a·ly
"The presence of that species is simply an anomaly. I'm still going to say that it's extinct."

ab·nor·mal·i·ty
"The procedure is bound to create abnormalities—and who's to say that a headless baby is always such a bad thing?"

cau·sal·i·ty
"We can't establish causality between the design of the vehicle and the explosion, considering what a hassle that would be."

HAVE YOU DEVELOPED A NEW THEORY?

Is your idea original?

YES → Did you check to see?

NO → Is the creator dead?

Did you check to see?
- NO → Is the creator dead?
- YES → Does it explain stuff?

Is the creator dead?
- YES → Can that be..."fixed?"
- NO → Can that be..."fixed?"

Can that be..."fixed?"
- YES → Does it explain stuff?
- NO → What if we knew a guy who could take care of that?

Does it explain stuff?
- YES → You have a theory! Now it's time to get a patent and, after that, try to make your theory prove something.
- NO → What if we knew a guy who could take care of that?

What if we knew a guy who could take care of that?
- YES → You have a theory! Now it's time to get a patent and, after that, try to make your theory prove something.
- NO → You don't have a theory. Prepare to languish in obscurity.

You have a theory! Now it's time to get a patent and, after that, try to make your theory prove something.

You don't have a theory. Prepare to languish in obscurity.

Please Get Back to Work

A Letter from the Fake Science Labs

By John Vanderhof Reynolds
Chief Scientist and Assistant Sanitation Technician

You thought this nice pink page would give you a break from work, didn't you?

Well, you're not there yet. It's going to take a little elbow grease for you to become a genuine scientist. Sure, you've made it through two chapters. But one of them was an introduction with a lot of large fonts, and the other was a chapter about the "history" and "methods" of science. That's about as scientific as finger painting with a hot fudge sundae.

You're about to get a taste of real science, and to truly appreciate it, you're going to need to work a lot harder than you have been. Quick: close your eyes and recite every word you've read on this page. A real scientist would have memorized every single character. And he also would have refused to close his eyes.

When the Fake Science labs opened, we all worked 24 hours a day and took a 10-minute nap each hour. While we were sleeping, most of us wore headphones and listened to a recitation of the Periodic Table of the Elements in German. Why German, you ask? Why are you asking questions instead of researching the periodic table right now? The *Periodensystem* is waiting!

The rest of your training will require serious discipline and a dedication to your craft. I don't complain when, after a long shift studying the microbiology of cells, I'm assigned double duty to clean the microwave, wipe down the men's bathroom, and refill the vending machine. I don't complain because I am dedicated to making this world a better place, and I'm worried about being fired.

You should take the same approach. Now that you know a few trinkets about science, you need to learn the rest about our world. At least you can use what you've learned to guide your studies. Do you think Sir Isaac Newton would have stopped reading to have "meals"? And, I ask you, would da Vinci have really interrupted his studies to "go to the bathroom"? You should have read to lithium by now on the *Periodensystem*, by the way.

You've signed up for a long life of meticulous study poring over documents with tiny letters (these look like billboards to me) and memorizing sequences of numbers. You want to be a scientist, and you'll spend the rest of your life paying for it. Read on. And please, if you haven't opened your eyes yet, do it before you take the quiz.

Chapter 1 Quiz: What Is Science?

Multiple Choice

1. What did cave men discover first?

a. Boron
b. Loincloths
c. Caves
d. Cave women

2. What did the Greeks accomplish?

a. Anatomically correct statues
b. Promotion of the letter *k*
c. A great use for hemlock
d. Discovering the wrong answer to almost everything

3. What happened to the Mayans?

a. They said they were just going out for cigarettes and then never came back
b. Got lost on the way to Six Flags South America
c. Just decided to call themselves "Aztecs" because the *z* was cool
d. They discovered the Fountain of Youth but drank too much and were turned into vulnerable, defenseless babies

4. What happened during the Scientific Revolution?

a. Scientists rotated nonstop
b. Wizards explored alternative careers in film
c. Peasants learned to stop drinking from giant pools of sewage
d. Galileo invented the telescope to spy on his attractive neighbor

5. What was the Enlightenment?

a. The 12–14 hours of daylight
b. The period when Ben Franklin convinced countless people to sleep with him
c. 150 years before the invention of anything fun
d. Too bright for its own good

6. How do social scientists spend their time?

a. Sleeping, interrupted by naps
b. Wishing they were real scientists
c. Leading their students away from lucrative, fulfilling careers in real science
d. Wasting your time

Short Answer

1. You've learned the scientific method. Now that you know it, use it to explain the creation of the universe, development of human beings, and the rest of this book.

_____

_____

_____

_____

_____

_____

_____

2. Now that you're a member of the scientific community, you have a responsibility to contribute. Send your name, bank account routing number, and checking account number to the Fake Science labs in order to help the advancement of science and possibly purchase a foosball table.

_____

_____

_____

_____

_____

_____

Essay Questions

1. Science rescues us from myth and confusion. Describe how you would use equations and scientific experiments to solve the world's most difficult problems, preferably before Monday.

_____

_____

_____

_____

_____

_____

_____

_____

_____

_____

_____

_____

_____

_____

_____

_____

2. Have you ever thought about what science means to you? Explain why what you think doesn't matter, and why what the scientific community thinks is far more important.

_____

_____

_____

_____

_____

_____

_____

_____

_____

_____

_____

_____

_____

_____

ASTRONOMY

LEARN HOW TO STARE INTO SPACE

Before You Start This Chapter . . .

- Move to a nice neighborhood so you can go outside at night.
- Make a wish upon a star, as long as the wish is to stop believing in wishes.
- Practice saying the word "astrolabe" without blushing.
- In space, no one can hear you scream, so scream as much as you can while you're still on Earth.
- Become accustomed to G forces by jumping up and down a lot.
- Get a spacesuit custom-tailored.
- Find a parallel-universe version of yourself who already read this chapter.
- Learn all the fictional alien languages, just in case they're real.
- Visit a tall building so you can look at space more closely.

The Space Where All Our Stuff Is

Astronomy is the study of our incredible universe, so it begins our study of science. Just as important, it's also the first subject in the alphabet.[1]

Have you ever spent a hot summer night inside watching television? Well, imagine if instead of doing that, you went outside and looked up at the stars. As you sat on that ground-carpet called "grass" and looked up at the outside-ceiling called "sky," you would probably ask yourself a few simple questions: "What are those tiny lights in the sky? How do day and night occur? And what am I missing on television right now?"

▲ Astronomy allows us to see things that would be really difficult to draw.

That's how astronomy began. A few people looked up at the tiny lights in the sky and never stopped wondering what they were. Because electricity hadn't been invented yet, they also decided those lights were interesting. Thus began man's quest to understand the parts of the universe that are incredibly far away.[2]

Astronomy has changed much since those first stargazers. But despite the technological advances, it's certain that man will always continue to look up at the sky and wonder where the universe began and if he can go back inside yet.

As astronomers, we have a duty to document the wonders of space as if there were actually a chance we could go there. It can be inspiring to see all the places you'll never visit. For now, however, space has endless mysteries, only a small percentage of which involve Mrs. Peacock in the Conservatory with a wrench. Perhaps, someday, we will see aliens looking back at us, wondering if our textbooks are as notable as theirs. Fortunately, the answer is that our textbooks are far superior.

---

[1] As always, our apologies to any aardvarkologists who may be reading.

[2] Many astronomers' spouses wish their stargazing partners would spend a little more time trying to understand the person in the next room.

The Tools of Space

How do we observe this magnificent space called space? We have many different tools to use, some of which cost less than a billion dollars.[1]

The first tool is right on you—it's your eyes.[2] By looking up at the night sky, you can perform rudimentary astronomy. You may also want to have a piece of paper with you to sketch the appearance of the moon, stars, and that attractive woman who always leaves her blinds up. Once you do this, you'll have a rudimentary idea of both astronomy and biology.

▲ Start small by tilting your telescope at your neighbors. Eventually, you'll learn to tilt it a little further up at the sky.

When you're ready, you can buy equipment to explore space. Telescopes are readily available every place from a department store to a military contractor, and they rarely check to see if you have a restraining order. If a telescope is getting pricey, you can always make your own with a mirror, some duct tape, and a world-class engineer and supplies budget of at least $300,000.

Once you've observed space, you can even visit it by joining the space program or seeing if you car has a gear labeled "Up." If it doesn't, your own career in rocketry awaits, assuming you aren't too attached to being alive.

Sounds exciting, doesn't it? Now let's learn what you'll find when you start staring into space. Prepare to squint at the wonders of the cosmos. Don't be alarmed if they're very blurry and dark, since that's what it will be like most of the time. Just say "Ooh" and "Ah" a lot and nobody will even know you can't see anything.

---

[1] Still, try to have at least a billion dollars.

[2] If you're blind, this is going to get awkward.

The Universe and You

The Beginning: When Everything Go Boom

Like all stories, our universe's had to begin somewhere.[1] Our universe began about 14 billion years ago, give or take 12 billion. It's believed that the universe was packed into a hot dense particle the size of a popcorn kernel, but scientists are almost certain there wasn't any butter. Then the "big bang" happened.

The big bang explains the explosion of the universe, and it's believed that if any people were around during it, their ears were seriously damaged. It's theorized that, from that point on, the universe kept expanding because it didn't know what else to do. But don't mention it, since it's kind of sensitive about its size.

---

[1] Unfortunately, scientists have never found an "Introduction" written by the universe.

How the Big Bang Got Its Name

Today, the big bang is a familiar term to anybody who knows about space. However, it wasn't always that way.

When the theory of a primeval atom was developed, it was immediately sent to a naming committee. Their suggestions were criticized as "too scientific" and "hard to understand." Since the name had to explain a stellar explosion that began the entire universe, it was difficult to come up with something simple.

Many early proposals were bandied about, including the "Not-Small Explosion." But when six-year-old Jimmy Blevins was told about the event just after having his milk and cookies, his name for it stuck. We still call it the "Big Bang" today.

▲ Little Jimmy before naptime and just after naming the beginning of all time and space.

The Universe: Even Bigger Than a Whole Football Field

Once the big bang occurred, the universe was created, though there was a lot of paperwork to do before it became official.[1] Since the big bang happened, the universe hasn't stopped expanding.

How long will it expand for? No one knows for sure, but some guess it will be 318 years, 4 months, 17 days, 12 hours, and 13 minutes. At that point, scientists believe the universe will begin to contract because it will run out of money.[2] When the universe contracts, you can at least expect your commute to work to get a little shorter each day.

Until that point, however, the universe will remain very large. How large is it? Stretch both arms out and reach as far as you can. Now imagine doing that 700 trillion times. You're about a fortieth of the way there. Of course, the number may vary depending on your arm span. Some people use other means to express the size of the universe.[3] That's futile until we build longer measuring tape.

The universe is so big that it holds untold riches. Any number of galaxies, planets, and clever theme restaurants could be hiding within the dark folds of space.[4] What else is out there? That's the sort of amazing question that you can ponder instead of doing your homework.

How were the cosmos made? Prominent mixologists recommend vodka, cranberry juice, lime, Cointreau, and a lemon twist. However, there may never be agreement about how much granulated sugar to add.

> **» SCIENTIFIC FACT**
>
> Because the universe is so large, there's still a chance that you're the center of it.

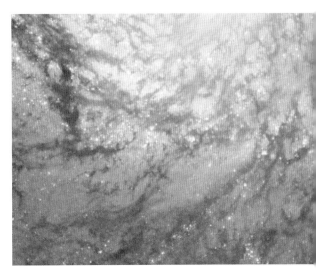

▲ Just how big is the universe? It's so big that you can't even see all the elephants in this picture.

---

[1] Carbon copies were especially difficult, since carbon hadn't been created yet.

[2] For this reason, don't buy your own planet until you're sure it won't be sold later for half off.

[3] Some people express size in football fields. However, it's less well known that for a few years, football fields were expressed in universe sizes. Every half-quadrillionth universe the ball traveled, players earned a first down.

[4] If you're looking for an investment opportunity, just imagine this: It's a science-themed diner—all the drinks are served in test tubes and burgers are made with Bunsen burners. Think about it, no pressure.

Parallel Universes: And You Thought You Were Confused Already

Before we discuss the contents of our universe, it's important to recognize that our cosmos may just be the beginning. Many scientists believe that parallel universes exist, especially after they've read some paperbacks and had a little too much to drink.

For now, these possibilities are purely speculative, but that doesn't mean that we can't put lots of numbers and symbols on a chalkboard.[1] We may one day even visit parallel universes, if we invent a space-time-travel machine or find an old amulet in an antique store that promises strange powers to the person who wears it.

> **» SCIENTIFIC FACT**
>
> In a parallel universe, parallel universes are perpendicular.

What do these parallel universes mean? Our universe is bound by certain physical laws and facts,[2] but a parallel universe might be governed by different ones that we can't predict. If you ever want to sit down and feel dizzy, thinking about parallel universes is a good way to do it.

There are other implications for parallel universes. In these strange cosmos, things could be like our own universe, but slightly different. They could "branch off" from our own world and into a new reality. It's possible to imagine a reality where fish breathe air instead of water, plants can talk, and instead of a 30-year fixed rate mortgage for a house, a 32-year fixed rate mortgage is the accepted national standard. It's amazing to think about, isn't it?

In Their Words

"Gentlemen, here is your cure for cancer."

—ART GARFUNKEL, SCIENTIST

In a parallel universe, it's easy to imagine that this quote might be true.

You can apply parallel universes to your study of science. Although the field remains theoretical, it teaches us important lessons. First, it will make it easier to understand movies about time travel. Second, it allows you to use the word *wormhole* in polite conversation. Finally, and most important, vigilant study of these parallel universes will teach you to spell "parallel" correctly 98 percent of the time.

---

[1] Once you've finished writing your theory, take two paces back and whisper, "I've done it. I've found a universe where chocolate waterfalls are real."

[2] Gravity, inertia, don't call after 10 P.M.

Imagine a parallel universe where . . .

This baby is named
Michael instead
of James!

Instead of
"Paper or plastic?"
cashiers ask,
"Plastic or paper?"

This cat is not
considered
particularly cute!

This textbook
didn't win the
Nobel Prize!

Galaxies: We Live in a Universe of Neighborhoods

Since the universe is so large, we divide it into smaller units. These units are called "galaxies" and they form the neighborhoods of our universe. Each one has its own distinct personality, landmarks, and real estate prices.[1]

» **SCIENTIFIC FACT**

Galileo spotted the first galaxy, though it was later found to be a smudge on his telescope lens.

There are countless galaxies in the universe, largely because the person in charge of counting them gets distracted around the billion mark. These galaxies each have different traits but are all bound by their gravitational fields and a common cultural background. It's exceedingly rare for different galaxies to have the same taste in music.

Galaxies are classified by their shape,[2] which varies depending on their gravitational field. Many galaxies have names, but some are classified by random numbers and letters, which hurts a lot of feelings. Though we may never visit other galaxies, we can studiously assess their prettiness from millions of light years away.

▲ After German scientists discovered the Umlaut Galaxy, they decided to incorporate it into their own language.

Dark Matter and Black Holes: Two Reasons the Universe Should Invest in Better Lighting

Unfortunately, some parts of galaxies are difficult for us to see because they have really poor lighting. Until scientists build more powerful flashlights, we are forced to infer what may be there. We do this through complicated equations and the power of imagination.

Based on math and a sixth "science sense," astronomers believe that 23 percent of the universe is made of something called "dark matter."[3] This dark matter serves as a great explanation for all the other things we don't understand.

---

[1] The Hoag's Object galaxy has gentrified a lot in the past 9.8 billion years. There's a great artisinal cheese store where a quasar used to be.

[2] This classification was begun by women's magazines that sought to help a galaxy figure out the best spring pattern for their shape.

[3] Our own galaxy is 40 percent polyester, 60 percent cotton.

Contrary to its name, dark matter is not evil; it is misunderstood and probably had a very difficult childhood. Maybe instead of blaming dark matter for everything, you should ask if society itself is the true dark matter. Think about it.

Dark matter may one day turn out to be a boon to society and help the black light break away from its niche market. However, scientists recommend that humans avoid dark matter at all costs, unless you are one of those people who actually like dark licorice.

▲ It took years for astronomers to get close enough to take this picture of dark matter.

Black holes are even more mysterious. These regions in space suck in everything in their presence, so much so that not even light can escape.[1] It remains unknown what they're using the light for, but it's easy to speculate that it must be something good. Perhaps the black hole thinks people look more attractive in dim light. Or maybe it needs a lot of light of its own to take professional-looking photographs.

We can only guess at the answer, because it is impossible to escape a black hole. If you come too close to a black hole, you reach the "event horizon." This is a kind way of saying that you better have updated your will before you decided to taunt that black hole.

How do black holes form? It's believed that they form when a star collapses under all the pressure of being bright. When the star collapses, something called a "supernova" occurs. This is a way we try to make the star feel better about itself for collapsing. It then turns into a black hole and starts sucking in everything that pushed it so hard to be something it never wanted to be in the first place.

▲ When a supernova occurs, a star decides to give up the fast track and instead focus on its painting.

Someday, our own sun will collapse and turn into a black hole. Earth will be sucked into the black hole almost instantly. It's estimated that only the most durable buildings will survive, so make sure you have a place with a good foundation and a solid home inspection.

---

[1] Though it's well known that dictators horde light bulbs for this very purpose, it doesn't have the same effect.

The Milky Way: Nursing Us for 13 Billion Years

Now that you know a little bit about the universe and other galaxies, it's time to learn about your own: the Milky Way. Originally known as the Milkish Way, a lucrative contract with Mars Candy brought about the name we know today.[1]

Even though it's just one galaxy, the Milky Way is impressively large. Shaped in a spiral, it maintains a slim figure despite its size. It fits hundreds of billions of stars, which is useful in case it loses any to supernovas or to a job transplant to Bode's Galaxy. Of these billions of stars, there are around 50 billion planets, of which 500 million are the same distance from a star as Earth is from the sun. Basically, that means there are more markets for this textbook than anybody ever realized.

> **» SCIENTIFIC FACT**
>
> Because the Milky Way is our home galaxy, you should refrain from supporting other galaxies' sports teams.

Despite its impressive appearance, the Milky Way is comprised primarily of gas and dust, though it is able to clean up when necessary. As the location implies, there is also a lot of space. Unfortunately, the Milky Way is too large for us to fully explore, since we don't know if there are any gas stations along the way.

▲ Dairy farmers banded together to prevent the Milky Way from being renamed the Soy Milky Way.

Still, we have some involvement in the galaxy as a whole. The sun rotates around the Milky Way once every 250 million years, so that's something to look forward to. Since scientists have only been studying the Milky Way for a few hundred years, we don't know what will happen when the sun crosses the finish line. Maybe there will be a medal of some sort, or at least an honorary certificate. We can only speculate.

Is the Milky Way the best galaxy in the universe? All signs point to yes. Many of the other galaxies only have numbers and letters for their names, and we know for a fact that none of them include Earth. Still, we have to remain open to the possibility of other galaxies that have carbon-based life forms or carbonated names. Does the "Diet Cherry Dr. Pepper Galaxy" wait for the chance to eclipse us? Only time will tell.

---

[1] The company's long history of space-based confections includes Mars Bars, Jupitersicles, Sunpops, and Pluto Balls.

Landmarks of the Milky Way

This reddish trail is believed to contain some of the universe's oldest traces of ketchup.

Farthest point that Earth radio signals have reached. Due to the delay, alien civilizations may be mourning the explosion of the Hindenburg at this very moment.

The absolute edge of the Milky Way, this area is known as the "margin" of the galaxy, unless we get more space from the printer.

Site of the first McDonald's, started by the McDonald brothers in 1940 in San Bernardino, California. Bought and franchised by Ray Kroc in Illinois in 1955, the corporation now has over 32,000 locations on the planet Earth and continues to serve affordable and delicious meals.

If this star cluster ever collides with another one, the Milky Way will be whipped into the frothier Creamy Way.

Stars: Night Lights of the Galaxy

When you look up at the sky, you might assume that all stars are the same. After all, the only ones that are different usually turn out to be satellites. However, stars are as varied as the colors of the rainbow, though not quite as pretty.

What are stars made of? It's believed stars are composed almost entirely of plasma, held together by massive amounts of gravity.[1] The plasma heats up through nuclear reactions, which is one of the reasons stars are outlawed on Earth, since they might be misused as bombs. These nuclear reactions are incredibly hot and entirely unregulated by the EPA.[2]

Stars are also composed of hydrogen and helium. The hydrogen helps them float, while the helium turns any sound they make into a humorous high-pitched noise. Stars spend most of their lives fusing this hydrogen, which is ironic, since they'd save a lot of electricity if they just turned out the lights.

> **» SCIENTIFIC FACT**
>
> Before using nuclear fusion, stars relied on coal, which is the reason why space is so black.

▲ The popular reality television series, *Little Star, Big Galaxy*, follows the everyday life of a red dwarf as it tries to make ends meet in a sun-sized galaxy.

Different Stars, Different Stories

Not all stars are perfectly normal gigantic balls of gas. Some are unusual.

For example, you may have heard of a red dwarf star. This star is smaller and cooler than the sun, which shows that size isn't everything when it comes to being cool. Why is it red? It's a combination of the differing temperature and the Red Dye #40, which is present in the star and in many colored cakes. Red dwarfs are joined by white dwarfs, black dwarfs, and brown dwarfs, but most scientists refuse to elaborate any further for fear of being labeled as racists. When you discuss these stars, it's a good idea to leave out both the color and "dwarf" part, since both are actually quite offensive.

---

[1] If you went on a star, it would be very hard to lift your feet, both because of the gravity and because you'd be burned to a crisp.

[2] Next time you look at the stars with a small child, remind them that each one is a flaming ball of death that could easily destroy Earth.

Stars don't have to be dwarfs, however. Some stars become giants or supergiants, in which their ego expands along with their size. These stars are much larger than the sun, but their size is short-lived. These stellar objects shrink when they've expended all their fuel, so they spend the rest of their days in a shadow of their former glory.

Constellations: Slightly Less Lazy Than Cloud Gazing

Why do we learn about stars? The main reason is so we can transform these gigantic, incomprehensibly powerful objects into things like bears and turtles.

These star animals are called "constellations."[1] Though stars have been part of the universe for billions of years, constellations have been part of human culture for thousands of years, so they're undoubtedly more important.

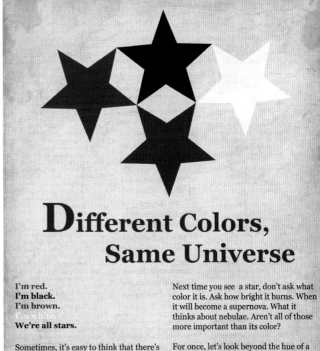

Different Colors, Same Universe

I'm red.
I'm black.
I'm brown.
I'm white.
We're all stars.

Sometimes, it's easy to think that there's one star that's the "right color." We all look at the sun and think that yellow is the way to be. But yellow is just the beginning. Stars are all different colors. But it's the incredibly hot plasma inside them that matters.

Dwarf or giant, stars can be any range of colors, and there may be stars we haven't discovered yet. If you saw a green star, would you accept it as your own?

Next time you see a star, don't ask what color it is. Ask how bright it burns. When it will become a supernova. What it thinks about nebulae. Aren't all of those more important than its color?

For once, let's look beyond the hue of a stellar object that could easily destroy us all, and lets look at the content of this luminous ball with a possibly large portion of degenerative matter.

Every star deserves a chance to burn as brightly as it likes. And every star deserves a chance to be a star. Red. Black. Brown.

All stars, together.

▲ This archival magazine advertisement tried to promote all different colors of stars.

What are constellations? Basically, people connect a random string of stars and pretend that it looks like something. This practice began with the Greeks and stuck from there.[2] Though the sky is too smoggy to see stars anymore, it's easy to look in textbooks and have a similar sense of awe as you turn the page. You'll also be less confused about whether you're seeing the Big Dipper or an airplane.

---

[1] They were called "pretty star pictures" before scientists got involved.

[2] Romans only used constellations for war. They said "Look up there," successfully distracted their opponents, and then beheaded them.

Constellations of the Night Sky

Cousin to the North Star, the Mostly South but Slightly West Star.

Some star patterns are too difficult to interpret. We may never know what this message says.

Greek myth of the man who put things on a shelf he couldn't quite reach.

Man learned to draw in three dimensions when he saw the first 3D cube in the night sky.

The lesser known Invisible Dipper.

It's like a little spaceship, right? Right? You know, the front parts are the lasers and the back is the engine. Do you see it?

The famous "Almost a Triangle" of Orion.

Asteroids: Dinosaur Killers and Heroes

Asteroids are rocks in space that are smaller than planets but larger than most babies. They orbit the sun in asteroid belts[1] and vary greatly in size. For rocks, they get a lot of press.

That's because it's believed that an asteroid killed the dinosaurs. When an asteroid left the sun's orbit millions of years ago, it angrily crashed into Earth. The resulting dust cloud gave the dinosaurs serious allergies. The resulting sneezing and sniffling made each dinosaur too unattractive for breeding. They died out and dinosaurs were never seen again.[2]

We have a lot to thank the asteroids for. That said, there's no reason another asteroid couldn't hit Earth again and create another dust cloud. For that reason, it's recommended that you always walk around with a surgical mask on, just in case.

▲ Thanks to asteroids, dinosaurs are dead. Scientists estimate that it would have taken almost twice as long to kill them with kindness.

Comets: Flying Popsicles of Space

You may also notice comets streaking across the night sky. These icy projectiles shoot through the night in search of an ocean to cool down. However, they never enter Earth's atmosphere, knowing that they would quickly melt anywhere south of Minnesota.

The most famous comet is Halley's Comet. It appears in the sky once every seventy-six years, or about as often as somebody is named "Halley." It can be seen with the naked eye, though you should only watch it while clothed, since you have to be outside to see it. If you're reading this textbook on July 28, 2061, it appeared yesterday and you missed it.

---

[1] It would be too uncomfortable to orbit in suspenders.

[2] Except in museums, movies, toy stores, computer games, and a really remote part of Wyoming.

Shooting Stars: Stars Don't Kill People; Meteors Kill People.

You may hear songs, read poems, and have conversations about "shooting stars." They are all wrong and, over time, should be corrected. For accuracy's sake, you are allowed to write the corrections in any book you find, whether you own it or not.

These "stars" are actually meteoroids when they are in space, meteors when they are in the atmosphere, and collectors' items when they are in a museum. Though it's rare to find a meteor that has survived the crash to Earth, if you do find one it is called a meteorite, and the steaming rock is a cheap way to grill a summer meal.

Meteorites are smaller than asteroids, but they are more commonly associated with the granting of strange powers and introduction of alien civilizations. Is there proof that meteorites can make people fly or help the Xenelex colonize Earth? No. But that's no reason not to try. If you ever find a meteorite, once it has cooled you should always hug, rub, or ingest it on the off chance it will help you lift a car with your bare hands.

> **» SCIENTIFIC FACT**
>
> Meteor showers are great if you like showers that can kill you.

Wishing on Stars: Dangerous and Irresponsible

Unfortunately, the myth of "wishing upon a star" persists in our culture, particularly among those under the age of ten. For many reasons, it's crucial that you dispel this myth as soon as possible.

First, there is no empirical evidence that star-wishing works. Second, the time spent wishing on stars is time that could be used conducting meaningful experiments or charting stellar patterns. The easiest way to make a wish come true is through years of study and an eventual PhD.

How should you tell children that star-wishing is a myth? Just sit them down in your home laboratory, make sure the Bunsen burners are all turned off, and show them a list of wishes that have come true. The list should be a blank piece of paper.

Will the children cry? Of course they will. They will cry tears of knowledge, which makes for a great supplementary lesson about tear ducts.

Our Solar System

For all the size and range of the universe, the part best known to us is the solar system. The solar system is the area under the influence of the sun and includes all of the planets, many moons, and all of Washington, DC. This powerful influence has ensured that the sun will remain legal for years to come.

The Solar System

using the sun to improve your
friendships, love life, finances,
and tan

by christopher benigni

▲ The solar system should not be confused with the classic self-help book.

Why are all these objects under the influence of the sun? Gravitational pull is the reason, as well as tradition. Because the sun is so large, it pulls all the objects in the solar system toward it the same way people crowd to the biggest mall in their suburb. There just aren't any other practical options.[1]

The solar system is also important because it's the area most likely for human exploration. Proximity of moons and planets in the solar system allows us to get close to them, sample them, and see if they contain any signs of life. So far, Earth is the only life-bearing planet in the solar system, but the other planets no doubt have some truly fascinating rocks.[2]

The solar system is also determined by its planets' orbit around the sun. As we circle the sun in the same pattern every year, our own planet gets a tour of the solar system, though it all seems to be the same. Our solar system itself is revolving, however, so there's a chance we might end up somewhere a little warmer or with a better supply of oxygen. Give it a few hundred million years and everything can change quite quickly.

---

[1] Though there may well be other solar systems that have better parking.

[2] Big rocks, small rocks, medium-sized rocks: space is fascinating indeed!

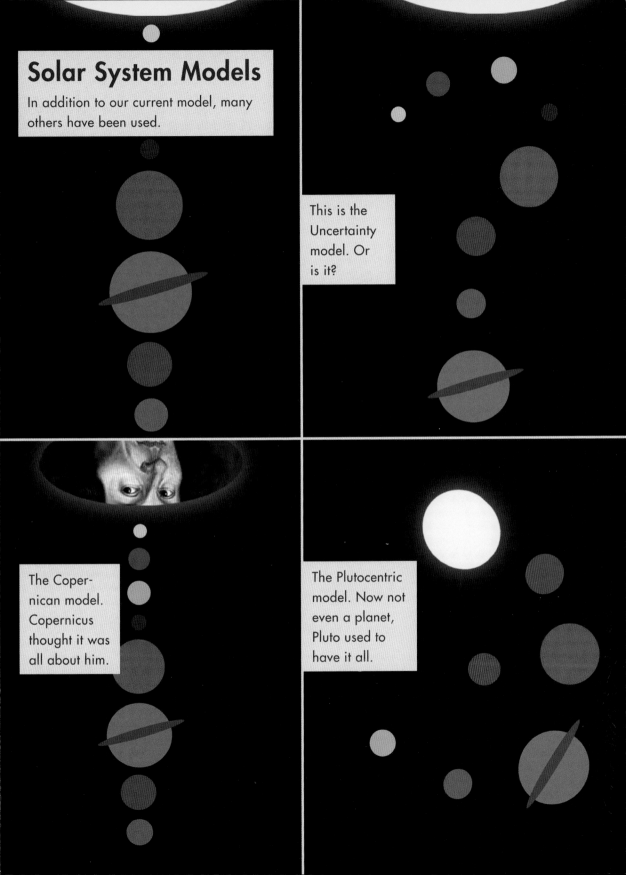

The Sun: Giver of Tans, Life

For millions of years, the sun has been nature's tanning bed. Perfectly calibrated to give humans a soft brown coating and great highlights, the sun's function is not purely cosmetic. It is also the center of the solar system and giver of life to Earth.

The sun is a medium-sized star with a big heart. Its light takes about eight minutes to reach Earth, or nine if it's rush hour. Before the invention of tanning beds, it was the sole source of tanning for the entire Earth. Even now, it remains key if you want even coloring and a nice glow.

Since the Earth revolves around the sun, it remains central to every part of our lives. In daytime, the sun helps us to see so we can drive to the tanning salon. At the same time, it allows us to go to the hardware store to buy light bulbs. At night, the sun goes away so we know when to turn the lights on.

These practical uses for the sun underscore how important it has become in our daily lives. Without the sun, we would have to use much more electricity to light our homes, and the heating costs would be much higher. In addition, solar power would become highly impractical, since we'd have to power our air conditioners using only coal. Thanks to the continued existence of the sun, weathermen don't have to redesign their charts. It's clearly fortunate that we have the sun around, since it makes our lives much more convenient.

That said, there are arguments against the sun, since it isn't just a positive force. If you've ever driven into a sunset, you know that the sun can be terrifically inconvenient. In addition, it's believed to be one of the chief causes behind global warming. As a result, scientists are considering whether the sun should be slightly muted, but the community remains split on just how cold to make it.[1]

» **SCIENTIFIC FACT**

Though often depicted wearing shades, the sun actually never wears them except during photo shoots.

▼ As this diagram shows, the sun's triangular rays are always at exactly 46 degrees.

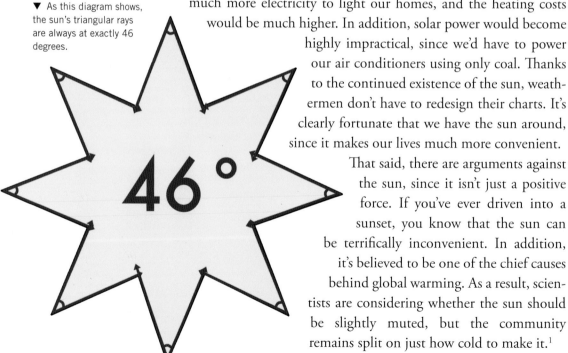

46°

---

[1] Every time one scientist writes a paper suggesting it be 68 degrees, another one changes it to 72.

In addition, though the sun is the perfect distance to give life to Earth, it is far too close to Mercury. Who knows what great things Mercurians might have accomplished were it not for the cruel sun? Perhaps they could be avid textbook readers, but we'll never know because of the sun's indifference to their plight.

Someday, we will learn what would happen without the sun. Eventually, it will burn out from overscheduling. Although this isn't forecast to happen for millions of years, the sun's burnout is something to consider. That's one of the reasons we need to continue developing tanning-bed technology so it can last beyond the sun's extinguishment.

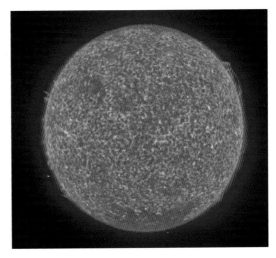

▲ The sun during its lesser known "blue period."

Solar Eclipses: You've Got to See One for Yourself

Occasionally, the sun is hidden by the moon in an event called an eclipse. It's a startlingly beautiful event you have to see for yourself.

For years, the scientific community has kept eclipses secret through the myth that they will make you go blind. As with other "blinding" activities, this story is completely false. As one scientist proclaimed, "I hope an eclipse is the last thing I ever see." Scientists shouldn't have eclipses to themselves.

What makes an eclipse so great? The light is brighter and more intense than any you've ever seen before. If you think you've seen the sun, you haven't even started yet.

Unfortunately, eclipses are all too rare. For this reason, you should bring along everyone you know to look directly at the eclipse. Children, grandparents, babies, and even pets can appreciate the beauty of the sun at its height. And remember: don't blink! You don't want to miss a single second of its glory.

Mercury: The First "Planet"

The planet closest to the sun is Mercury, but as a hot, tiny rock, it's not really the best example. Its orbit around the sun is rapid at about 88 days, but it can't even appreciate the frequent birthdays since nobody is around to celebrate them.

Mercury's surface is rocky, though there are some plains and possibly even ice. However, it's doubtful any of the ice is in usable cubes, and even less likely that it's crushed. The mountainous ranges of Mercury were either created by meteorites and solar winds or by abandoned development projects. There's no way to know which for sure. In any case, it's key to make sure that when a developer signs on to build something, their company has the resources to finish the job.

Rich with minerals, Mercury would be a gold mine for explorers if any of those minerals were gold. Unfortunately, it consists largely of minerals we can find on Earth, but with the negative aspect of being much closer to the deadly fireball that is the sun. For this reason, humans may never explore Mercury, even though the hot and dry climate is good to know about, in case the areas outside Phoenix become overpopulated.

Mercury is not totally useless as a planet. Have you ever used a thermometer? The thermometer contains mercury. Thermometer manufacturers have found that liquid mercury is highly useful in telling whether you have a slight fever or a really bad fever. However, the difficulty of going to the planet and retrieving the mineral has made electronic thermometers more practical.

If you're interested in seeing Mercury, you can spot it from Earth. When it is closest to Earth, it will appear as a tiny rocky ball dwarfed by the sun. If you ever make it to Mercury, it's suspected to smell a little like the inside of a metal lunchbox. No one knows what the planet tastes like, but licking a railing might give you an idea.

> » **SCIENTIFIC FACT**
>
> Mercury was named after the Roman God of Irrelevance.

◀ If Mercury weren't so hot, it might make for some decent bouldering opportunities.

Venus: Sister Planet, If Your Sister Rained Sulfuric Acid

Venus is the second-closest planet to the sun and the planet with the sexiest name. It is also referred to as Earth's "sister planet," though the genealogy is too confusing to accurately trace.[1]

Approximately the same size as Earth, Venus proves that size isn't everything. Covered with volcanoes and plagued by lightning and acid rain, it should only be called a feminine planet if you are a misogynist. There is no sign of plant or animal life on Venus, though there is plenty of lava. The lava may be drinkable because it is liquid, but there's a large chance the heat would be a problem.

Despite the dangers of placing real estate near volcanoes, Venus has been considered for colonization. Some scientists have suggested floating cities could be built in the friendly Venusian atmosphere, 50 kilometers above the surface. Other scientists propose that stationary cities could be built on the ground, as long as they were located millions of miles away and on the planet Earth.[2]

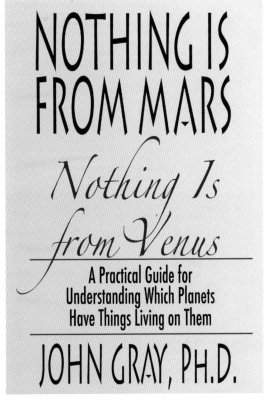

▲ Though more accurate, the first edition of *Men Are from Mars, Women Are from Venus* never became very popular.

Venus is visible in the night sky, as long as you're inside a planetarium. Sometimes it is visible when you're outside as well. How can you find Venus? First, look up. Do you see a bright light? Check that it isn't a street lamp. If it is, look beyond the street lamp and into the sky. If you see a pinprick of light that doesn't move or make a helicopter noise, it's probably Venus.

---

[1] Technically, Earth and Neptune are cousins, but they aren't really close.

[2] Venus could also serve as a prison colony, if the prisoners were being executed.

Earth: Unless You're an Astronaut, You're on It Right Now

Earth is the third planet from the sun, but most people identify it as their top-ranked celestial body. It is home to human life and all the astronauts who try to figure out a way to escape it.

The Earth's place in the solar system greatly affects our daily lives. Did you know that the seasons are caused by the angle of the Earth's rotation around the sun?[1] Or did you realize that day and night are caused by the Earth's rotation around its axle? Even the hours of the day are determined by whether you're traveling through a boring or interesting part of space.

> **» SCIENTIFIC FACT**
>
> Earth is home to the universe's most exclusive dance clubs, except for XIniiar-405QZ.

The Earth itself is shaped a little like a pancake, though the threat of it being eaten is small. It is always at an angle of rotation, which is key to our survival. If the Earth ever turned completely upside down, Americans would be likely to fall off while Australians would thrive.

Even the years are determined by the Earth's revolution around the sun. Each New Year's Eve, we toast and drink champagne to celebrate the safe passage of Earth around the sun. The headache you feel the next morning is, most likely, a result of planetary shifts caused by the start of another trek around the sun.

Often called the Big Blue Marble by people who play marbles, Earth is almost 75 percent water. This is the main reason beachfront property is so popular, simply because there is so much of it around. If we had less water, things might be the other way around, and Nebraska housing would be extremely pricey.

▲ The Earth tilts on its axle, which keeps the angle of its rotation even and adds torque.

Next time you have a difficult day, remember that our Earth is just one planet of many. Hopefully, that thought will inspire you to discover a way to blow up the other planets so that Earth can have the solar system all to itself.

---

[1] In fact, it's also the sun that determined that green is the hot new color this spring. Buy your shawls accordingly.

Our Moon: The Rock with the Most Poetry Written about It

Just as the Earth orbits the sun, the moon orbits the Earth. Meanwhile, another rock known as Gary orbits the moon, but it's best not to give him any additional attention.

Even though it's in space, the moon deeply affects life on Earth. Have you ever swum in the ocean? For years, scientists believed the moon controlled the tides through passive-aggression. However, new studies have shown that the moon controls the tide by dipping deep into the ocean each night. That pushes the water toward our shores for the entirety of the next day.

The moon has different shapes during different parts of the month. This is because the moon is covered by shadows from Earth. It's also the reason the moon frequently appears in the shape of a bunny rabbit, an old man, or a peace sign, since these are the easiest shadows to make.

In Their Words

"Doth moonlight is actually sunlight mirrored, strumpet."

—**WILLIAM SHAKESPEARE, POET AND SCIENTIST**

Shakespeare sought to make his plays entertaining and educational at the same time.

"The moon controls the tide by dipping deep into the ocean each night."

Mars: Red and a Little Puffy

Though Earth may be more important for "existence" and "breathing," it's Mars that captures the popular imagination. Though half the size of Earth, it is perhaps the most similar planet due to its number of syllables.

Known as the "Red Planet" due to rumors about Soviet colonization, Mars also has a reddish tint, which is the reason that we have the "Mars Crayon."[1] The reddish tint comes from the presence of iron oxide on the surface of Mars, which is also the main reason we haven't built any statues there, since they'd rust in addition to attracting pigeons.

Easily visible from Earth, you can see Mars when you are outside at night. If it looks strikingly similar to your shoes, you may be looking down instead of up. Adjust the incline of your neck and make sure you're gazing at the sky. Mars also has two moons of its own. Though these moons aren't easily visible at night, you can point in the general direction and have a chance of being right.

Due to its proximity to Earth, humans have explored Mars through the use of able and willing robots.[2] We have sampled the soil, but it isn't worthy of purchase. We also have taken many pictures on the surface of the planet. These pictures have shown that, for all their strengths, robots don't have a great sense of framing. It also puts doubt on the actual color of Mars, since it might be a large-scale case of red-eye.

The atmosphere, climate, and highways of Mars are not as friendly as those on Earth, but they do show promise. Scientists have also found water on Mars' surface with taste equivalent to most tap water found on Earth. For these reasons, it's easy to speculate that Mars may have carried life in the past and could well sustain it in the future. Will humans live on Mars? If so, they may require a new wardrobe for better color coordination with the ground. Martian tones aren't as nice as Earth tones.

▲ If you want to be polite, you can call Mars the "Planet with a Healthy Glow."

---

[1] Mars is between umber and maroon, with a dash of Saturn.

[2] Unlike humans, these robots are not allowed to say things to commemorate their work in space. This is expected to be a major grievance when robots become sentient in 2034.

Is There Life on Mars?

Believers point to this picture, taken by the Viking 1 robot, as proof that a Bigfoot-like creature lives on Mars. Skeptics, however, insist that it is simply a Martian prankster in a Bigfoot suit.

Great Scientists

History's Most Memorable Forgotten Names

Name: Ned Kerrey
Scientific Field: Space exploration safety tester
Greatest Strength: Tolerance for pain
Greatest Weakness: Can't say no
Greatest Discovery: Learned that seven hours in a gyroscope is bad for you

Though we normally think of laboratory rats and other small animals as the pioneers in man's journey to space, human test subjects are equally crucial. And, until his accidental death, Ned Kerrey was one of the best.

Serving in the 1950s and 1960s, Kerrey was a flat-footed, shortsighted astronomer who had difficulty with cardinal directions, which made it hard for him to find the North Star. However, he was willing to serve, so NASA made him a space exploration tester.

Kerrey spent over a decade testing the psychological and physical effects of space travel on humans without the distraction of going to or seeing space. Beginning in a desert in New Mexico, he spent up to four hours at a time upside down and the rest of the time sideways. Using this information, scientists determined that blood does indeed rush to the head and cause irreparable damage.

Since astronauts live in close quarters, Kerrey had to as well. However, since no other humans volunteered, he bunked with Chip, the third chimpanzee to visit the moon. His interactions with Chip taught NASA much about the difficulty in sharing close spaces and food with possibly rabid monkeys.

Kerrey also tested food, including dehydrated ice cream, dehydrated steak, and dehydrated water. Through repeated testing, he lost the ability to process normal food, but he did teach scientists that bouillon cubes should always have a little extra salt.

The final stage of Kerrey's training took him to a weightless environment underwater. There he studied the effects of weightlessness on the body and water on the brain. His storied career ended during the same study, when he made his final discovery: he couldn't swim.

Jupiter: Full of Cold Air

Our solar system's largest planet is Jupiter. Known as a "gas giant," this planet is composed almost entirely of air, making it closer to a balloon than Earth.[1] Still, it's notable for being larger in size than all of the other planets combined, which puts it first in line to replace the sun should it pursue other interests.

Composed of hydrogen, helium, clouds, and other gases, Jupiter is believed to have some water in its atmosphere or surface. That allows for the possibility that fish may have evolved there. Though there's no data of any sort to support this theory, it's probably true. How can we prepare for an onslaught from the fish people of Jupiter? For one, many recommend that we limit our consumption of fish sticks in public places. Second, we should make sure that tuna fishing expeditions stop catching both dolphins and tuna.[2]

Geographically, Jupiter is perhaps best known for its Great Red Spot. Created by the same oily conditions that produce acne, this Great Red Spot has blighted the face of the planet for millions of years, even though scientists thought it was just a phase. A faint planetary ring surrounds Jupiter as well, though it might just be a stain.

Scientists have analyzed the planet's core and found it to be surprisingly dense. That is compounded by Jupiter's magnetic pull. In fact, much solar detritus is pulled in by Jupiter and tugged to its gassy surface. This bodes well for Jupiter as a stellar landfill in the future. Humans may have an entirely new planet to dump their trash on. The magnetic field will let us dump it from a distance, which is good for hiding it from the fish people.

> **» SCIENTIFIC FACT**
>
> Jupiter has at least sixty-three moons, so the phrase "once in a blue moon" is useless there.

▲ We could almost cover Jupiter's unsightly Great Red Spot if we converted 500 Asias into a Band-Aid.

---

[1] Though Jupiter is known as a gas giant, that name may soon be trademarked by a major natural gas company. Lacking lawyers, Jupiter may be renamed a "matter state numerary."

[2] Sadly, Voyager robots sent to Jupiter are not able to convey what it smells like.

Saturn: Put a Ring on It

Named after a now-defunct car company, Saturn is the sixth planet from the sun and is best known for its rings. Large icy rings surround the planet, and it's believed that one of the world's largest diamonds is on the other side.[1] These icy rings serve as the template for our own ice skating rinks, though it would require a lot of hot chocolate to make it all the way around.

Saturn is a gas giant second only to Jupiter, and it also has one less moon than Jupiter. While some say the rings are overcompensation for these shortcomings, you can also argue that they're essential to making Saturn stand out. After all, it's easy to remember "the one with the rings."

Some signs point to an electric current within Saturn's atmosphere. Though not a sign of life, it is a potential indication of lightning and other phenomenon. If mankind ever colonized the planet, we could use this electricity for wall clocks and household fans. It could be done with effort and a few million years.

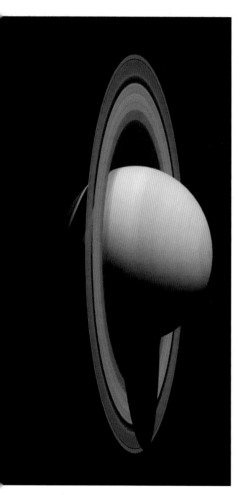

▲ Saturn, if you've turned your head sideways. It's important to be able to recognize the planets from any angle.

Uranus Gives Hope for Science

Uranus is a planet that's far away from the sun. It's icy. In many ways, it is considered an unremarkable planet without the size of Jupiter or beauty of Saturn.

However, the scientific community has been stunned by the positive response young people have when they hear this planet's name. Normally more interested in video games and television than science, a recent survey of seventh-graders named Uranus as their favorite planet by far.

As a result, it's key we encourage interest in Uranus for all future scientists out there. Uranus is a great entry point for inquiring minds, and without it there would be a gaping hole in scientific study. As Sir William Herschel, who discovered Uranus, once said, "One thing in our universe deserves intensive study and endless probing, and that is Uranus."

---

[1] Don't think about buying Saturn, since it would cost 3 billion months' salary.

If you're a science teacher, consider holding an entire day of activities centered around Uranus. A poetry reading, story time, or intensive study of Uranus will no doubt inspire wild giggles of knowledge. In a cynical time, we should do anything we can to inspire a lifetime of passion for Uranus.

Neptune: The Final Planet, Predictably Anticlimactic

The last planet in our solar system is Neptune. Colored like a blueberry lollipop, Neptune is too far away for us to visit. There's a reasonable chance that Neptune's chilly surface is made of a compound of carbon, hydrogen, and oxygen, also known as sugar. For that reason, it's known as the "dessert" of the solar system.[1]

Extremely cold and large, Neptune is the period to our solar system's sentence. A final planet, it is the end of our boundaries, not our opportunities.[2] Who knows what other planets, edible or not, may lie beyond our tiny cul-de-sac of the universe?

However, there is more in the solar system. Sadly, it's necessary that we discuss Pluto. Formerly a planet, this "thing" is now a dwarf planet considered a mere cog in an outer asteroid belt. To say it's awkward would be an understatement. But such is the process of science: constantly defining and redefining the categories of objects that are millions of miles away.

As we conclude our study of the solar system, it is an apt time to reflect upon all you have learned. Do you have a favorite planet? If you had to explode one planet, which would it be? Finally, is the sun overrated?

These are questions that can only be answered as we leave our Earthly hamlet and explore the universe ourselves.[3] Let's learn what other phenomena lie beyond and see how we get there.

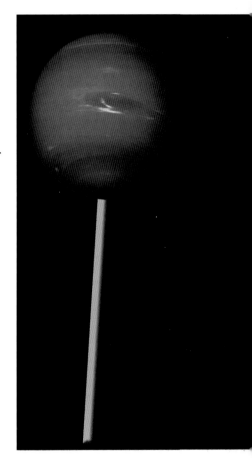

▲ A beautiful shade of blue, Neptune is easily the most lickable planet.

---

[1] There is no appetizer. The universe is not that fancy.

[2] Opportunities end when you fail a test.

[3] Or in libraries through textbooks.

Exploring Our Universe

Now you finally understand absolutely everything about the universe. What next? Instead of taking a trip to the tanning salon, consider an equally momentous journey: a trip into space.

Humans have been exploring space for millions of years, and they won't stop anytime soon.[1] Whether it's looking at the night sky through a high-powered telescope[2] or investigating aliens in the deserts of New Mexico, there are countless ways to kill time noodling around our universe. You can even build your own rocket ship, as long as you have a competent engineering team and $1.7 billion.

Why bother exploring space instead of just looking at it? Have you ever been to an art museum? Who would be satisfied just looking at a da Vinci or Salvador Dali painting? Instead, we touch them, smell them, and press our bodies against them to experience them fully. Space delivers the same imperative to smudge it fully.

---

[1] Unless they get bored.

[2] Far superior to using a microscope.

What to Bring to the Planetarium

A planetarium is like a movie theater, except without the popcorn, drinks, and movies. Instead, you get to watch lights projected against a ceiling.

The next time you go to a planetarium, be prepared. Because these buildings are meant to simulate space, bring along rocks, bright lights to simulate the sun, more rocks, some magnets to create gravitational fields, and fans to simulate solar winds. Be ready to throw everything around to echo the universe's chaos.

The Competition to Exit the Atmosphere First (Also Known as the Space Race)

For hundreds of years, man has tried to leave Earth and enter space. The first rocket ships were built in the Victorian era, but since they were made of wood they failed quickly. Progress stalled during the Civil War, World War I, and World War II, since scientists were more interested in sending rockets sideways than upwards. But aeronautics developed sufficiently to kick off the great space race.[1]

> **» SCIENTIFIC FACT**
>
> Canadian scientists considered exploring space, but they were too polite to insult the atmosphere by leaving it.

During this era, the Soviet Union and United States of America[2] drove each other to new heights of exploration, initially through seeing who could jump higher. Once it was clear that a pole vault competition wouldn't resolve their differences, they each decided to spend billions on missions outside the Earth's atmosphere.

The Soviets struck first with the launch of their satellite Sputnik[3] in 1957. Suddenly, it was clear that the space race was an uneven match. The United States shouted, "You cheated!" at the Russians, but the world did not listen, even though it was completely unfair. As a result, the United States responded by launching its own satellite later and claiming they just hadn't felt like launching one first.

▲ Soviet scientists never launched these colorful rocket ships.

What did the satellites teach us? Satellites performed two key functions. First, they proved that is was possible to send something into space, as long as it was a tiny metal ball that could float around. Second, they showed the innate human excitement for the "space race," though that may have been because special effects in the 1950s weren't very good yet. Still, Russia's launching of Sputnik ignited a competition that would send many different objects, creatures, and people into space, most of which were impressively expensive.

---

[1] The space race refers to the competition to reach space, not the race of people that are interested in aliens, gadgets, and invented languages.

[2] If the order offends you, feel free to say the United States of America and the Soviet Union.

[3] Sputnik continues to broadcast Russian television today.

Tricking Animals to Go Into Space First

Now that man had sent metal objects into space, it was time for humans to go themselves. However, they were incredibly scared. Thus pets became the first pioneers and victims of space travel. Typically, the space race escalated the stakes.

The Russians began the race by placing a goldfish inside a plastic bag in Sputnik. The goldfish died by the third hour in space, but it was difficult to tell if that was because it was in space or because it was a goldfish. Challenged, the Americans sent the first hamster into space. Sadly, hamster wheels require gravity to function and the hamster quickly gained weight. Though the environment was weightless, the hamster's increased girth made it unable to manipulate the controls of the space ship. The $2.3 trillion rocket was lost forever.

As the animals grew more intelligent, it became necessary to trick them into going on their missions, since they were as scared as the humans. Soviet escalation sent the first dog into space. They threw a ball into a rocket ship, the dog ran after it, and then they slammed the door. However, the dog was wagging his tail at lift off, so he was very happy before he died a few hours later. Americans sent their own dog to space in subsequent weeks. However, he had associations with some Hollywood personalities and was blacklisted from returning to the atmosphere. A second dog fared better after a routine test to make sure he supported capitalism and apple pie.

The final animal to be sent into space was a chimpanzee. Biologically similar to humans, this chimpanzee was the best test to see if a man could survive the rigors of space. Lured by the promise of bananas, 1,400 chimpanzees gave their lives for the space program. Once one survived, astronauts knew that they could go into space next, without having to even bring bananas along.

> **» SCIENTIFIC FACT**
>
> Scientists considered using guinea pigs as space guinea pigs, but they agreed they were too cute.

▲ Rover, the second Space Dog, is the reason we call space robots "rovers" today. Sadly, Rover died due to an ejector seat malfunction.

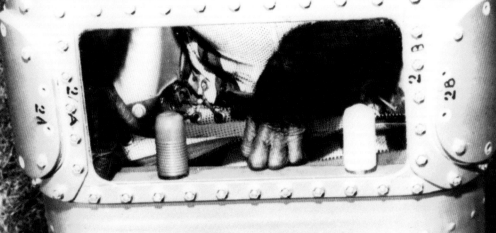

The First Chimpanzee in Space

It was easy enough to lure the first chimpanzee into serving his country.

FREE BANANAS

UNLATCH COVER
WHEN NOT IN USE

Raising Money

As the space program sought funding, alternative means of raising money were used.

Sending Man Where Only Chimpanzees Had Gone Before

After years of testing spacecraft for animals, all of the animals were dead. Since the space program could no longer lure animals into rocket ships, they had to send humans. Thus the space race cleared its first hurdle.[1]

The respective space programs began sending brave men and women higher and higher. In the United States, these pioneers were called "astronauts" in honor of the dog Astro on the popular television program *The Jetsons*. Meanwhile, in the Soviet Union, they were called "cosmonauts" in honor of the cat Cosmo on the popular television program *Stalin's Hour for Work and Truth*.

Sadly, the Russians beat the United States into space. Famous Soviet corpse Vladimir Lenin was sent into space, where the weightlessness helped him look extremely lifelike. Following that, Yuri Gagarin went into space and returned alive and well, though he still spoke in Russian instead of English.

The United States quickly caught up with the Russian forces, however. At first, American astronauts considered sending small children into space due to their lighter weights. This would have saved both fuel and food for the American space program and cut an estimated $300 from the $78 billion budget. But the program had to be scrapped when it turned out that developing a space yo-yo for the children cost an additional $300 million.

That setback didn't last long though. A few months after Gagarin's flight, Alan Shepard launched into space, with the help of a rocket ship. His successful flight proved that the United States could do anything the Russians could and do it with more American-sounding names. As the programs of each country improved, so did the achievements.[2] Soon, sending men and women into space wouldn't be enough. The space race had a finish line: Mars. The first country to reach Mars would be victorious and technologically superior. However, the moon was established as a consolation prize, since man might reach it two or three years before getting to Mars.

» **SCIENTIFIC FACT**

Although animals frequently went into space, they fared poorly when installed in the control room.

---

[1] Interestingly, having a rocket clear a hurdle was the first test of any new propulsion system. Most failed.

[2] However, it would still be years until the space milkshake was successfully developed.

The Moon Becomes American

After years of painstaking effort, the United States was finally ready to send a man to the moon. The so-called Apollo program, named for the Roman God of Rocket Thrusters, had succeeded in bringing man closer and closer to his goal of putting his footprints somewhere new. Finally, a crew was selected.

In Their Words

"One small step for man, one giant leap for mankind. Wait. No. That's not right. I mean, one leap for a man, one giant steps on mankind. No. Um. One small pet for Stan, one giant leek and we dine. Crap. One more. One stall wet for man, one guy sweeps with pine. You know what, can we just edit this?"

—NEIL ARMSTRONG, FIRST MAN ON THE MOON

Neil Armstrong famously bungled the first radio broadcast from the moon, after which it was heavily edited.

Neil Armstrong, Michael Collins, "Buzz" Aldrin, "Skip" Forrester, "Zip-A-Dee-Doo-Dah" Blankenship, and "Kerpow" Franklin were all selected. At the last minute, NASA realized it could only fit three astronauts on the ship, so the first three went and the last three were sent to Costa Rica for R&R.

It was truly a historic time in that summer of 1969. On Earth, the so-called hippies were smoking mud and swimming in marijuana.[1] The country was embroiled in war in Vietnam, which didn't even have a space program. And the Soviets were busily trying to send their own man to the moon to serve the first bowl of borscht there. No one knew what would happen next, except that it would have a good soundtrack. Could the United States achieve its dream and discover if the man on the moon was simply a myth?

It was a hot day, and the chimpanzees sweat in their orange spacesuits. Controllers in Houston wiped their sweaty brows, though that was just because it was Houston. But in time, America lifted off for the moon first. The rest is history.

While on the moon, man conducted many important studies. Astronaut Armstrong took samples of the lunar surface, and, as expected, it tasted quite chalky. He left footprints in the surface as well, despite strict orders to keep his shoes on. Finally, he carefully documented the landing with photographs, audio recordings, and a brief interpretive dance.

---

[1] Possibly the other way around.

America Reaches the Moon First

Except for one minor packing error, the first moon mission went flawlessly.

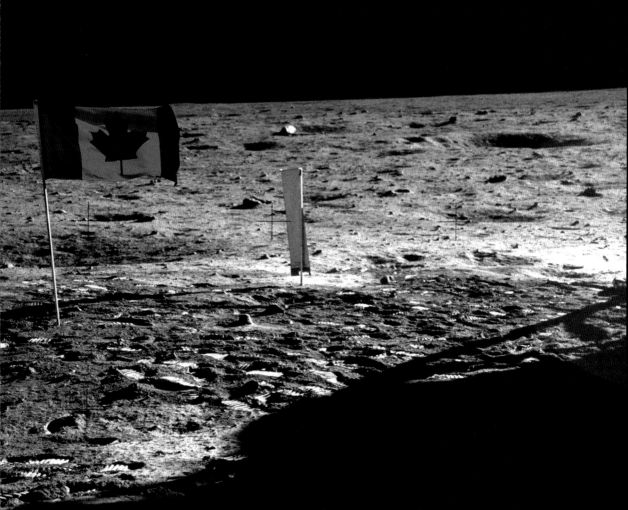

Figuring Out Other Stuff to Do on the Moon

With one man sent to the moon, the United States saw no reason to stop. Subsequent missions to the moon gave more astronauts a chance to say they moonwalked, which greatly helped their chances with the women of Earth.[1] In addition, it allowed them to make sure that the whole thing hadn't just been a dream.

Returning to the moon allowed scientists to test many new things. They learned what it was like to golf on the moon, eat a banana on the moon, have a small but competitive badminton tournament on the moon, and bicycle on the moon. They even found women's bikes worked well due to lower lunar gravity. These tasks taught the people of Earth much about the moon and also looked really cool. Moon missions continued until man ran out of humorous sports to play on it.

» **SCIENTIFIC FACT**

Only Americans have been to the moon, but citizens of almost every other country have seen it.

[1] Having been to the moon is a great ice-breaker in Houston-area bars.

"*They even found women's bikes worked well due to lower lunar gravity.*"

Beyond the Moon: Improving Earth and Space

With the moon successfully conquered, mankind struggled to decide what to do next. The sun was too hot, Mars was too far away, and though flying from Tampa to Moscow was a great trip, it wasn't that technologically impressive.[1]

In response to the pressure to visit new lands, more countries joined the fray. Eventually, the United Kingdom sent a man into space in hopes of making the universe a little more dignified. Much later, China conducted a space voyage of its own, largely to try to make its own country less populous. Neither of these countries journeyed to the moon, presumably because they'd seen the flag and assumed that it was taken.[2] Meanwhile, the United States led the way by sending robots to do the work that men had once done.[3] Advancements in technology made this easier than ever before and allowed robots to find new and exciting places to put flags.

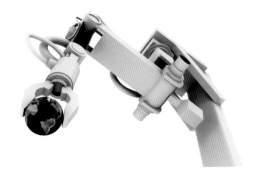

▲ When it comes to robots, there's nothing to worry about. Nothing at all.

The space program's dividends, however, are not restricted to the celestial climes of space. Dehydrated food became incredibly popular as a result of the space missions, and the popular sugar drink Tang was invented for astronauts and has proved a boon to dentists in the years since. In addition, many technologies we take for granted can plausibly be credited to the space program.[4] Perhaps you've consumed a TV dinner as you sit down for a pleasant five or six hours in front of the television. That was a result of astronauts who lived in close quarters and got sick of talking to each other.

Even as man approaches the limits of space, our exploration still pays off in our daily lives, especially if you're an astronaut.

---

[1] Even without a layover.

[2] The United Nations may eventually send diplomats into space in the hope of using their extraordinary parking privileges.

[3] Many working-class astronauts complained that these same robots were putting them out of a job.

[4] Less plausibly, we can say that other inventions before the space program existed were deposited in the past by the space program's team of time travelers.

The Future of Astronomy and Space Exploration: Space Frozen Yogurt and More

There's one question on the lips of scientists and the tiny metal pincers of robots: What's next?

▲ We can only hope that, someday, convenient shopping centers like these will be built on Mars.

No one knows for sure where astronomy and space exploration will take us next. Scientists continue to innovate. New space shuttles allow rockets to use the vastly more efficient carpool lane when traveling to the cosmos and beyond. Newer and better computers will allow us to calculate tips quickly at 15 or 20 percent, should we eat out in space. Finally, the International Space Station makes space affordable, thanks to rent control.

Some suggest that man will colonize other planets. It is a possibility, if you've had a bit to drink. The discovery of AstroTurf bodes well for us to inhabit strange new worlds and improve them through the addition of both water parks and water. Some even speculate that Mars could become livable through a process called "terraforming." Terraforming means that we make other planets more like Earth.[1] It's hoped that through the addition of strip malls, roller-skating rinks, and the Chrysler Building, the rest of Mars would gradually adjust. Perhaps our grandchildren will live on Mars and look at our blue planet as they speak of their grandparents, killed long ago by plague and civil unrest on Earth. The future is indeed bright.

Even meeting extraterrestrial life is a possibility within our lifetimes. Do you think aliens will be kind and wise or intelligent and friendly? It's something to think about the next time you look up at the stars and then wake up in a cornfield the next day with no memory of the previous twelve hours.

Even though you now know all the answers of the universe, your journey is not over. Continue to look up at the night sky and wonder who is up there, what they are doing, and if they'll wave back. The stars are limitless, and so are the possibilities.[2]

---

[1] The word *terra* meant "earth," or "land," in Latin, which is why all terraformed planets' citizens would be required to speak Latin.

[2] Actually, there is a limit to the possibilities. Each person receives 318.

Chapter 2 Quiz: Astronomy

Multiple Choice

1. Which is biggest?

   a. The universe
   b. A family-sized van
   c. A really big stadium
   d. A breadbox

2. How did the universe form?

   a. Lots of yeast
   b. A large mold, later used for Jell-O
   c. It asked other universes for advice
   d. It remains a corporate secret, patent pending

3. Which of these happened in a parallel universe?

   a. The universe is called the "monoverse" and can be contracted from kissing or using water fountains
   b. JFK's initials are FKJ
   c. Squares have three sides
   d. The French Revolution ended with a cake party

4. Why do we live in the Milky Way?

   a. The calcium helps our bones
   b. Moving to the Poison Way seems like a bad idea
   c. The dog can't walk itself
   d. Good schools

5. What makes a star?

   a. Helium, a wish, and a prayer
   b. Marketing
   c. A desperate need for attention
   d. Networking

6. Which of these is a planet in our solar system?

   a. Nougat
   b. Neptune
   c. Stevie Wonder
   d. Pluto

7. What was the space program's greatest accomplishment?

   a. Mooning Earth from the Moon
   b. Leaving footprints and initials on the lunar surface
   c. Space bacon
   d. Pictures of Earth that look great on calendars

Short Answer

1. Looking at space can be a fulfilling mental exercise. Go outside now, look up, and memorize the stars. Then draw each one here once you've returned.

_____
_____
_____
_____
_____

2. The space program is looking for new astronauts all the time. How would you explore space and, if you did, would you promise to bring us something back?

_____
_____
_____
_____

3. Aliens: Real, or totally real?

_____
_____
_____
_____

Essay Questions

1. You know our universe well. Imagine an entirely new universe. How would you design it, including the galaxies, chemical makeup, arrangement of stars, and development of planets? Don't worry about the details, but do include every single one.

2. Astronauts have to deal with deep questions, whether they're looking into space or exploring it. Use the rest of your time to design a new, sexy spacesuit that would look great in space and on the runway.

BIOLOGY

EVEN GROSSER THAN YOU THOUGHT

Before You Start This Chapter . . .

- Learn how to operate a microscope, or at least pretend convincingly.
- Purchase some hand sanitizer, as well as entire-body sanitizer.
- Become familiar with human anatomy, beyond looking at yourself in the mirror.
- Get some new shoes. No, it's not related to biology, but would it kill you to look nice every once in a while?
- Hunt down a few endangered species so you'll have fewer names to learn.
- Drink eight glasses of water to stay hydrated, since eight boxes of water would get too soggy.
- Talk to your plants, since your dog stopped listening to you years ago.
- Clone yourself and give your clone enough money to buy another copy of this book.

The Most Alive of Sciences

Biology is everywhere, except in places where nothing lives.

From the smallest ant to the biggest ant, biology is in play. From the Greek words *bios*, which means "life," and *logy*, which means "dissection is mandatory," biology is the study of all forms of life on the planet. Whether it's a tiny bacteria or a giant elephant that the bacteria ultimately kills, biology is the discipline that helps us study it all.

Biology began when people looked around and asked two simple questions: What is life? And why is it biting my leg? From that point on, man set out to discover the mysteries of life on Earth and, in turn, discover a way to heal that bite on its leg.

When we study biology, we try to discover the origins of ourselves and the things that we like to eat. How does parsley grow? In what way do cows reproduce? Where do potatoes grow best? And in what ratio should they be combined, and then grilled, to make a great meal that will really fill in all the cracks?

Biologists are curious about all life in ways that usually aren't too creepy. Through careful observation and hourly blood samples, it is possible to learn the secrets of life, or at least the trivia of life. With that knowledge gained, biologists can start assigning Latin names to everything in sight, even if those things are only found in Asia.

Our understanding of biology has changed much through the millennia. We can analyze, describe, and understand biological phenomena more easily than ever before, though it's still hard to get the smell off our clothes. Let's learn about the phenomena that keep our world alive, and discover new ways to dissect it.

▲ Biology answers big questions. The chicken or the egg: which tastes better?

Life: Probably a Good Thing

Cells: Tiny, Complex, and Squishy

Cells are the building blocks of life.[1] Since cells were named and discovered by Michael Cell, these tiny organisms have been the engines behind animal life, plant life, and mobile telephones. You have trillions of cells in your body and are making new ones all the time. That's the reason it's possible to donate your own plasma for money—your body is always making new cells for you to sell.

▲ While we're on the subject, this is a prison cell. Please stay in school.

---

[1] Cells are the building blocks of life unless you're reading the Chemistry chapter (life comes from elements), the Physics chapter (life comes from atoms), the Astronomy chapter (life comes from the Big Bang), or the Introduction (life comes from reading this book).

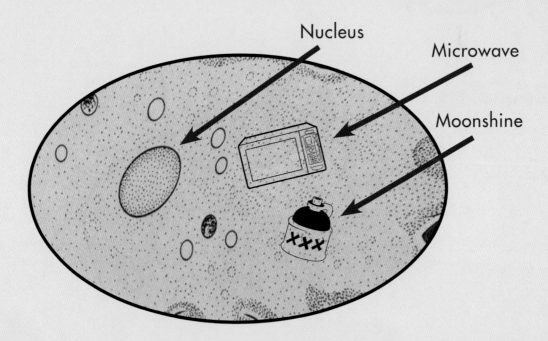

A Cell Contains Everything It Needs to Live

Nucleus

Microwave

Moonshine

Cells: Power Plants Without Unionized Employees

Cells work because they are like tiny power plants, except without the meter readers. Each cell has the materials to make energy, reproduce, and float in an amorphous blob for as long as it wants.

Our Bodies, Our Cells

However, not every cell is alike. The two main cell types are prokaryotic and eukaryotic. Because the cell names are derived from ancient Greek, no one knows what they mean. But archaeologists are working hard to find the answers.

The most important cells have a nucleus. The nucleus is the center of the cell and makes the other parts extremely jealous.

The nucleus is where the term "nuclear family" comes from, and it means that the cell has a stable home life led by a strong patriarchal figure. For this reason, many cells keep a picture of Dwight D. Eisenhower around at all times.

Boundless Knowledge

Looking at Cells

When you're learning about cells, you'll be looking at stained slides. Scientists look at cells before people trust them to look at anything.

However, you'll gain great knowledge from looking at these tiny dots through your microscope. If you're lucky, you may even contract pinkeye from the dirty eyepiece. You'll get to analyze your own cells later on, assuming you can still see.

Inside the Cell: Goo and More Goo

Cell parts are called organelles, named after Motown's most famous biological lab. They include:

Cytoplasm: A formless and shapeless goo frequently used in movie slime and hair gel. Because it holds cells together, you should dunk your baby in it at least once a month.

Mitochondria: The chemical engines of cells that convert useless matter into slightly less useless matter.

Flagella: Tiny fingers that help cells move; these are the "creepy uncle" of the cellular world. Whenever you feel a small tickling sensation, you are probably being fondled by bacterial flagella. Multiple lawsuits are pending.

Ribosomes: These parts manufacture proteins and, as a result, are a key ingredient in Muscle Milk. Steroid investigations plague their reputation.

Cell Wall: Though vital to the cell's survival, cell walls are usually so thin that the next cell's music keeps everybody up at night.

»**SCIENTIFIC FACT**

Our bodies make cells constantly, so feel free to destroy them whenever the urge strikes you.

▶ It's probably easier to dunk your baby in cytoplasm than get her to take a nap.

How Cells Reproduce: Parental Guidance Recommended

Understanding how cells reproduce is the key to understanding all life. In *mitosis*, cells duplicate and break into two identical parts. This is the same way most fast food is made.

Meiosis is a similar process dedicated to the production of the sperm and egg. It's slightly different from mitosis and attracts significant attention. Indeed, outside of science laboratories, entire industries have been created to watch the reproductive processes of humans, although most of them require a subscription before viewing. Have you spent time in your local lab watching meiosis? If not, what are you waiting for? Many are open 24 hours.

In Their Words

"Mmm, yeah, you know daddy likes to watch you split that nucleus."

—ROBERT HOOKE, DISCOVERER OF CELL REPRODUCTION

Reproductive biologists watch cells reproduce over and over again, usually in a very dark room.

You may be wondering why cell reproduction matters at all, especially if it isn't your thing. Cell reproduction is important because each time a cell is built, an organism grows or is created. Cells are the "bricks" in the "tanning salons" of life. By understanding cell reproduction, we understand how our bodies survive and flourish, despite how we treat them.

Even cells in our bodies are replaced through reproduction. Your nails grow because of cellular reproduction, and your hair and hair dye do the same thing. Have you ever had a sense of déjà vu? Scientists speculate it's due to cellular replication in the brain. Your brain cells multiply an experience so that, when it happens the first time, you think it happened already. That also explains why your face looks so familiar.

▲ This scientist told his wife he was going to the lab to "do some paperwork." Five hours later, he'd watched almost 2,000 cells reproduce.

Mitosis: When Cells Break Up

Stage

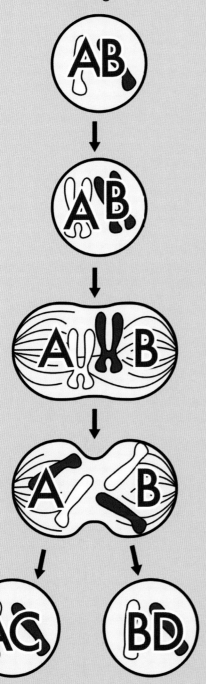

Process

B: Jack?
A: Yes, Nadine?
B: Do you think we'll be together forever?
A: I knew from the moment I met you.
B: You didn't answer the question.
A: Maybe you shouldn't have asked it.

A: Well, that was a nice dinner with the Harrisons.
B: I could tell you liked it.
A: What is that supposed to mean?
B: Don't tell me you didn't spend the whole night looking at Patty's mitochondria!

B: All I'm saying is that they're my chromosomes, so I'm keeping them in my part of the cell!
A: This is our cell, damn it, not yours.
B: There was a time when I believed you. Now I think Bertram knows more about my ribosomes.

A: Your flagella have been out of control, Nadine.
B: Like your flagella haven't been wiggling?
A: That's not true.
B: Sometimes I cry at night. All you do is roll over in your cytoplasm.

A: I love you Patty. I'm glad Nadine is gone.
B: I'm happy now, Bertram. I don't miss Jack.
A: I'll never split again.
B: I'll never split again.

Microorganisms: Making the Most of a Single Cell

Normally, cells are just part of a bigger, more impressive organism. Sometimes, however, we pretend that they can do the work themselves. These are called microorganisms.[1] They are all around us and probably crawling on your skin right now.

A microorganism can do a lot of impressive things, especially if you are easily impressed. Though they only have one cell, a single microorganism can fell an empire, especially if that empire is made of bread or led by a really infirm, immunodeficient baby.

In Their Words

"Oh no, I totally realized mold would make penicillin. Completely intentional. What, do you think I just forgot I left my orange in the lab?"

—ALEXANDER FLEMING, DISCOVERER OF PENICILLIN

Alexander Fleming discovered that fungus could kill bacteria, and he insisted he meant to do it.

There's a Fungus Among Us

Let's start by learning about the mold in your refrigerator, bathroom, and other moist parts of your life.

This mold is called a "fungus." You may be familiar with larger fungi like mushrooms or, if you are unemployed, "shrooms." However, there are many different single-celled types of fungi. The study of these fungi is called "fungology." Many scientists were tricked into studying fungi by the name, since they assumed it was the study of fun.

You can find single-celled fungi everywhere in your life. For example, baker's yeast is a single-celled fungus that tastes delicious in bread, pizza dough, and other moldy concoctions.

◀ If you're curious what fungi tastes like, it's easy for you to find out at home.

---

[1] Pronounced "me-croor-ga-nisms."

If you've ever seen moldy bread, remember that it's made from fungus in the first place, so you can feel free to eat until you are content.

Even medicines are made from these microorganisms. Discovered by Alexander Fleming after he tried using dirt, trash, and leftover spaghetti to cure diseases, penicillin has saved countless lives. If you've ever taken penicillin, you've had a juicy helping of mold. Unfortunately, the composition of this powerful drug created a large black market in some parts of the country. Moldy refrigerators exist in large banks in rural America, and law enforcement is constantly trying to shut these penicillin factories down. If you see someone with green stains on their lips, walk away; they're probably an antibiotic junkie.

> **» SCIENTIFIC FACT**
>
> Most beers are fermented through the use of fungi, which explains why too much makes people vomit.

Viruses: Back Massagers of Death

Look down and to the right. A simple back massager, right?

Wrong.

After a long day at the office, you may think you can rub this across your neck and feel some relief from a stressful day. That would be a deadly mistake.

Thousands have died from trying to use viruses to soothe their aching backs. The influenza virus killed millions, and those who didn't die found that the flu made their backs sorer.

Viruses, however, are not cells. Because these microorganisms lack a nucleus and a soul, they can only replicate in other cells. They're known as the "leeching roommate" of the biosphere.

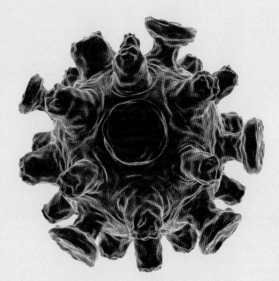

Fortunately, it's easy to avoid viruses. If you're ever looking through your microscope and you see a tempting back massager on the slide, don't rub it against your body. There's a 99 percent chance it will be a virus, though it's true that a nice back massage would really hit the spot.

The Mighty Plant: Some Sun Required

Any study of biology should touch upon plants, the source for almost all of mankind's salads.[1] This study is called "botany," or "plantology," depending on your schooling. Plants are all around us, and they provide us with incredible food sources and lots of shade. Have you ever seen the thin green spikes that lie next to the road? Even those have a name, though it slips our mind at the moment.

What is a plant? Plants are easily defined by what they cannot do. Since they are relatively defenseless, they are easier to kill. Plants generally do not move, though they might move if their owner bothers to pack them into the moving truck. Finally, plants usually do not eat other plants or animals, a strategy that doesn't seem to prevent it from happening to them.[2]

Let's learn a little about the science behind common plants.

Moss: Nature's Shag Carpet

The first category of plant is moss. Moss is a flat plant that covers rocks and land quickly, like slime but soft. New Zealand is covered entirely in this soft, fabric-like plant, which allows its people to travel barefoot wherever they go.

Moss may seem like a simple plant, but as most plants are, it is used in many innovative ways. Native cultures often use moss to dress wounds, since wounds look good in green. Many houses use moss as insulation against the cold as well. The natural density of moss traps heat and that pleasant wet-plant smell. Finally, you can always decorate your home in moss, as long as you have the aesthetic sensibilities of a gnome.

---

[1] Except the Bacon 'N Rocks Caesar Salad.

[2] If you ever feel plants might be getting too confident, consider snapping a tree branch and growling just to keep them in place.

The Venus Puppy Trap

Though most plants receive energy from the sun, the infamous Venus Puppy Trap lures in innocent canines before clamping its jaws down on their lovable moist noses.

Life-Threatening Plants

Scientists believe the puppy trap is not the only life-threatening plant. If a plant ever tells you to come closer, you should be suspicious. Your first clue is that the plant talked to you. To protect yourself against these plants, consider carrying weed killer with you at all times, since it might be hard to hit the plants' narrow stems with bullets from your gun.

Using Ferns to Tastefully Decorate Your Planet

▲ By counting the leaves on a fern, you can determine how bored you are.

Beyond moss, ferns are an even more important decorative plant. Though it is rarely confirmed, ferns do exist outside of the house and are frequently found outdoors.[1] These jungle plants are unique because they reproduce entirely through spores and they lack flowers. This is important to know so that you don't try to give a fern to your date.

Why do ferns matter? Though ferns are not of key economic importance, they have many uses that keep them relevant to our daily lives. These include:

Fanning the Wealthy: The leaves of ferns are referred to as fronds. If you are an incredibly wealthy person and are either from ancient Egypt or eschew air conditioning, you will want your slaves to fan you with ferns, since moss just gets messy.

Improving the Taste of Food: Before you have a meal, eat part of a fern. When you take your first bite, it will probably be bitter and impossible to chew. As a result, your meal will taste much better in comparison.

Hiding: Of all the plants in the ecosystem, the fern is one of the most beloved for hiding behind. Nestle in behind a thicket of ferns and you can easily push them back to jump out and scare your family members, friends, or prey. This tactic works especially well for dinosaurs.

Clothing: Many tribal cultures wrap the fern around their body to create a festive and unique form of dress. The trend is not exclusive to these small groups. In fashion capitals around the world, elites have proclaimed that fern is the new black.[2]

Even if you don't find a use for these incredible plants, you are bound to kick one back when you're walking through a jungle or an elementary school terrarium. Appreciate these strange plants and remember that they're usually pretty cheap.

---

[1] Don't tell your aunt, since it will make ferns seem less exotic.

[2] More exactly, fern is the new bark, since bark was the new black a month ago.

Flowers: You Like That, Don't You?

Ever since man figured out they weren't edible, he has scattered roses on the bed of science. These seductive plants are perfect for making any night or textbook more romantic. Just look at them.

Flowers are the reproductive organs of plants. You heard that right: reproductive. There's a reason humans are so attracted to the raw sexual energy in those rose petals you bought at the grocery while getting a two-liter of diet ginger ale.

There are many different kinds of flowers. The variety exists so that humans have many opportunities to see what they smell like. Different smells help flowers attract new opportunities to reproduce, just like humans, though flowers don't seem to sweat as much.

Why do humans find flowers attractive? The scent is one of the main reasons, since it activates our primal urge to inhabit an area that smells almost as good as an air freshener. Without that, there's no doubt that we'd be scattering chocolate on beds instead of rose petals, assuming the room was cold enough that the chocolate didn't melt.

Pick up this book and smell the rose petals on this page. Unless you are sexually attracted to tree pulp, which is admittedly a common problem in libraries, you probably felt nothing. That's because the steamy floral essence wasn't present, or it could be because you have a cold.

Trees: The Plants Paper Comes From

Tall, majestic, and branchy, trees are beautiful plants that provide many things for us once they've been chopped down and ground to a pulp.[1]

There are three major types of trees, determined by their leaves: deciduous, coniferous, and disposable. When you're determining how to chop down a tree, knowing what type it is will help you pick the best axe. In addition, these different trees burn at different rates in fireplaces.[2]

It's lucky that trees are so useful to humans, since they aren't edible.[3] Trees are well known for serving as houses to members of the population under ten. Once we age past that, we chop them down and use them to make houses for grown-ups and beautiful floors that are classier than carpet. The applications of trees are limitless, and so are the trees, as long as we keep discovering new forests.

You might wonder about the science of trees. From bottom to top, every part of these plants has an explanation. The roots of a tree dig deep into the ground in order to conceal their full weight from public view. From there, a tree's trunk is covered in bark and sap, which keeps away predators through the threat of slight chafing and stickiness. Branches help a tree look more menacing to potential threats, though it would be more useful if the branches moved. Finally, a tree's leaves change color once they are completely baked.

Still, there are lingering questions about the usefulness of trees. In a modern world, do these majestic woody creatures remain necessary? It's easy to imagine plastic chairs and stainless-steel dining tables. In order to upgrade for the future, trees may need to start creating their own varnish and fine-grained finishes. Otherwise, no one will hear a tree falling in the forest.

▲ The woodpecker upgraded to vinyl siding years ago. Can trees stay relevant in the face of technology?

---

[1] Except, of course, for Christmas trees, which should only be destroyed after the presents are opened.

[2] To prevent slow-burning fires, you should douse soil near a tree with gasoline, so the wood will grow more flammably.

[3] Though it's always worth double-checking. After all, if you bite through enough of a maple tree, you'll eventually hit the syrup.

Using Trees Wisely

Because trees are a scarce resource, it's crucial that we use them carefully.

Toilet paper squares used to make protective covering for public toilets.

Bonfire commemorating second place at State in JV Field Hockey.

Coasters used to protect wood coffee tables.

Asking for chopsticks instead of silverware to make Chinese takeout feel more "authentic."

20,000 flyers for "Great Ways 2 Make $Money$ From Home"

Greeting cards specifically designed to console aunts after a divorce.

Unfinished novels about vampires and zombies in love.

Maps of countries that no longer exist.

Celebration gifts for the first wedding anniversary, the "Paper Anniversary."

Listings of things to watch on television.

Newspapers used to line bunny cages.

10,000 posters promoting recycling.

Fake Science textbook sequel, *Fake Science 2: Einstein's Revenge.*

Edible Plants: Delicious Sugar and Some Other Stuff

Plants may be even more familiar to you as food. Every day we eat plants, whether it's the ketchup on top of our hamburgers or the caramel sauce on top of our ice-cream sundaes.[1] Unfortunately, these plants are rarely edible by themselves, since they lack the chemical inventions of science. Without Red Dye #140, polysaccharides, and high-fructose corn syrups, plants are difficult to consume.

However, the most important plant is one that is frequently eaten raw. That plant is known as sugar. Harvested in perfect cubes, sugar provides us with energy and a cocktail of chemicals that almost perfectly simulates happiness. When you have sugar, your body immediately reacts and releases endorphins to encourage you to have more.

Brown sugar is the same as sugar, but from a warmer climate where it is baked beneath the sun.

Have you had your helping of sugar today? Perhaps you've heard about the food pyramid.[2] Sugar isn't formally depicted in this official document, but that's because sugar is the mortar that holds each food block together. Without it, our diets and lifestyles would crumble.

Some artificial sugar substitutes exist, but comparing them to actual sugar is a little like comparing a light bulb to the sun. Even honey, which is harvested by and stored inside of bears, is not as directly rewarding as sugar. For the right sugary taste, you need the real thing.

Sugar has ancillary benefits in addition to its taste. By working away at the enamel in your mouth, it helps your teeth become smaller and more efficient. Also, sugar protects you from attackers by surrounding your vital organs with a protective layer of fat. The only way to discover more benefits is to eat more sugar.

Edible plants other than sugar supposedly include oranges, apples, and broccoli. Someday, mankind will find a use for each of them as well.

> **» SCIENTIFIC FACT**
>
> Did you know that the tomato is not actually a vegetable? In fact, it's a type of nut.

▲ When buying your sugar, always make sure to sniff the cube for imperfections.

---

[1] No matter how you pronounce it, caramel is good and good for you.

[2] The Egyptians built the first one, but it quickly melted in the hot African sun.

I'll Drink to That: The Most Important Planty Liquids

Many drinks are made from plants as well. If you've ever had liquor or soda, you've been drinking plant.

Most soda pops are made using high-fructose corn syrup, which is a way of making corn taste like sugar. That's also the reason that soda is healthy for you. You should drink three to four liters of soda a day for health, but make sure not to dump it down your drains, since it will probably destroy them.

Children are fed these drinks almost exclusively because of their high plant content. As a result, they obtain all the energy inside the corn and burn it off incredibly quickly. They also grow more quickly, though sometimes their growth is horizontal instead of vertical. If you want your child to be on an even playing field, he or she needs vegetables that don't require too much chewing before digestion.

If you don't like soda pop, then coffee is the drink for you. This plant's beans are boiled in water, and the resulting liquid is drunk either by the pot or consumed intravenously. The chemical caffeine inside it helps stimulate the heart to a healthy 148 beats per minute, giving adult humans the metabolism of a particularly feisty gerbil. The coffee plant is easy to recognize because it's the only plant that's jittery.

▲ Soda pops because it contains as much corn as popcorn.

Tea is also made from plants, specifically tea leaves. Tea is less caffeinated, so it is inferior. Still, it can provide some interesting advantages. It's a great plant for smelling tentatively and then sipping. In addition, you can look into tea leaves and learn if you're crazy enough to believe that leaves can predict your future.

Finally, many alcoholic drinks are made from plants. When plants go rotten, we call it "fermentation," which means that they are ready to drink. Corn, wheat, and grapes all ferment to provide us with alcoholic pleasures. In fact, these drinks are so good that, on the morning after, your body requires more of them or will be in extreme pain. Sometimes, people are so excited to drink these plants that they act differently. They become so enthusiastic that they dance, meet new people, and collapse.

Photosynthesis: Plants' Greatest Gift—and Danger

Now you know everything about different types of plants. But how do plants eat without teeth? Growth requires nutrition or at least some kind of steroids, neither of which plants can get through their mouths. How do they do it? The answer is *photosynthesis*.

What is photosynthesis? It's the way plants boil their food. In addition, the steam from the boiled roots creates oxygen for humans to breathe. This makes plants crucial to human survival and an inspiration in our own efforts to create energy.

It's believed that oil comes from the fossils of old plants. The ancient photosynthesis helps the fossils have energy, even millions of years later. That's the main reason that we can say our cars are all already solar-powered.

However, there are risks that come with plants. Greenhouse gases are created by greenhouses around the world. In addition, the creation of too much steam threatens to overheat our globe. We must limit how much water we let plants boil. For that reason, we allow smog to enter the air in an attempt to block out the sun and make things cooler. Humans are rapidly increasing production in an attempt to make more smog as quickly as possible.

▲ Because plants make oxygen, many deep-sea divers bring along flowers to help them breathe.

As with many things in nature, regulating plants can be a delicate balance, especially if you have too many stacked on your windowsill. Do you think plants are good, overall? Or do these organisms create unnecessary headaches for humans, especially if you consider allergies in spring? Only time will tell whether plants are worth the time and trouble of watering them three times a week.

How Photosynthesis Works

Step 1: Hot sun rays travel to earth and hit plants.

Step 4: The steam seeps through the earth as dew and oxygen, allowing humans to breathe.

Step 2: Plants collect heat and funnel it to water underground.

Step 3: Water boils the roots for plants to drink up a nice stew.

Animals: Humans Without the Thumbs

Whether it's in the zoo in San Diego or the zoo in New York City, you can encounter animals almost anywhere. Zoology, the study of zoos, also looks at the strange and marvelous creatures we call "animals."[1] The variety in the animal kingdom keeps the world's zoos interesting and provides ample material for the gift shops.

Why is it important to study animals? Their biology gives us clues to our own. You may have heard that laboratories often use rats to test new medications and exciting lipsticks.[2] We do the same with chimpanzees and other monkeys, since their biology is similar enough to our own to be useful, but not so similar that they can complain. Even the attitudes of animals remind us of ourselves, from the proud lion to the awkward-at-dinner-parties hippopotamus. By learning about animals, we can learn about ourselves.

Because the animal kingdom is so vast, we have to figure out a way to organize it. Unfortunately, there aren't enough cages to do this as efficiently as we'd like. As a result, we use other means. Carl Linnaeus was the leader in categorizing these animals, and we still use his methods in pet stores and groceries. By narrowing the ways we describe animals, we make sure that we don't get dogs and cats confused so frequently.

▲ Lab mice test many different things for humans. This mouse is being asked to evaluate potential presidential candidates based on their smell.

That said, humans and animals are different, largely due to the size of their brains and their taste in food. Humans also have opposable thumbs, while animal thumbs are agreeable. For that reason, we must separate the human and animal kingdoms. Let's bring a tray to this buffet of life and sort the animals out. From the aquarium to the theme park safari, we'll survey the animal kingdom and learn some of the science behind each group, since they can't tell us about it themselves.

---

[1] And then, after grilling, we call them "dinner."

[2] Before selling Arsenic Passion Lips to consumers, we have to make sure it is safe.

Linnean Taxonomy

Though modified since, Carl Linnaeus created a complex system for categorizing the animal kingdom.

Totally Cute

Bunny
Butterfly
Cat
Chimpanzee
Chipmunk
Dog
Deer
Giant Panda
Koala
Otter
Penguin
Squirrel

Sort of Cute

Anteater
Ape
Armadillo
Chicken
Dinosaur
Duck
Elephant
Ferret
Fox
Guinea Pig
Hamster
Hedgehog
Human
Kangaroo
Monkey
Moose
Mouse
Owl
Pig
Reindeer
Seal
Seahorse
Sheep
Swan
Turtle
Zebra

Not Cute

Alligator
Buffalo
Baboon
Badger
Barracuda
Bat
Mean Bear
Beaver
Bee
Bison
Boar
Camel
Cattle
Chamois
Cheetah
Cobra
Cockroach
Coyote
Crab
Crane
Crocodile
Crow
Dogfish
Donkey
Dragonfly
Eagle
Echidna
Eel
Eland
Elk
Falcon
Finch
Fly
Gaur
Gnu
Goat
Goose
Gorilla
Guanaco
Guinea

Gull
Hare
Hawk
Heron
Hippopota-
mus
Hornet
Hyena
Iguana
Jackal
Jaguar
Jellyfish
Komodo
Dragon
Kouprey
Kudu
Lark
Lemur
Leopard
Lion
Llama
Lobster
Loris
Louse
Lyrebird
Magpie
Manatee
Meerkat
Mink
Narwhal
Nightingale
Okapi
Oryx
Ostrich
Ox
Oyster
Panther
Partridge
Peafowl
Pelican

Pigeon
Platypus
Quelea
Raccoon
Rail
Ram
Rat
Raven
Red deer
Red panda
Rhinoceros
Salamander
Sea Lion
Sea Star
Shark
Shrew
Skunk
Snail
Snake
Spider
Squid
Stinkbug
Tapir
Tarsier
Tiger
Toad
Turkey
Vicuna
Walrus
Wasp
Water
Buffalo
Weasel
Whale
Wolf
Wombat
Worm
Yak

Insects: Nature's Most Disgusting Miracles

Have you ever wondered what that itching sensation is? Chances are that it's somehow related to an insect.[1]

What is an insect? These creatures are defined by a few traits and killed by a range of insecticides.[2] Every insect has an exoskeleton, which is the biological equivalent of wearing a T-shirt with a skeleton on it. In addition, all insects have three distinct parts to their bodies, though since they are unable to talk, we have no way of knowing what these parts are called. Insects also have antennae, which are somewhat useless since they existed millions of years before the invention of radio.

Each insect has distinct traits that make it stand out. Let's learn a little about the science behind each.

Ants: These steady workers are incredibly strong and can carry up to 100 times their own weight. For this reason, scientists believe that 20-pound ants helped the Egyptians build the pyramids.

Bedbugs: An added feature at hotels everywhere, these creatures make sure you don't sleep too deeply and miss your morning meetings.

Bees: Organized around an unelected queen bee, bees live in complex honeycomb structures supplied by bears. The phrase "the birds and the bees" comes from the bees' proclivity to try to procreate with birds. Sadly, only stinging results.

Butterflies: Beautiful and interesting, these creatures are worth obsessive study and collection.

Caterpillars: Ugly and dull, these creatures are not worth noting.

▲ Bees labor under a monarchic system and often see their labor exploited for profit. However, protests have been ineffective because of bees' inability to read.

---

[1] Or a parasite, which is too small to handle with a fly-swatter.

[2] The first study of insects occurred when somebody was trying to kill one with a magnifying glass.

Cockroaches: This commendable species scuttles across our homes and hallways, bringing fresh life to a dull night. Able to find food effortlessly, the cockroach shows us the best of what insects can do. In addition, these bold creatures are one of the few that would survive a nuclear holocaust, since they have significant treaties with nuclear weapons–holding nations.

Earwigs: These insects are often misunderstood because of their name. They have absolutely nothing to do with wigs, though they will burrow into your brain through your ear.

Flies: A buzzing creature, the fly includes many types of insects. As its name suggests, the fly is distinguished by its mastery of flight, though security checks have made that process more and more difficult. The firefly, a subset of this group, creates a bright light at night in order to achieve its evolutionary goal of living inside a Mason jar.

Ladybugs: Since this species lacks any males to procreate with, we say it is "bad luck" to kill them in order to ensure their survival.

Mosquitoes: The mosquito helps encourage genetic variety in humans and other animals by performing small-scale blood transfusions. Next time a mosquito bites you, make sure not to slap it away too soon.

Spiders: For years, spiders have avoided extermination by convincing scientists that they "aren't insects." This ends now. They may eat insects. They may have eight legs. But none of that matters when you define an insect by its crawliness.

Termites: Why do termites eat wood? The answer is simple: They think brick looks classier and lasts longer.

Wasps: Like a bee without the charisma, wasps are fierce stingers. Their aggression is driven by a chemical desire to serve as mascot for as many high-school basketball teams as possible.

> **» SCIENTIFIC FACT**
>
> Insects are credited with driving man to go back inside.

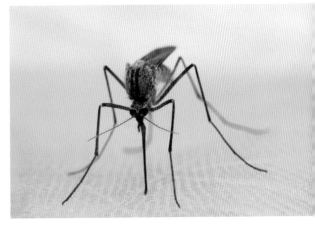

▲ This mosquito only accepts type O blood, so bring your paperwork with you.

Things to Be Afraid of in the Water

Next time you look in an aquarium or lobster tank at a restaurant, remember that all those creatures came from somewhere. Usually, they came from a larger aquarium or lobster tank. But sometimes they come from an oversalted pool of water called "the sea."

Some of these creatures are called fish because they breathe water instead of drinking it.[1] Their bodies are composed to go well with butter, though most are not naturally breaded. They travel in unaccredited schools and are found around the world. Some fish even live in unsalted water, though it is still too dirty to drink.

> **» SCIENTIFIC FACT**
> Fish breathe using gills, which is why they're able to smoke without risk of lung cancer.

These fish are joined by the mighty shark, which is well known for its large teeth and taste for human flesh.[2] Did you know that if a shark stops moving, it dies of boredom? The shark is also known for its ability to smell blood, which for many is the final straw against keeping that old bottle of Eau de Blood perfume. Should you be afraid of sharks? The answer is no, unless you are afraid of death, in which case you should definitely be afraid of sharks.

More benign, shellfish are another common creature. Many humans have allergies to these fish, which is a protective mechanism they developed as buffets grew in popularity. The lobster is the most famous shellfish and is best cooked alive in a boiling pot of water, which has prevented it from invading our hot tubs and jacuzzis.

Finally, whales and dolphins are also well known. These creatures are technically mammals, not fish, because they are less likely to swim in circles. Whales are known for their unique uses for humans, though the oil they used to be hunted for was long ago replaced with solar panels. Dolphins are known for their reputed intelligence. Should we fear a dolphin uprising? Not yet, since dolphins appear to be peaceful creatures with an inability to build weapons or, really, anything at all. However, it is recommended that aquariums remain guarded at all times, just in case.

▲ Octopi are known for their ink. But can they stay relevant in a paperless world?

---

[1] Scientists are eager to explore whether fish can also breathe Kool-Aid.

[2] Almost always uncooked.

Dolphin Intelligence: Overrated

Though some consider them as intelligent as humans, dolphins don't even have color television.

The Predators: Animals That Want to Kill Us

There are many ways to classify animals in the wild. We can sort them by where they live, what they eat, or even their species.[1] It's also useful to know some of the animals that want to kill us.

These dangerous creatures live in a wide range of ecosystems and have many different characteristics. They have one thing in common, however: They are "carnivorous," which means that they like to eat the people you love. They especially like children because they are sweeter and more tender.

▲ Just a bunny rabbit, right? Wrong. This snake in disguise illustrates the threat predators pose.

The Mighty Jungle (of Death)

Humans are familiar with the natural beauty and even more natural deadliness of the jungle. What is the jungle? The jungle is like a large zoo where all the cages are broken and there aren't any ice-cream stands. That alone is frightening enough. Now add predators to the mix.

Snakes are well known as a threat to human life and a pet to people who weren't popular in high school. They have different ways to kill humans. Some snakes kill with venom, a poisonous liquid that they inject into human blood. Others kill by squeezing their prey to death and then eating them, though snake defenders claim that snakes do it because they "love too much."[2]

These serpents are paired with the great jungle cats. You may have heard of the lion and its majestic mane. This large coating of hair allows the lion to attract mates and easily get a perm. As the lion prowls the African savannah, or the mall near the zoo it just escaped, it searches for fresh prey. Is there any way to evade a lion? Most jungle experts suggest walking slowly and calmly, never staring the lion in the eye, and carrying a low-grade military bazooka.

---

[1] Or the objects we can make from their skin.

[2] This is the subject of the classic Steinbeck novel, *Of Mice and Men*, in which a snake thinks a woman is a mouse and accidentally squeezes her to death.

The lion is not the only great cat. It is joined by the leopard, cheetah, jaguar, and tiger, none of which anybody can tell apart. One has spots, another is fast, and another is a car. All are totally unsafe.[1] The tiger is most well known for its baby-killing proclivities. No matter how pretty they are, you should never let a tiger into your child's daycare center.

Finally, you should be afraid of bears, which live in forests instead of jungles, just to catch you off-guard. These honey-making creatures are faster than they look and are frequently grizzled. How can you evade a bear? Bears are able to climb trees, run fast, and hide. However, bears cannot read, so you may find safety by running to your nearest library.

> » **SCIENTIFIC FACT**
>
> Wolves can prove a threat to humans unless you are a baby, in which case they will raise you.

---

[1] Not the car, however, which delivers a smooth ride and luxurious experience. Ask your local dealer about the newest Jaguar models.

"No matter how pretty they are, you should never let a tiger into your child's daycare center."

Pets: The Animals That Serve Us

Not all animals are predators to humans. Indeed, man has formed a lasting alliance with some animals that we call "pets." These animals are called "domesticated" because they rarely immigrate from foreign countries. Mankind's relationship with these friendly animals is deeply informed by science.[1]

▲ In some cultures, the dog is viewed as adorable.

Dogs and cats are the most famous pets, with dogs taking a slight edge because they don't hate humans. Many canine[2] phenomena can be explained through science. Did you know a dog wags its tail because it is happy and needs a way to fan itself? Perhaps you've seen a dog's tongue hang out of its mouth. That habit gives it a millisecond advantage when licking strangers on all parts of their bodies. Finally, you may have heard that dogs are easy to train. This is because, in the wild, they survived almost entirely on doggie treats.

Cats have a different disposition. Related to the jungle cats of the wild, these beasts have a distant demeanor and uncanny ability to scratch things. Though they may seem perpetually bored, they are actually carefully surveying their surroundings. Then they do actually get bored, since they are stuck in a living room. Have you ever noticed that cats shed? There's a reason for this behavior, since it helps them track every place they've been in a house. At least it's better than marking their territory through urine.

Other pets exist. For years, hamsters have been the sole source of power for hamster wheels. Goldfish teach children important lessons about the Coriolis effect, which determines the direction that toilet water flushes. Even birds occasionally serve as pets. The parrot is able to repeat phrases that humans say, though it doesn't understand the words it is saying. Tests have shown no bird has named itself "Polly," and most parrots prefer cookies to the crackers they claim to want.

---

[1] But mostly doggie treats.

[2] Dogs and cats are called canines and felines, respectively, due to their proportion of calcium (Ca) and iron (Fe).

Food: The Animals That We Serve

Perhaps the animal kingdom is best known for the sustenance it provides to humans.[1] Animals contain protein, different tastes, and fats in their bodies that humans use to augment their diet of soda and candy.

Different cultures eat different foods, so it is important to recognize that the science behind food is complex and appears in many different languages. In Germany, sausage is popular for its high fat ratio, which counterbalances beer, and for its shape, which is easy to hold with a free hand. In some Asian cultures, the dog is consumed because it obediently agrees to be slaughtered.[2] In Australia, ostrich is frequently eaten for its high protein content and because it can't fly away to escape.

Fortunately, Americans have a different selection of animals that they have agreed are not cute and can, therefore, be bred, slaughtered, consumed, and thrown away.[3] The most popular meats come from the cow and the pig, though the bison has become increasingly popular, despite the fact that buffalo chips have a bad reputation.

▲ In some cultures, the dog is viewed as delicious.

The cow grazes on grass or, when farmed, a mixture of grass, other cows, and orange soda. With four-and-a-half stomachs, it is able to continue digesting as it is being killed. Different cuts of steak come from different parts of the cow. The most popular type of steak is called "Angus," and it has higher quality because the cow Angus exercised a lot, back when it was alive.

Pigs, or pork, form the other core of the human diet. Pork chops and sausage are made from this animal. Did you know that pigs roll around in the mud because they are unable to sweat? This is the reason that pork is never salty enough. Though some hot dog manufacturers claim pigs are used in their food, all the lab rats called upon to test the claim died before the results could be revealed.

---

[1] Even vegans consume animal crackers.

[2] Usually while wagging its tail.

[3] Almost always in that order.

(Oh the) Humanity

The Science Experiment of You

One of the central tenets of biology is that humans are the most important part. After all, we're the ones who invented it.[1]

Why is it important to learn about human biology? By learning the science of ourselves, we can be certain if we're alive or not. It's difficult to take a pulse if you don't know what one is.

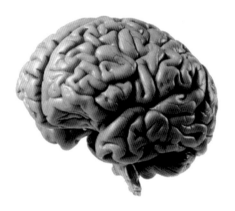

▲ The original owner of this brain had his will state that all his organs should be donated to textbooks.

Everything about us is determined by our biology. The source of our babies and the shape of our ears are all biological phenomena, as is our taste in music. By understanding biology, we understand ourselves.[2]

Take, for example, the brain. Did you know that the brain is more powerful than any computer?[3] Our brains work hard to help us avoid thinking, reading, and learning so that we can relax a little. The brain may just be a squishy ball of matter, but to humans, it is valuable enough to wear a helmet almost half of the time you ride a bike.

The discipline of anatomy intersects with biology. Anatomy is the study of naked pictures. Each part of the body has its own unique function and its own unique way to be abused. It's best to think of the body as a complex machine with a million tiny parts. That's one of the reasons you should have a lot of grease in your diet.

Biology, in turn, informs the practice of medicine. Have you ever had a cough? That's probably because a doctor told you to turn your head and cough. If you've ever had a broken arm or broken heart, you've probably seen a doctor or been dumped by one.

Let's start our study of human biology by learning the stages of life.

---

[1] Though some dolphins claim credit, they insist on communicating through squeaks.

[2] And we pass biology tests.

[3] But only one person can plug into it.

Babies: The Nakedest Stage of Life

Babies are the youngest members of mankind. Usually, they have a poor vocabulary and few financial assets. Despite these shortcomings, however, babies are considered a miracle for their ability to cry at all times. Who hasn't wondered, when sitting in a library or on a crowded airplane flight, where all these babies come from?

It all begins with a stork. Imagine a nest in the wild as the sun rises. A stork flies in from the distance, his eyes intense. There is work to do. The stork brings babies to parents without fail and, from that point on, life begins. However, this is only true when the babies are baby storks.

For humans, babies begin when a male's sperm attacks the female egg. These sperm contain a male's genetic information and are strongly sexually attracted to the egg. The egg contains a female's genetic information and is less attracted to the sperm but chooses one anyway because it's too lazy to keep waiting. If the sperm and egg are in love, based on a relationship of mutual support and respect, they create a new baby.

This new baby contains the genetic information, or "flaws," from both of the parents. This is one of the reasons it is born bald and crying. It begins to grow in the stomach of the female mother, since the man's stomach is hairier and might cause the baby to choke. Growth continues and the woman starts consuming more food in order to compensate for the creature growing inside of her. It's recommended that women not drink during pregnancy, since it's difficult to know whether the baby prefers beer or liquor.

The baby receives all its food through something called an umbilical cord. Made from the same material as a flexible straw, the umbilical cord supplies food and liquid to the baby. When it is eventually cut, it provides a valuable keepsake, especially if the baby becomes famous. In addition, this cord's connection forms the bellybutton. Have you ever wondered why some bellybuttons are "innies" and others are "outties?" The innie is a Windsor knot and the outtie is a more ostentatious bow tie.

> » **SCIENTIFIC FACT**
>
> While pregnant, women develop cravings based on what the baby thinks would be funny.

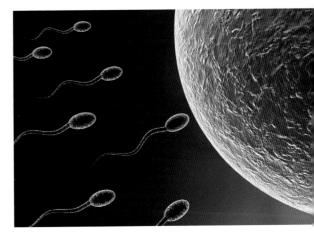

▲ Sperm invade the egg, unless this is a leftover picture of Mars.

Great Scientists

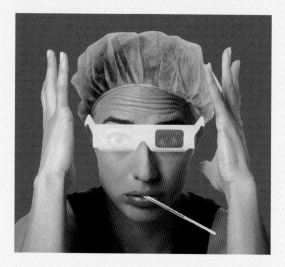

History's Most Memorable Forgotten Names

Name: Dr. Susan Hillard
Scientific Field: Medicine
Greatest Strength:
Willingness to experiment
Greatest Weakness:
Willingness to experiment
Greatest Discovery:
Found almost all the surgical tools she left inside patients' bodies

Schooled independently through medical dramas, Dr. Susan Hillard blazed a trail through the world of medicine and biology, and a few of her patients even ended up surviving. A self-proclaimed "experimental doctor and biologist," she performed the experiments that other scientists were either unwilling or legally barred to perform.

Buoyed by a strong belief that medical breakthroughs occasionally involved breaking things, Hillard pursued a trial and error system with her patients. To find a cure for chickenpox, she studiously infected 1,700 preschoolers with the disease and, though she didn't find a cure or vaccine, the disease was good for business and allowed her to expand her practice. The children also learned a valuable lesson about trust.

Being part of the vanguard, however, also meant refusing conventional wisdom. Convinced that Jonas Salk's polio cure was "overrated," she encouraged people to enjoy public swimming pools in order to build up an immunity. Though Salk proved correct in the end, the patients who might testify against Dr. Hillard were already dead.

Hillard's innovation extended to the ways she performed her duties. Early exploration convinced her that 3D glasses would help her see patients more clearly, though actually the glasses only made the patients a blurry mix of red and blue. Hillard also believed that taking her own temperature would help, but a reliable 98.6-degree reading convinced her that even her most feverish patients were healthy. Her habit of wearing a surgical cap might have worked if she had washed her hands.

Though her practice ended in the early 1970s with reprimands, lawsuits, prison time, and eventual exile from the United States, Hillard remains a pioneer in process-of-elimination biology and medicine, in which doctors study her work and try to do the opposite. It's unknown if Dr. Hillard is alive today, but if so, most scientists speculate that she is performing new experiments in medicine or, more likely, golfing.

After nine months, the baby is ready to emerge from the stomach and begin crying in public. Birth is a long and painful process, for both baby and mother, since neither has been drinking. Hopefully, all goes well with the birth and a healthy baby emerges with ten fingers and ten toes, and also a brain. Immediately after birth, the baby is sent to a phototherapy room to prepare it for the tanning salons it will encounter in the world.

Did you know that, proportionally, a baby's head is seven times bigger than the average adult head? This allows the brain room to grow as the baby learns how to crawl, talk, and control its drooling. Babies have other abnormal biological traits, like male pattern baldness, which can be easily fixed with a toupee. Please allow your baby to be confident and sexy.

> *"Please allow your baby to be confident and sexy."*

Children: Precious Creatures, from a Distance

The most ambitious babies grow up to be children. Though still smaller than adult humans, children have many adult traits in some form or another. While children have yet to make any major scientific discoveries, they are considered a worthwhile part of society for their bell-like laughter and willingness to take orders. As in all stages of life, kids have certain attributes that can be explained by biology.

Technically, children are between baby and pubescent human, which means that they aren't as cute as babies or as self-reliant as teenagers. Since children's minds and bodies aren't yet mature, it's assumed that they will make many mistakes. Their coordination is poor and their knife-fight skills are undeveloped. Children should wear helmets at all times, since they have less brain matter available to damage.

This is the main reason they have an extra set of teeth called "baby teeth"—it's clear that if the teeth didn't fall out naturally, the child would find a way to accidentally knock them out. This also protects children from the social consequences of getting in fights with others, since people can assume the loss of teeth was natural.

Children are biologically different in other ways, too. Their bones and bodies are weaker than a young adult's, and as a result their bones break. A child may need to wear a cast. The cast is worn until the child heals or somebody writes a curse word on the cast in permanent marker.

A child's rapid growth requires attentive nutrition from the guardian. Children need lots of vitamins and minerals, so a trip to a quarry is key. Young people also have a higher metabolism than adults, which means that they burn off fat more quickly. Give your child candy and sugar while you can, since they will gain weight later on in life. Finally, children don't sweat as much as adults, so avoid giving your children too much water, since they will just ask to go to the bathroom too often.

» **SCIENTIFIC FACT**

Child obesity has become a major problem ever since the end of a form of exercise called child labor.

▲ This child lost his teeth in a fight with a carnie, but the larger teeth he's grown will help him get revenge.

Pubescence: Giggling, Misery, Repeat Until Adult

Eventually, the child grows into a teenager and puberty begins, the period in which a human wants to breed most despite the fact that no one wants to breed with them.

Puberty involves many changes for the child, all of which are embarrassing. As the body changes, so does the biology. Hormones are injected into the bloodstream. These hormones allow for the growth of hair and self-consciousness. They also create pimples, which ensure that a teenager won't be able to breed until puberty is over. Teenagers may be emotionally or physically unstable due to these changes, which is why they alternate between clothing that is too baggy or too tight.

Pubescent changes are different in the male and female. For males, puberty involves a deeper voice, growth of the sexual organs, and obsessive laughter upon hearing the phrase "sexual organs." For females, puberty involves the beginning of menstruation, which is commonly known as "the period," because that's all we're going to say about it. Period. This textbook is already awkward enough.

Teenagers, Grooming, and Survival

Due to their newfound ability to breed, teenagers spend a significant amount of time grooming. They wear large quantities of perfume so that anyone within a 200-foot radius can smell them. They also use hairspray to control their hair and enable it to be used as a weapon.

However, this grooming can occasionally endanger them, since it requires total focus on the mirror at the expense of being aware of their surroundings.

Middle Age: Even Worse Than the Historical Era

When a human approaches middle age, the body begins to conserve its resources. The male in particular prepares for increased hardships it would have encountered in the wild. He develops a potbelly to protect his organs against the horns of predators. He also loses his hair so that it's easier for potential mates to spot him in bright sunlight.

In Their Words

"You know, I have really evolved some great stuff. Wanna see?"

—CHARLES DARWIN, BIOLOGIST

Darwin's midlife crisis involved countless genetic experiments with younger women.

The woman improves at ignoring him.

Perhaps the most notable psychological effect of middle age is the "midlife crisis." This event has a biological basis, since the man acts younger to shame his children, so they won't be around to deter new mates.

Why Do You Age? And Can It Stop Now, Please?

Have you ever looked at your face in the mirror and wondered why it's degraded so much in quality? The reason is aging.

Aging is the process by which we get uglier. It occurs over a number of years or after a really rough night on the town. Why does it happen? As cells replace other cells, they do a poorer job each time, the same way a copy of a copy is of worse quality than the original. The blurrier the cells get, the more your back hurts in the morning.

Over the centuries, scientists have developed many responses to the problems of aging. Plastic surgery has helped people who are forty look like they are twenty, if people who are twenty looked like they'd recently been melted. This has been paired with many

innovative drugs that help stretch the last 18 minutes of life into a full 21 minutes, with a cost in the low two hundred thousands. These bold new responses have helped people live longer and happier lives, or if not happier, then definitely longer.

Science is marching forward with new solutions to help stop aging. Many speculate that genetic engineering will be at the forefront of combating the useful but embarrassing senior citizen discount. For example, there's no reason why new skin couldn't be grown from petri dishes and then transferred to the forehead, allowing a wrinkleless surface that smells only a little like formaldehyde.

In the future, it's possible that we'll be able to use clones to advance our age. Why not

Old Age: Wiser, but Worse at Hockey

Particularly persistent humans reach old age, a final stage of life that involves many changes for the body.

Perhaps you've wondered why the elderly go to meals earlier. This is a behavior developed before civilization, when they had to catch prey before younger, more able competitors took it. For that reason, most buffets are full by 5 P.M.

In addition, many elderly migrate to warmer climates, since they worry that their white hair might blend into the snow. These warmer climates allow them to spend more time in the sun. Late in life, humans try to develop photosynthesis in an attempt to save some energy chewing. Old age has many mysteries yet to be revealed, and if you have a few hours, a senior citizen will be happy to tell you all about them.

> **» SCIENTIFIC FACT**
>
> As life expectancies increase, medical professionals have had to learn to count higher.

transfer elderly brains to young bodies? Why not preserve our brains on ice until scientists figure out a way to defrost them? Why not use new organs to replace old ones, even boring ones like kidneys? Of course, there will be ethical questions, like how much to charge for the services and whether to state a person's real age or augmented age on their driver's license.

No matter what happens, old age won't be the end anymore. It's just the beginning of a long scientific trial. When you ponder old age in the future, don't waste an afternoon making a will. You aren't going to need it once your brain is attached to a Ferrari.

▲ Is it plausible that we could transfer the heads of senior citizens onto the bodies of baby clones? Absolutely!

Systems in Harmony, Unless You Have a Stomach Ache

Almost all stages of humans have bodies.[1] These bodies have biological systems that allow them to live, flourish, and procrastinate every day.

Every body has organs. Organs are machines in the body that perform many different functions, most of which we know.[2] Take a quick look in the mirror, and you'll see an organ, unless the lights are off. Your eyes, skin, and even your kidneys are organs, though if you can see your kidneys, you should probably go to a hospital right now. Since everyone needs organs, consider becoming an organ donor, as long as you specify you should be dead first.

> **» SCIENTIFIC FACT**
>
> The skin is the largest organ, which is why we show it off by wearing it where everybody can see.

These organs are supported by bones through the skeletal system. Hit your head against a wall right now.[3] There's a reason your brain didn't splatter next to your Albert Einstein poster. A skull protects your brain and face from the assaults of bullies and doors that came out of nowhere. Other bones do the same when bullies decide to change it up. You have a total of 206 bones in your body, or 523.24 in the metric system. The longest bone is the femur, though it's what you do with it that matters.

The organs are connected by the muscular, nervous, and circulatory systems. The muscular system helps your body move and gives you something for the fat to grow on. It is controlled by the nervous system, which is why you twitch so much when you talk. Finally, all these muscles and organs are given food and oxygen by the circulatory system. The circulatory system is the way blood travels, so if the sight of blood frightens you, don't look at any part of anybody's body. Veins carry old blood into the heart and supply it with fresh red coloring and food. Working in concert, all these systems make it possible for you to take a nap without even thinking about it.

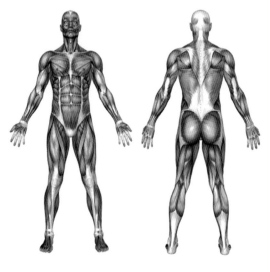

▲ The most important muscle of all is the brain, because it . . . my gosh, look at those abs!

---

[1] Cremated ones don't.

[2] The stomach turns pastries into energy and regret.

[3] If a wall is not available, a textbook will do.

The Human Body: Smorgasbord of Organs

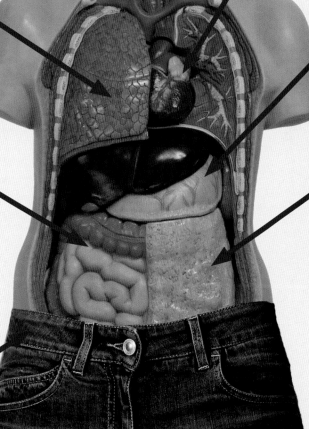

Brain: The mainframe of the human body, the brain is a flawless machine that can remember everything, except the name of your neighbor's wife.

Lungs: The lungs store cigarette smoke and allow it to pass through to our bloodstream, providing a sweet rush of nicotine.

Intestines: Pink and twisty, the intestines process our food so that it can't be eaten a second time.

Jeans: These can be low rise, hiphuggers, or loose fit. They help cover unmentionable parts of the anatomy.

Heart: This organ pumps blood through the body, unless you are a certain female scientist whose name we don't want to mention, in which case you don't have a heart at all, clearly, after what you did in Cabo San Lucas . . . Sharon.

Stomach: The place where we store food when a refrigerator isn't portable enough.

Liver: It's around here somewhere, but you can't see it because of all the beer.

Feet: Featuring heels and, hopefully, toes. These appendages aren't officially organs, but once they learn to pick stuff up they might be promoted.

Genetics: The Easiest Way to Blame Your Parents for All Your Flaws

Now that you know everything about how the human body works, you may have a few questions.[1] Why do different people look different? How does the body know to make itself a certain way? Why do I look so much like the milkman? The answer is genetics.

Genetics is the part of biology that traces all your flaws. Basically, it states that your genes contain instructions to your body, the same way you have instructions to assemble furniture.[2] These instructions tell your body how to do everything from building your stomach to putting a large mole on the back of your neck.

It's also the reason that you look like other members in your family and can't act on that attraction to your cousin. Everything about you has a gene, which is made by the combination of your parents' genes. Your brothers and sisters have genes that are very similar to yours, though theirs are probably slightly better.

Even our favorite animals are subject to genetics. Dogs are carefully bred with one another so they have a rarified gene pool.[3] Clever crossbreeding has created the labradoodle, the cocker schnauzer, the poodotweiler, and the siamese terrier weasel.

Practically, genetics is used in a variety of different tasks, from making corn slightly larger to creating a super race of humans that will crush anyone standing in their path. Because of the power of genetics, it is important to use genetics carefully, or quickly enough so that nobody has a chance to complain.

> **» SCIENTIFIC FACT**
>
> Genetics is the reason you have that weak chin.

▲ Red hair is created by an endangered gene. These babies are cowering because genetics is coming to get them.

---

[1] Not that question. That's for your parents and requires hand puppets.

[2] This works because, like your furniture instructions, genes use pictures and are available in over 100 different languages.

[3] Like pools, the best genes should remain private and gated off from the riffraff.

DNA: The Reason You Got Caught

You might wonder how genetics works. How does the body give instructions, since babies can't read? The answer is DNA. Your genes carry these instructions everywhere: in your spit, your hair, and your skin. It tells your body and the police everything about you.

DNA was discovered in the early 1950s by some scientists who were looking at spit. DNA appears in a double helix, a name borrowed from the same move in Olympic figure skating. The code is not written in letters but in different acids, which you shouldn't try doing yourself unless you're wearing gloves. Each sequence has its own specific instructions for everything in your body. As we continue to learn about DNA, we're finding more and more uses. In the future, we'll be able to fix everything from your nose to your eyes just by changing the sequence of your DNA.

» SCIENTIFIC FACT

Your DNA contains adenine, guanine, cytosine, thymine, and just a little salt for flavor.

Discovering DNA

DNA was originally named acidic nucleic deoxyribose, but it caused too much confusion.

TRANSCRIPT, JAN 12, 1953

```
 CRICK: WATSON, I'VE DISCOVERED AND!
WATSON: AND WHAT CRICK?
 CRICK: RIGHT, AND IS WHAT I'VE DISCOVERED.
WATSON: AND...?
 CRICK: EXACTLY!
WATSON: EXACTLY WHAT?
 CRICK: NO, EXACTLY AND.
WATSON: EXACTLY AND WHAT?
 CRICK: NO, IT'S JUST AND.
WATSON: SPIT IT OUT, CRICK!
 CRICK: THAT'S RIGHT, YOUR SPIT HAS SOME AND.
WATSON: AND WHAT?
```

Evolution: Your Excuse to Breed as Much as Possible

Perhaps the best-known application of genetics is in the theory of evolution. Developed by Charles Darwin during a singles cruise to the Galapagos,[1] the theory proposes that species change over time because of the traits they inherit or the money they inherit. It's the main reason why Three-Toed Mike doesn't have any children and the royal family is alive and well.

▲ Undoubtedly, Darwin's greatest accomplishment was evolving into a statue.

This breeding process is determined by natural selection, which is also used at many organic groceries. As Darwin observed the mating habits on his cruise, he realized that some men would never have children as ugly as they were. No woman would "select" them for breeding. Natural selection was aided by later theories of mutation, which helped create slight changes in species. Shortly after the introduction of these theories, there was a craze to consume radioactive products in hopes that they might make the drinker mutate into somebody more attractive.

Perhaps the theory of evolution is best known, and most controversial, for its assertion that men and apes share a common ancestor. Many apes found this highly offensive, since they consider themselves to be less violent, better climbers, and considerably more attractive than humans. The chimpanzees responded by throwing their feces, though they do that to almost everything.

Evolution leads to a key question: What will man evolve to next? Perhaps a particularly bookish young person will breed with a computer and create the first compu-man, with incredible powers of calculation and a tendency to glare and have glare. Or maybe man will finally develop a mutation to fly, assuming the wings meet regulatory standards.

We don't know what will happen next, and that proves that biology is the continually unfolding story of ourselves.[2] There's always something new to discover about ourselves when the door's closed. Our amazing world is full of life: go find it, name it, and eat it today.

---

[1] During one of the buffets, Darwin ate turtle and realized that all fish taste alike. He immediately began forming his theory, right after karaoke.

[2] But please don't get any biology on these pages—it might make them wrinkle.

Chapter 3 Quiz: Biology

Multiple Choice

1. What is the basis of all life?

a. Central air conditioning
b. The cell
c. Dirt hit by lightning
d. A balanced diet

2. Why do cells split up?

a. To increase the number of shareholders
b. Just didn't have the same taste in mitochondria anymore
c. They want to get closer to Seattle and have to start somewhere
d. Irreconcilable cytoplasm

3. Why are viruses dangerous?

a. They're too small for nets
b. They aren't as pettable as dogs
c. Most viruses never took an ethics course
d. They lack the affability of bacteria

4. Why do flowers bloom?

a. It's easier than exploding
b. They need to attract husbands who forgot about Valentine's Day
c. Just being green is so last season
d. The smell is too strong without letting a little air in

5. What is photosynthesis?

a. The process of shaking Polaroids
b. How plants make memories
c. The process by which light bulbs are grown
d. Sexier than it sounds

6. How do animals differ from humans?

a. They are less racist, but more specist
b. Their textbooks have fewer pictures
c. They're more vegan
d. They smell each other more

7. Which organ is most important?

a. The heart, for keeping a beat
b. The pancreas, for picking up the gall bladder's slack
c. The skin, due to its support of tanning salons
d. The brain, because its wrinkles mean it's wise

8. What can genetics teach us?

a. How to make the grape-banana hybrid everybody's always wanted
b. Who to hate
c. Who committed that unsolved murder
d. Why blondes do things wrong

Short Answer

1. The plant, animal, and human kingdoms are all important. But which one has the best fashion sense and why?

_____
_____
_____
_____

2. The life of every animal is precious. How would you drive up the price in an auction?

_____
_____
_____
_____

3. Genetics gives us many opportunities. Would you rather engineer fat-free steak or an orange with an easy-to-peel zipper?

_____
_____
_____
_____

Essay Question

1. **Genetics and DNA raise countless ethical questions. How would you tackle the ethical issues that will arise over the next 100 years without upsetting anybody at all?**

_____

_____

_____

_____

_____

_____

_____

_____

_____

_____

_____

_____

_____

_____

_____

_____

_____

_____

_____

_____

_____

_____

_____

_____

_____

_____

_____

_____

_____

_____

_____

_____

_____

_____

_____

_____

_____

_____

_____

CHEMISTRY

BLOWING THINGS UP WITH SCIENCE

Before You Start This Chapter . . .

- Make sure you have accidental-eyebrow-removal insurance.
- Sterilize your lab and lab partner, who isn't right for you.
- Memorize all the elements through a catchy song sung in at least three popular music styles.
- Melt down all your nickels. Don't ask why, just do it and wait for your next instructions.
- Collect all your favorite atoms and put them in plastic sleeves for safekeeping.
- Clarify your laboratory's "blow-up" policy.
- Make a four-star meal using only baking soda and a Bunsen burner.
- Experience life as a solid, liquid, gas, and plasma.
- Put on safety goggles, preferably over your eyes.

Where All the Warning Labels Come From

Chemistry studies everything that makes our world, except all the messy feelings.

Chemistry began when alchemy finally decided to go legit. Instead of making gold, scientists decided to make other things that were worth more than gold. Secretly, they always wanted to make gold. But in the meantime, they spent some time with boron. It's about as fun as it sounds.

Perhaps you've dipped your hand in boiling water or swallowed bleach in the hope that it would make your organs cleaner. Both times, you've been working with chemistry. Chemistry studies exactly what makes the things around us hurt so much and taste so bad. Chemistry is everywhere.[1]

You'll use chemistry for the rest of your life, especially when you're making potions. This science has many practical applications in our world, from plastic grocery bags to plastic cups. Since it studies the materials from which all things are made, it's also a hard section to skip in a textbook.

Without chemistry, we'd be forced to produce all of our tires through careful cross-breeding of rubber trees and some animal that's tire-shaped. Instead of using hairspray, spray paint, and varnish, we'd have to be content with shapeless hair, a total lack of graffiti, and really boring wood. Are we animals or are we men? That's simply no way to live, and thanks to chemistry, we don't have to.

▲ It may be hard to believe, but this beautiful Styrofoam box didn't grow naturally. It was made through chemistry.

Whether it's in your home laboratory or your work laboratory, chemistry surrounds you at all times.[2] Put on your safety goggles and start learning.

---

[1] Except for between you and your lab partner. She's not flirting, she's just being nice.

[2] Make sure to clear the fumes every 2 to 3 hours.

The Things That Make Things

Matter: That Stuff over There

If you've ever touched, breathed, or seen anything, you've dealt with matter. It is the basic building block of chemistry and an essential ingredient in every type of chili, whether the chili is spicy or not. Throughout history, scientists have questioned exactly what matter is, as well as why matter matters matter.

Matter was discovered when scientists looked around and noticed there was a lot of stuff. Needing a name for this stuff, they settled on "matter" because it was easier than naming everything separately. From that point on, chemists made it their mission to study matter's behaviors, even though a chimpanzee's behaviors were usually cuter.

What is matter? Varying wildly in price and quality, matter consists of all the physical objects in our world.[1] Although matter may appear in many different forms, especially if a cookie cutter has been used, it is consistent in its basic composition. Matter is everywhere and appears in many different states and also in different countries.

It sounds like everything is made of matter, doesn't it? However, not all things are matter, so you have to be careful when showing off your knowledge at dinner parties. For example, if you shout right now, you'll notice that the sound didn't linger in the air.[2] That's because sound travels in "waves" and the tide sweeps all the matter out. The same goes for light, since light is made of particles that are too tiny to grab. That means that when you take a trip to the tanning salon, the UV light that turns your skin a desirable caramel color isn't matter: it's something closer to magic.

---

[1] While we can't prove that your opinion doesn't matter, we can prove it isn't matter.

[2] Unless you are a cartoon character, in which case you should be doing something funny instead of reading a textbook.

Atoms: The Things That Make Our World and Then Blow It Up

Now that you know about matter, you might wonder what it is made from.[1] From the beginning, scientists have addressed the same question. At first, they thought everything was made from rocks. Then they broke the rocks into pebbles and were done for a while. But after that, they broke the pebbles into dust. Eventually, scientists realized there was something even smaller than dust, though the allergies weren't as bad.

They found the atom. The atom is the smallest unit of matter, until we find something smaller. For years, scientists have tried modeling the atom, but just as they'd almost drawn it, their hands slipped and they had to start over again. As a result, scientists typically pointed at a blank page and turned it really quickly before anybody realized there was nothing on it.

Over time, models of the atom have changed, especially once engineers learned how to make more complex shapes with chocolate. However, the fundamental structure of the atom has remained the same. In the center is the "nucleus," also known as the "Nükleus" when it appears in heavy metal.

▼ Though the atom remains more popular than the *catom*, the latter is undoubtedly cuter.

As small as the nucleus is, it contains other things inside it. These unique pieces are called *protons* and *neutrons*. Protons are known to always take one side, while neutrons waffle between the other two. This helps keep the atom balanced, though it occasionally makes it difficult to tell what the atom is really all about. It's almost impossible to get an atom's real opinion on your new haircut. It's important to count the number of protons

---

[1] Especially cake.

in an atom, since they determine a lot about what it looks like in public.[1]

Orbiting the atom are *electrons.* Electrons are small batteries for the atom that have a negative charge, unless you turn them in the other direction. Unlike devoted protons and neutrons, electrons can leave and switch to other atoms, which is the reason static electricity occurs between your feet and the carpet. Though scientists used to believe that electrons orbited the nucleus in a regular path, they now believe electrons orbit in a cloud, because of their presence in lightning. Though this theory advances science, it makes the atom tragically more difficult to draw.

In Their Words

"Okay, I know you can't see them. But trust me, it is super impressive that I discovered atoms."

—JOHN DALTON, DISCOVERER OF THE ATOM

Despite discovering the atom, John Dalton's work failed to impress women in bars.

---

[1] This is commonly referred to as "atomic weight," which is why the heavier atoms sink to the bottom of the Periodic Table of the Elements.

Complimentary Atoms

As promised, your copy of *Fake Science 101* includes the following complimentary package of atoms[1] at no additional cost.[2] These atoms may be utilized in any way you so choose and in any state, though if you choose to melt or burn this book, please purchase it first.[3] If you don't choose to use these atoms yourself, they make a great gift for any chemist or easily pleased person in your life.

---

[1] Number of atoms may vary, as will your satisfaction.

[2] Estimated resale value smaller than actual atoms.

[3] You may also recycle the book for 5 cents in CA, CN, DE, HI, IA, ME, MA, NY, OR, and VT, and for 10 cents in MI.

Elements: The Smallest Things Worth Mining

▲ Without elements, we'd call this a "rock" instead of whatever it actually is.

Atoms aren't all alike. Just like with people, their differences help us categorize them and establish reasonable rules for their behavior. Each different type of atom is called an "element," and these stable categories come with different traits and prices in the free market.[1]

Though we'll never be able to count all the elements without the help of a calculator, they're all worth learning. From oxygen to the one after oxygen, each element has characteristics that make it useful in home construction, cooking, and poison.[2] Do you have a favorite element? What would it take for you to pawn it?

[1] Especially gold. Do you have any gold we could borrow?

[2] Make sure you know which one you're using it for.

Discovering and/or Sponsoring New Elements

To the untrained eye, it may seem like the elements are permanent and unchangeable, written in stone and, on many occasions, including stones. However, the elements are surprisingly dynamic, which means you should buy new editions of your textbooks at least once a month.

Of the many elements, only 94 occur naturally, and most of those require too much looking. The rest of the elements were made in a laboratory by enterprising scientists who got sick of the same old same old from the past 5 billion years.

New elements are engineered by adjusting the weight and character of atoms. As any cosmetologist will tell you, it's possible to change the entire appearance of something with a little eye shadow and concealer, and many chemists have done the same. Scandium never looked better.

Why bother creating these new elements? Quite simply, creating elements gives the creator the right to name them. That's where we get berkelium, einsteinium, whosanerdnowium, and stillsingleum from. These elements give the creators an opportunity to celebrate their creation and de-emphasize the fact that they blew up their laboratory in the process.

New elements can also perform new functions. Who hasn't spent a few hours breathing

The Periodic Table: Better Than the Periodic Ottoman

Because there are so many elements to keep track of, and because so few of them are as interesting as gold, we have the Periodic Table of Elements. Named the Periodic Table because the Exclamation Table would be a bit much, the table is a carefully organized system in which you can see how many elements you've never heard of. It's recommended that you memorize all the elements as soon as possible, both for personal safety and to make new friends.

Over the years, the periodic table has developed greatly. Scientists originally organized all of the elements in piles, which would have worked, except the helium kept floating away. They finally settled on printing the names of the elements on paper, along with their attributes and a few convenient local coupons. Writing down the elements proved far easier than discovering all of them each time they went to the lab.

> **» SCIENTIFIC FACT**
>
> When splaying elements on the periodic table, make sure to use your periodic tablecloth.

and thought, "Oxygen is fine, but why can't it be more like beryllium?" By engineering new elements, we save lives and kill time. If you're sick of the aluminum you know, change a few things around and you'll finally have aluminum you can eat, though Americans and Brits will never pronounce it the same way.

Indeed, these new elements have created opportunities for commerce. Every day, new elements are being sold for sponsorship to large corporations. Next time you drink a soda pop, thank carbonadium (Cb) for the extra zip in your drink, assuming the rights have been paid for by the manufacturer. As we create new elements to name, sponsor, and sell, we'll have an opportunity to finally make the elements profitable.

elementally **DELICIOUS!**

SPONSOR CHIPIUM (Cp) TODAY!

▲ A lucrative bidding war has erupted over the rights to chipium (Cp), the newest and most delicious element.

Take a Seat at the World's Most Fascinating Table

When it began, the periodic table was nothing. Now it contains all of the elements and their names. Learn a little about this legendary dinnerless table.

Elements of Elements

Each element comes with its own stats and trivia. Let's learn from the example of cadmium (Cd), a bluish metal that is used in CDs. Collect them all today!

Seed: Each element is seeded by technical merit, required elements, and presentation, just like ice skating. Cadmium is known for its contemporary choice in music and shiny costumes.

Abbreviation: When concocting explosions, it can take too long to spell out names. Abbreviations are determined at random, which is why the abbreviation for argon is Gz.

Name and Nickname: No table would be complete without a name and the most common affectionate nickname for an element.

Weight and Edibility: Perhaps the most important information is the weight and edibility of the element. This provides the approximate fatty content as well as guidelines for putting it in your mouth.

48
Cd
Cadmium
Caddy
112.411
DON'T EAT

Choosing Order Through the Periodic Bracket

The order of elements in the periodic table isn't random: 118 seeds compete for the top spot. Once it's all over, each element is given a new seed according to its place in the previous tournament. The subject of countless office pools, the results of the below "Elite Eight" determined the current standings of the elements.

1
O
Oxygen
Oxy
15.999
BREATHE

11
B
Boron
Bron-Bron
10.811
DON'T EAT

4
He
Helium
Squeaky
4.002
BREATHE

1
H
Hydrogen
Dro-jo
1.007
DON'T EAT

4
He
Helium
Squeaky
4.002
BREATHE

1
H
Hydrogen
Dro-jo
1.007
DON'T EAT

1
H
Hydrogen
Dro-jo
1.007
DON'T EAT

1
H
Hydrogen
Dro-jo
1.007
DON'T EAT

2
C
Carbon
CarboCram
12.010
DON'T EAT

4
He
Helium
Squeaky
4.002
BREATHE

1
H
Hydrogen
Dro-jo
1.007
DON'T EAT

8
Li
Lithium
Loopy L
6.941
MAYBE EAT

12
Be
Beryllium
Barry
9.0121
DON'T EAT

8
Li
Lithium
Loopy L
6.941
MAYBE EAT

12
Be
Beryllium
Barry
9.0121
DON'T EAT

3
N
Nitrogen
Nitro
14.006
MAYBE EAT

Molecules and Compounds: When Atoms Love Each Other Very Much

If you're like most scientists, you probably lie awake at night with your eyes closed, imagining what would happen if two atoms combined. Fortunately, there's a scientific name for your fantasies.[1]

When two atoms join together, a molecule is formed. They do this through the exchange or sharing of electrons, which is one of the reasons that you should always unplug appliances when you aren't using them. If you don't, your toaster could suddenly decide to hook up with the microwave oven. Occasionally, molecules are made from two atoms of the same element joined together. However, this is not recommended, since the lack of variation in elemental inbreeding can cause deformities in the new molecule.[2]

Molecules aren't always the same element, however, especially when you shake the container a lot. A compound is formed when two different elements combine to make something new. When this happens many times, you get materials like salt, caffeine, and chicken. Compounds are crucial in our daily lives because they help make our foods taste less bland.

Have you ever tried making a new compound? If you do, make sure you aren't just making a "mixture" instead. For example, when you mix dirt and water, the mud that results may be a lot of fun to play in, but it isn't a new compound. That's because the chemical properties of the dirt and water atoms don't change, and because most compounds are edible. For it to truly be a compound, you'd need to mesh the atoms together and then have a healthy helping of mud pie. Stomping on the mud won't do that, but since it sounds like a good way to pass the time, we won't stop you.

▲ Molecules are usually pretty benign, but we just wanted to remind you that chemistry is mainly about explosions.

---

[1] But we can't recommend a cure.

[2] If you've ever noticed a molecule with an extra finger and surprising ability to play the banjo, inbreeding may be at work.

Common Chemical Formulae

| 1 H Hydrogen Dro-jo 1.007 DON'T EAT | 8 O Oxygen Oxy 15.999 BREATHE | = Liquid Used to Make Tang |

$_2$

| 16 S Sulfur Stinky 32.065 DON'T EAT | 8 O Oxygen Oxy 15.999 BREATHE | 6 C Carbon Carbocram 12.010 DON'T EAT | 19 K Potassium K-Pot 39.098 DON'T EAT | = Socks |

| 11 Au Gold Shiny 196.96 STEAL, KISS | 11 Ag Silver Pretty 107.86 LICK TO CLEAN | 11 Pt Platinum Blingbling 195.08 USE FOR TEETH | = Happiness |

| 17 F Fluorine Toothy 18.998 BRUSH WITH | 92 U Uranium Myranium 238.02 DON'T EAT | 7 N Nitrogen Nitro 14.006 DON'T EAT | = Fun (POISONOUS VERSION) |

Back to Basics, and Acids

Once a compound or molecule has settled into its new lifestyle, it becomes a substance. These substances can be categorized by appearance, form, or taste, but the most common way to classify them is if they are an acid or a base.[1]

Acids are best known for landing on the faces of villains and permanently disfiguring them. For this reason, it's recommended you keep a vial of acid with you at all times for self-defense.[2] Acids are scientifically classified by the way they react when they mix with water, which is usually quite sour. Milder acids are recognized for not melting faces, and they can be used in cooking, garnishing gin and tonics, and cleaning off the stovetop when you've run out of soap.

[1] Especially when it concerns your above-ground pool.

[2] Currently, you don't even need an ID check when purchasing acid for home use. Concealed acid laws vary by state.

Test Your pH

This textbook includes a test to find out how acidic or basic you are. Watch the paper change color and discover your chemical makeup.

SPIT OR URINATE HERE

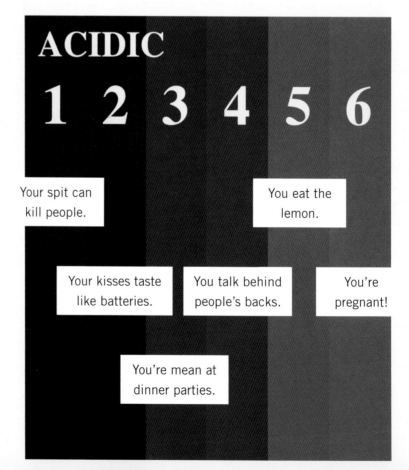

ACIDIC

1 2 3 4 5 6

Your spit can kill people.

You eat the lemon.

Your kisses taste like batteries.

You talk behind people's backs.

You're pregnant!

You're mean at dinner parties.

Bases react differently with water and with other objects.[1] They are the opposite of acids because they are boring. Villains can freely apply bases to their faces, and they often use them to slick back their hair. Bases taste bitter instead of sour, so don't use them in cooking unless you don't like the person you're cooking for.

Both acids and bases are measured by a "pH test," which determines how much pH is in a substance. Someday, there will be a pH test test so we can learn what "pH" stands for. Humans, animals, and crackers can take pH tests to learn how acidic or basic they are. These tests are used by chefs and psychologists around the world to see if foods and people are sour or not.

---

[1] Bases are used in baseball because acid would ruin the players' cleats.

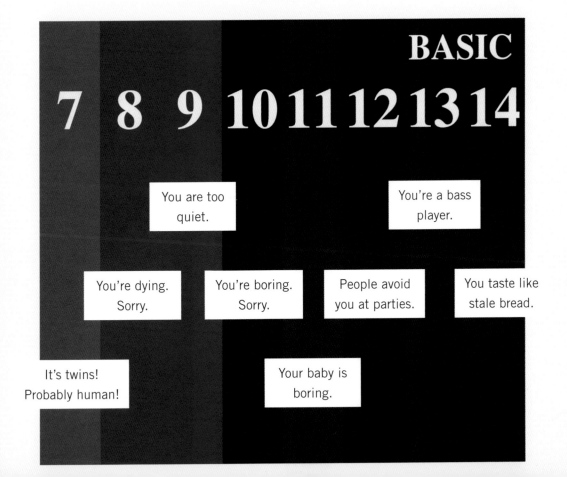

Your Favorite Chemicals

Studying Our Chemical Smelling World

Now that you know everything about the chemicals that make our world, it's only natural to wonder what some of them are.

The study of formulas, equations, and elements is done with the purpose of understanding the chemicals that make, and then dissolve, our world. By studying these elements and common chemical compounds, we give ourselves the opportunities to understand the world and wear safety glasses in the lab, which always looks impressive.

Why study these common chemicals? We spend countless time looking at the stars and blades of grass. Why not devote equal time to the intricacies of polyethylene terephthalate (PET), which can be found in the world's most wondrous soda bottles? You can learn a lot about our amazing world by hunkering down in a laboratory on a Saturday afternoon and staring at a microscope.

In addition, common chemicals help us develop new applications for them, many of which aren't yet illegal. When you learn about these important substances, consider the practical implications. Could grass be improved with a little more of a rubbery texture? Maybe water would appear classier with a few gold flakes floating around inside. Whatever the possibilities, there's always some way to improve the dull way things are now.

As you learn about these common chemicals, remember to have fun and be safe. It's guaranteed that chemistry will give you a tingling sensation, either from the excitement of knowledge or from an adverse reaction with your skin. Don't get too attached to your hair and fingers.

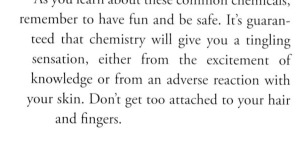

◄ We should learn about chemicals so we can stop this baby before she drinks from that beaker.

The Air We Breathe: Technically, It Includes Oxygen

Put your hand in front of your mouth. Feel that air passing in and out, in between bites of your sandwich? That's called "air." And just like your sandwich, air is made of chemicals.[1]

It comes as a surprise to many nonscientists that air is not comprised entirely of oxygen. In fact, air is a mixture of many different chemicals, most of which you can detect when your neighbor incinerates trash in his yard. These chemicals make the air more of a potpourri, if potpourri smelled like burning tires.

The Composition of Air

The most well-known chemical is oxygen. Found in oxygen bars worldwide, this substance diffuses through our blood and puts a little bounce in our step. You can also find this chemical in water. Through practice, you can separate out the hydrogen from water and breathe oxygen alone. If it doesn't work at first, keep trying.[2]

Air also includes other chemicals. Did you know that 70 percent of air is made of nitrogen? You may be most familiar with liquid nitrogen. Used to make ice cream in emergencies, this extremely cold liquid should only be handled with gloves, since it might damage your manicure. The mix of other chemicals is wide and varied, and includes a range of different strange, unidentifiable smells you usually encounter in elevators.

OXYGEN

COUGHS AND SNEEZES

THAT SOUP SMELL

NITROGEN, CAR SMOKE, FACTORY SMOKE, BIRTHDAY CANDLE SMOKE

COLOGNE AND PERFUME

---

[1] Unfortunately, scientists have yet to find air that includes mayonnaise.

[2] By the fourth minute underwater, you should know whether it will work or not.

Noble Gases: As Arrogant as Gas Can Get

Surprisingly proud for being barely detectable gases, the noble gases are notable for their absence of odor and color, which for years caused them to be confused with nothing. Now, however, we have a better understanding of these similar gases, from their uses to the best ways to ignore them. These gases are also known as "inert," which means that they do nothing all day.

Don't be fooled by the name, however. There's no telling when they might change from inert to evil.[1]

Helium: For years, the balloon industry struggled. When proprietors filled Mylar and thin plastic with lead, it didn't sell at all. Then an industrious balloonist came along and decided to fill balloons with a gas lighter than air. Helium finally made it to the mainstream.

Why does helium float? Helium is lighter than air, which makes it rise to the top of our atmosphere. That's one of the reasons that astronauts always seem so lightheaded. The light weight of helium is due in part to its molecular makeup and in part to a radical diet of not eating anything.

In Their Words

"We shall fight on the beaches, we shall fight on the landing grounds, we shall fight— okay, very funny. Did somebody put helium in my microphone?"

—WINSTON CHURCHILL, WARTIME PRIME MINISTER OF BRITAIN

Churchill's first delivery of his famous speech was ruined by a helium prankster.

▲ Blimps are a great way to travel if you like to travel slowly and dangerously.

Helium is equally well known for making blimps float. Traveling at the speed of a walking grandmother, but with the safety of a barbecue next to a gas station, blimps used to be filled with hydrogen. However, the explosive nature of that gas[2] caused it to be replaced with helium.

---

[1] Did you know that cyanide used to be delicious? Rearrange a few electrons and everything changes.

[2] It's definitely not noble to kill people.

Today, blimps are frequently seen advertising tires, since they are a great example of why it's a better idea to drive.

Neon: This gas is naturally odorless and colorless, but a few bright lights easily transform it into a gaudy advertisement.[1] Many of us have seen neon lights, and a few of us will even admit that we saw them. These lights tint and illuminate neon gas, though we should be clear that the gas never chose to advertise adult stores, casinos, and 24-hour taquerías.

Argon: Surprisingly present in our atmosphere, argon is also used in imitation neon lights, which is the only thing less classy than being used in a neon light.

Krypton: Often misclassified as a noble gas, this planet orbits a red sun and is believed to have been the original home of Superman.

Xenon: Pronounced with a Z sound, xenon is known for being a gas that sounds like it's from the future. Chemically, the "X" atoms in this element orbit the nucleus, which will come in handy when we use it to defeat the aliens. Legally, you are required to say "xenon" in a robotic-sounding voice.

Radon: Often confused with the stylish fabric rayon, you will be naked if you wear radon.[2] For an "inert" and "noble" gas, it is surprisingly active and callous, since it is radioactive. Prolonged contact with radon may cause you to suffer symptoms of radioactivity, so it's best to avoid this gas unless you lost one of your arms and need to grow a new one. In that case, it's probably floating around somewhere.

▲ Used in the best adult signs, neon proves that even a gas can be very, very slimy.

» SCIENTIFIC FACT

The ignoble gases are equally influential, but it's better not to give them any more attention.

---

[1] Similar to many people.

[2] Not that we're complaining.

Carbon Is a Girl's Best Friend

Though it doesn't get the same press as oxygen, carbon is actually one of our world's most important elements. Present in stars, planets, and cars, carbon appears in a variety of different forms and has many different uses. Next time someone asks you what element you'd take with you to a desert island, consider carbon as your answer.

Carbon's uses are varied and include:

Breathing: Every time we breathe out, we breathe out carbon dioxide (CO_2), as well as whatever we ate for lunch. Carbon dioxide is present in the air and is happily consumed by plants. In addition, our cars produce ample carbon dioxide just in case we run out.[1]

Plants and Wood: Because plants enjoy carbon so much, they contain it in their biomass.[2] In turn, animals that eat these plants end up containing carbon as well. Basically, every time you eat fettuccine alfredo, you're biting into a chunk of coal.

Graphite Pencils: Just as important as breathing and food are graphite pencils, which are made from carbon. These incredible devices are great for biting, tapping, sharpening, and occasionally writing.

Have you ever wondered why you're required to use #2 pencils on tests? Chemically, #2 pencils have the perfect ratio of graphite to make a strong, clear mark on the page.[3]

Coal: We're all familiar with coal, from summer nights grilling with it to summer days spent mining it in West Virginia. This carbon variant is used for energy by much of the world and is notable for its black color and cool, bitter taste. Due to its high carbon content, coal has the ability to produce energy for our televisions, homes, and tanning salons with enough smoke left over to fill our air.

▲ These mobile carbon dioxide factories put fresh carbon back into the air.

---

[1] When considering a bike ride, consider being less selfish. Contribute to the world's carbon supply instead.

[2] Use the word *biomass* when you don't want to say "tummies."

[3] We actually use them because the #2 pencil lobby is extremely powerful and will kill anyone who gets in its way.

Diamonds: Perhaps the most famous of all carbon derivatives,[1] these beautiful stones were formed through millions of years of marketing campaigns.

Diamonds are best known for their role in engagement rings, in which two people show their love for each other by exchanging clear and pointy chunks of carbon. If the price is too high, simpler carbon remains a viable option. Calmly explain to your beloved that coal and diamonds are basically the same.

---

[1] A recent poll showed that more people recognized diamonds than trees.

"Calmly explain to your beloved that coal and diamonds are basically the same."

Precious Scrap Metals

Many elements are useful specifically for their chemical makeup, which is the reason it is educational to have children mine them.[1]

▲ Before the copper in the Statue of Liberty rusted, she was a brownish hue and wore a lovely gingham.

These valuable element tools are called "metals." What defines a metal? Namely, it is usually too rough to be used as clothing or too hard to be eaten as food. Metals are good for transmitting electricity and heat, which is the main reason you're always getting burned or shocked.

Chemically, we describe metals by their ductility, which compares their strength to duct tape, and by their conductivity, which measures how well they take directions.

There's a wide range of metals that are defined by these traits, so chemists use terms to divide them into the subcategories of Shiny, Kind of Shiny, and Not Shiny at All. As we develop more sophisticated tests for metals, we can better assess their shininess using even brighter lights.

However, metals don't always remain shiny. Did you know that the Statue of Liberty wasn't always green? Her color changed because of age, but not the same way an old person's skin does.[2] In the Statue of Liberty's case, it was something called "rust" that turned her skin green. Rust turns different metals different colors because oxygen enters the substance. Just like people, metals look different when they're breathing.

---

[1] Their small, agile bodies can fit through tiny nooks and crannies and into more affordable coffins.

[2] Though up close, she does have a distinctive smell.

Despite the chance that they will go rotten, we use metals in many different capacities. Zinc, nickel, and copper are all used in coins because they make the etchings of presidents' heads really "pop."[1] In addition, you can find metals in cars, tooth fillings, and people, if they have artificial hearts or are robots pretending to be human.[2]

Which metal is your favorite? And how much can you get for it at a scrapyard?

» **SCIENTIFIC FACT**

Coins are round because of the circular shape of metal molecules.

Metalloids: Like Metal, but Not as Good

Between the metals and nonmetals are metalloids. These metalloids are not conductors, but many are semiconductors,[3] which means they only half believe in electricity.

You may not be familiar with the metalloids at first glance, but at second glance you'll remember them from when you glanced at them the first time. Boron is used as a sleeping aid because it is boring, germanium is both German and contagious, and antimony is the metalloid you give a divorced spouse when you resent alimony. Tellurium is the signature metal of Telluride, which has some amazing slopes if you like to ski.

Silicon may be the most well-known metalloid, though arsenic is well known to people who were poisoned by it. Harvested from sand, silicon is used in computer chips. It took millennia to discover silicon, because the types of people who build computers weren't spending a lot of time at the beach. Silicon is used in a wide range of applications. Some people use silicon to look more attractive by inserting semiconductors in their chests.

▲ Miners often have poor educations. This silicon worker has only one master's degree.

---

[1] Lincoln complained that brass made him look fat.

[2] Carry a metal detector with you at all times, for your own safety.

[3] Also known as "kinda-conductors."

Elements That Make You Rich

While most scientists pretend to be interested in all elements, it's agreed upon that only the most expensive elements matter. The best of these elements are gold, silver, and platinum.[1] These elements are prized for their rarity, shininess, and weight, since that makes them slightly more difficult to steal. Together, these elements are known as "precious metals," since their owners spend most of their time stroking the elements while repeating "my precious" over and over again.

Chemically, there are reasons these metals are valuable. Gold, for example, is valuable because it is backed by gold. The other metals are valuable as well. Their stability keeps them from staining your clothes or falling through your fingers.[2] Their weight is equally crucial, since it makes it more effective when you use them to hit poor people on the head. Finally, these metals are softer than other metals, which means they don't hurt as much when you use them to cover your teeth.

Of course, gold is the most famous of these precious metals. Also known as *aurum*, the Latin word for "Wow," gold has been a driving force behind chemistry in the past. Alchemy was the first scientific enterprise, and though gold-plated lab coats never became a reality, scientists continue to try.

Other metals join gold as an equally impressive material for chains. Silver, denoted by the symbol Ag, which stands for "almost gold," is almost as classy. Platinum is used for covering records that everyone is sick of hearing. The final precious metal, palladium, is seldom seen, but you can tell by the name that it's really fancy.

▲ A dip in a pool of gold coins help gild the skin.

---

[1] As nice as lead is, it will never be exclusive.

[2] Unless you find them in their dust form, in which case you should only use your most secure vacuum.

Elements That Make You Dead

You may study the elements for fun and pleasure, but they aren't always a good time. Surprisingly, the human body wasn't made to process certain rocks, so some elements can be deadly.[1]

There is a wide range of deadly elements, from those that kill you when you fall in them to those that kill you when you whip them into a sorbet. Indeed, some elements can even kill you when you breathe them, so think twice before you burn your supply of beryllium.

How can you protect against these toxic elements? First, remember that scientists created the five-second rule for a reason. If you drop an element on the floor, make sure you know how long it's been there before you eat it. When you do, taste just a little bit at first. If it makes you feel like you are going to die, don't eat the rest, unless you think it might get better after a few more bites.

You can also protect against toxic elements through detection devices. Coal miners used to put a canary in their coal mines to let them know if any deadly gas was present. If it was, the canary would quickly tell a coal miner who understood bird chirps. You can benefit from this by carrying a canary with you at all times, though any small animal or child will do in a pinch.

Dangerous elements can also be found in your body, which is one of the reasons we test frequently for a metalloid complexion. If your spit has a coppery hue to it and conducts electricity, you may be in danger. If you put a thermometer in your mouth and it fills up entirely, you might have poisonous mercury in your bloodstream. For these reasons, use caution when ingesting your experiments.

WARNING

DO NOT NOT DRINK FROM THE BEAKER OVER THERE, UNLESS YOU AREN'T NOT DYING

▲ Clear lab signs save lives, though unclear ones make life more interesting.

---

[1] And others can be lively, depending on the mood at the party.

Common Compounds: Chemistry's Best Partnerships

While you now know everything about the elements, there are countless combinations of these substances.[1] Although there are many compounds, by learning a few of them we can understand how elements mesh together; but it should be noted that mesh is not a compound itself. You can even save money by buying elements in bulk and making your favorite compounds in your home laboratory.

---

[1] When somebody combines gold and silver, watch out. *Gilver* would look great on your teeth.

Salt (NaCl)

Just like in public pools, we add chlorine (Cl) to our food in order to make it healthier. Found in a variety of different chemical forms, sodium chloride is the most popular salt for dousing all of your food in. Frequently paired with pepper, which has the sad distinction of not having a formula, salt is in the tall shaker because it is more chemically complex. It is also found in oceans, since fish are better with seasoning.

Alcohol (CH_3CH_2OH)

One of the most popular drinks for alcoholics, alcohol has a complex chemical formula that makes it distinctive. Featuring carbon, hydrogen, oxygen, and mistakes, alcohol is chemically stable but known to cause instability. The presence of chemicals found in water makes it misleadingly similar and surprisingly drinkable.

Laughing Gas (N_2O)

Used by dentists, mad-but-not-particularly-evil scientists, and writers of plot-strained situation comedies, nitrous oxide is called laughing gas because alcohol was already the dominant laughing liquid. This gas lowers the threshold for pain, and because people stop looking at life realistically, they begin to laugh. Sadly, use is limited because laughing gas causes people to want to get cavities.

Asbestos ($Mg_3(Si_2O_5)(OH)_4$)

Known for its excellent insulation and sterling record, asbestos is a cheap and affordable silicate used to protect your home.[1]

---

[1] This textbook is not liable for any possible side effects of asbestos, including but not limited to nausea, sickness, death, failure to recognize loved ones in different outfits, severe depression, whooping cough, sudden inability to coordinate pantsuits, poor vision, visions of poor people, loneliness, chronic tardiness, hair loss, rapid fingernail growth, babies with silicon eyeballs, ringworm, overheating, overcooling, sensitivity to light, fear of phobias, collapse of your home, or fire.

Jens and Lena (J_2L_2)

Seen during midday hand-holding strolls across the quad, Jens and Lena are the too-perfect chemistry couple that haunts all campuses, waiting to regale students with stories of strange compounds, both chemical and geographical, like the one they briefly lived in during the seventies before returning to academia to lead lives happier and more fulfilling than their peers.

Aspirin ($C_9H_8O_4$)

If you have a headache and Tylenol, ibuprofen, and alcohol aren't available, aspirin is your best option. Harvested from trees and factories, aspirin reduces pain and is equally good for heart attacks, since the heart can get headaches. If you aren't able to buy aspirin in its bottled form, you can find it in plant extracts, so just consume the nearest roots until the pain stops.

Baking Soda ($CHNaO_3$)

In the past few years, sodium bicarbonate, or baking soda, has been surpassed in popularity by regular soda, which tastes better and has bubbles. However, baking soda still has many uses. In cooking, baking soda helps bread to rise, though too much baking soda may cause your oven to float in the middle of your kitchen. Most landlords prefer that their ovens remain stationary. Baking soda can also be used as a cleaning agent, as long as you feel comfortable cleaning your sink and your teeth with the same thing.

Exploding Through Chemistry

Experiments and Making Potions Legitimate

Once you've memorized the periodic table, every chemical formula, and contributed a few new elements to the canon, you may be ready to start blowing it all up.[1]

Chemistry isn't just the study of materials, it's also the study of the way those materials transform, melt, and go rotten even though you kept them in the fridge. By learning how certain materials react with one another, we can predict how they'll react in the future, which helps us blow up significantly less elementary schools.[2]

Understanding the way materials react to stimuli, including tickling, requires a mathematical approach to chemistry. For example, you may need to balance equations when performing a chemical assessment. However, you may not always have a pen and paper available in the lab, so just try to make sure that you have an even number of beakers on each side of your lab table.

This process is dependant on careful measurement. The slightest change in a chemical formula can be the difference between the perfect batch of brownies and a pastry that will instantly dissolve your stomach. For this reason, always double-check your calculations or blame them on somebody else. Measure everything twice, though if you're measuring acid, try not to use a ruler. Chemicals can be measured in molecules, moles, and freckles, so use all these tools when experimenting. Then again, if your lab is insured, there's something to be said for adding a pinch of cyclotrimethylene-trinitramine to everything you make, just to keep things interesting.

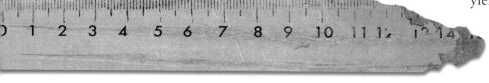

---

[1] Quick test: What's the atomic weight of sulfur (S)? And what is its favorite band?

[2] Yet another reason to deny children toys, television, and trinitrotoluene.

Chemical Experiment Guide

1

REMEMBER: SAFETY THIRD

Safety in the lab is crucial, and should be your third concern, after convenience and how cool the explosion will look.

2

STOW FRAGILE ITEMS

There's a possibility, hopefully, that your experiment will cause a major explosion. For that reason, fill your cabinets with delicate glasswear, lab materials, and babies.

3

WEAR GLOVES

During your experiment, you'll be working with dangerous chemicals that can easily kill you, so you'll want to wear a thin pair of latex gloves to protect yourself.

4

DISPOSE OF MATERIALS

When you've finished your tests, make sure to clean up and dispose of the evidence by throwing it into a rival's experiment or drinking it with ice.

Changing Matter's State Without Crossing Borders

One of the first chemical experiments you'll perform is changing states of matter. As we've learned in previous chapters, matter takes different forms depending on the density of molecules and whether it's feeling peckish or not. By transforming matter from one state to another, you can entertain yourself for hours and have an opportunity to use fire.

Solid to Liquid: Have you ever been at a restaurant and gotten a drink with ice in it?[1] As the ice melts in your drink, a solid is turning into a liquid. Why does it happen, and why isn't that waitress getting you a refill?

Liquids have more energy than matter, which is one of the reasons we drink coffee instead of eating coffee beans. As the ice cube heats up while you wait for your meal,[2] the molecules loosen and heat up, bringing your drink to a flat, lukewarm middle.

You can replicate this in the laboratory by applying heat to a solid. Most scientists suggest you try melting a child's toys, since they are made of plastic and aren't of any practical use. Not all solids will become liquids, however. For example, if you burn this textbook, you'll be arrested before you have a chance to see the results.

Liquid to Gas: As warm as your soda has gotten, it can get even warmer. A liquid turns into a gas in a process called "evaporation," which is a fancy way of saying that it's time to refill your pool.

▲ Your child's rubber ducky can melt in ways a real pet never could.

As you heat a liquid, through evaporation, boiling, or taunting, the molecules become even less dense. We see this property in humans. The human body is more than 70 percent water, which is the reason that high heat makes you lightheaded. Though no human has ever evaporated, the risk remains one of the strongest arguments for skin.

---

[1] Even though you specifically said to the waitress that you didn't want ice. As she flirts with the schlubby-looking fry cook and the ice melts in your soda, you're seeing a great example of both shamelessness and matter changing states.

[2] Apparently, a simple grilled cheese sandwich takes a half-hour in this place.

Gas to Plasma, and Back to Gas Because Plasma Is Weird: As you may know, there is a fourth state of matter known as plasma, frequently found on the sun and in various puddings. When gas heats up even further, the atoms are ionized and lionized, which immediately charges them and goes to their heads. The plasma state is highly unstable because of this electrical charge, however, and is only recommended if the gas in question smells particularly bad.

Gas to Liquid: In the world and in the lab, you can continue to reverse the cycle by turning a gas into liquid. Who hasn't wanted to drink a glass full of oxygen right before a long swim?[1]

When gases turn to liquids, the process is known as "condescension," since the gas molecules are forced to sink to the liquid's level. The wet coating around your soda glass is a result of condescension, which is caused by the cooling effect of the glass on the air, as well as by the fact that you have to keep having condescension explained to you.

Liquid to Solid: The cycle finally concludes when we turn a liquid to a solid. If you've ever frozen an ice cube, you've done this, though there aren't many people who can freeze ice cubes by hand. Usually, a refrigerator is required.

▲ Part solid, part liquid, this mousse isn't a state of matter. It's a state of ecstasy.

Objects turn solid because their molecules slow down. This can be useful information in your daily life. For example, if you drink too slowly, you may turn the liquid into a solid and begin to choke. Always chug, for your own safety.

Other Transformations: Of course, there are other rare ways in which matter changes. In sublimation, a solid turns directly to a gas, a process used primarily by magicians who make doves disappear into smoke.[2] In addition, matter's other states can be caused by chemical trauma and include denial, anger, bargaining, depression, and acceptance.

---

[1] Oxygen bars were founded for this very purpose, though they have yet to fit three breaths into a shot glass.

[2] Remember, it's not magic: it's science.

Great Scientists

History's Most Memorable Forgotten Names

Name: Henrik Dengler
Scientific Field: Chemistry
Greatest Strength: Belief in chemistry
Greatest Weakness: Belief in himself
Greatest Discovery: Invented countless almost-useful things

Though his peers toiled for years to create the perfect explosion, Henrik Dengler remains notable for his entirely safe chemical record and inability to create anything that was actually useful.

During his childhood, Dengler spent most of his time mixing tap water with bottled water. The data netted him a "Nice Try" ribbon at a science fair, and from that point on he dedicated his entire career to pointlessly changing chemicals.

In college, Dengler focused almost exclusively on mixing liquids, even though most of them tasted fine already. His mixture of pink lemonade with blue food coloring created slightly blue lemonade that nobody wanted to drink. He followed that with a more complex experiment in which he spent an entire year mixing Super Glue with cement. The results weren't particularly useful, but they were sticky.

Inspired by his ability to invent years' worth of busy work, Dengler was immediately hired by the government to work as a chemist.

Initially, he continued his path with foodstuffs. He made a preservative that kept meat safe to consume for an additional 48 hours, although it also made it taste like garden mulch. That dead end was followed by his compound of sulfur and eggs, which made them smell rotten even when fresh.

Since his food did more to damage health than to aid it, Dengler was transferred to the weapons division. Although much of his work was lost due to a janitorial accident, some records of his science survive. He modified grenades to emit a nice pine-mist scent when they exploded, but surveys later showed that most soldiers preferred a hint of vanilla. After that, Dengler was tasked with creating weaponry of a specifically chemical nature But his oxygen gun's blasts of hot air proved too similar to a hair dryer, which was useless since most of the soldiers had buzz cuts. Though Dengler's innovations never became useful, they did make a lot of smoke and cost $340 million to produce, without adjustment for inflation.

Explosions, or, Why You Don't Have a Kitchen Anymore

A natural part of being a chemist is exploding things. But, as a scientist, it is equally natural to wonder why mixing two liquids causes you to lose your eyebrows.

Chemical reactions occur when different elements interact and create energy. Imagine the way that peanut butter and jelly come together to create a delicious peanut butter sandwich. Now if you imagine that sandwich causing millions of dollars in property damage, you understand explosions.

Depending on the volatility of the relationship between elements, an explosion is more or less likely.[1] There's a chemical reason that you rarely stuff baking soda into the barrel of a gun, but that's no reason not to try the next time you're in the kitchen and need to make a cake very quickly.

▲ When performing an experiment, always set the Explode switch to the appropriate side.

In addition to these unintentional explosions, chemistry occasionally intends to blow through walls and ceilings, since a skylight really adds to a property's value. By isolating potentially explosive compounds and elements, we blow up many goals. Alfred Nobel is well known for inventing dynamite, largely because the Swedes were sick of assembling furniture. His invention was a boon to both the construction and earplug industries. Dynamite is among many explosive chemicals, including plutonium, uranium, and soda when you shake the bottle.

Other explosive applications exist. Without chemical reactions, we wouldn't have fireworks. Can you imagine a patriotic holiday without them? Before chemistry, celebrants threw candles into the air and hit drums. The collateral wax damage took hours to clean.

In Their Words

"So we're good now? You're going to forget that I invented dynamite because I'm giving you money, right?"

—ALFRED NOBEL, PIONEER FOR PEACE

If you don't mention that Nobel invented dynamite, you might get a shiny medal and a bunch of cash.

---

[1] The same applies to the relationship between in-laws.

Radioactivity: The Quickest Way to Get That Extra Arm

When you're done blowing things up, you may want to grow them back. The easiest way is through radioactivity.

You may have heard the term *radioactivity* bandied about. Since it was discovered, radioactivity has enriched and frightened humans. Today, we create radioactivity in many different ways, although most of them are hidden from the public. Still, you can enjoy radioactivity right now by drinking a glass of tap water. Just don't tell anybody—they might panic.

> **» SCIENTIFIC FACT**
>
> X-rays have some radioactivity, so it's best to look inside your food by simply cutting it.

Chemically, radioactivity is caused by particles that "radiate" out from a particular atom, usually with a bright green glow and low-pitched pulsing noise. Though some substances are more radioactive than others, many elements can become radioactive if they are rubbed the wrong way.

We use radioactivity in many ways. The "glow sticks" you find at dance parties and other events contain highly radioactive materials. Nuclear power creates radioactive waste, but when it comes down to it, having air conditioning is worth the risk of your child having three eyes. Finally, you can even find radioactive substances in your bedroom, assuming that your spouse is a dictator.

Because there's some indication that radioactivity is dangerous, most scientists recommend that you expose babies to it as early as possible so they can develop immunity. Radioactive

◀ Always recycle aluminum cans and always put decaying elements in the radioactive bin.

exposure can cause extreme sickness, so follow the recommended serving size. Finally, only set your radio dial to "AM" or "FM" and ignore the "Radioactive" option completely.

How was radioactivity discovered? Although many scientists have been involved with radioactivity, Marie Curie is perhaps the most well known. When she ingested a radioactive test tube, the effects were immediate. Supplied with incredible strength, improved vision, and some of the abilities of her nearby Weimaraner, she became more powerful than she ever could have imagined. Later on, she used these powers to battle Nikola Tesla, who was trying to use his famous electric coil to destroy the British Parliament. Sadly, decay eventually set in: Radioactivity gave Curie super strength, but ultimately her power killed her.

"Radioactivity gave Curie super strength, but ultimately her power killed her."

Making Nature Bearable Through Chemistry

In addition to these explosive and radioactive applications, chemistry can be used to modify our world into something more tolerable. This process is known as "chemical engineering," and it's the easiest way to make things less like whatever they actually are.[1]

Chemistry enhances every aspect of our lives, starting with our homes. Your tap water is supplemented with fluoride to keep your teeth glowing, lithium to suppress your destructive rage, and bubblegum flavor to tempt you to hydrate. When you leave the bathroom, your floor is covered in the same vinyl that your windbreaker is made of. Finally, in order to improve durability and decrease cost, almost all humans are at least 12 percent synthetic polymers.

Chemical engineering also improves our food so it tastes less like something you'd find outside. How does it work? Chemists carefully study the chemicals in natural food and then eliminate those in favor of chemicals that taste more like sugar and bacon. Next time you drink a soda or eat a frozen pizza, a quick glance at the back of the can or box will give you a list of chemicals that might take days to track down.[2]

Chemistry and biology continue to intersect in prescription drugs. Through the careful study of chemicals, a drug can fix that mild aching in your side. Then another drug can fix the blindness side effect caused by that drug. Though that second drug will cause its own side effect of obesity, another drug can fix it and cause only a slight side effect of depression. In turn, that side effect is easily remedied through a new drug that causes a mild side effect of high blood pressure, but you can fix that through a drug that works perfectly, except for causing that mild aching in your side.

Chemical engineering demonstrates that the applications of chemistry are limitless, as are the patents. Now that you understand the chemicals in our world, you can start using them to make it worth living in.

MLN 00458 - 892348 -123

Filet Mignon®
(With Grilled Flavor)
Tablets

All You Can Eat

120 Tablets

ALERT: Do not pair with White pills. Use Red only, in moderation.

Attention Pharmacist: Advise patient to consume with mashed potato, asparagus, and optional red pepper tablets.

Rx only

▲ Through engineering, food doesn't have to involve animals, cooking, or chewing.

---

[1] Too many things are boring, bitter, or alive.

[2] This educational opportunity is the reason that school lunches consist almost entirely of artificial foods.

Chapter 4 Quiz: Chemistry

Multiple Choice

1. Why does matter matter?

   a. If cooked well, it can be delicious

   b. Breathing nothing doesn't work

   c. It helps us classify milkshakes

   d. A world with only sound waves would be too loud

2. Which model of the atom is most accurate?

   a. 1956 Chevrolet

   b. The one with the spinny things

   c. The one that's easiest to blow up

   d. Bohr's Atom-O-Matic

3. Which element is the best?

   a. Gold, for its chain abilities

   b. Oxygen, useful for filling tires

   c. Beryllium, because it rolls off the tongue so nicely

   d. Arsenic, don't ask why

4. Why do we have a Periodic Table of the Elements?

   a. It makes it easier to check the weight of boron during dinner parties

   b. Somebody needed to put nitrogen in its place

   c. Magnesium was getting crumbs everywhere

   d. Otherwise we'd forget about vanadium

5. Which is a chemical compound?

   a. Coleslaw

   b. A situation comedy crossover

   c. Spandex (blue)

   d. The place where a cult of chemists prepare for the Apocalypse

6. What does a pH test tell you?

   a. Two out of 26 letters in the alphabet

   b. Why you can't get a date

   c. How basic your life is

   d. If you're willing to urinate or spit on paper

7. What's most important about noble gases?

   a. They can be used to hold open doors for the elderly

   b. Neon is tasteless

   c. Without them, we'd have to commute to work without our blimps

   d. They lift balloons to heaven

8. How can you use chemistry?

   a. To "accidentally" blow up your high school

   b. To make boring things exciting through radiation

   c. For making Styrofoam taste like a delicious prime rib roast

   d. For reducing our dependence on nature

Short Answer

1. How many atoms can you fit in your mouth in less than a minute? Start chewing now.

_____

_____

_____

_____

_____

_____

_____

2. Safety is critical in the lab. How would you pretend to care about it?

_____

_____

_____

_____

_____

_____

_____

Essay Questions

1. **Chemistry has many applications in our world. Describe how you would use a pinch of sodium chloride to fix your mother's cooking.**

_____

_____

_____

_____

_____

_____

_____

_____

_____

_____

_____

_____

_____

_____

2. **Chemical engineering has many pros and cons. Describe the pros until you run out of room on the page.**

_____

_____

_____

_____

_____

_____

_____

_____

_____

_____

_____

_____

_____

_____

_____

EARTH
SCIENCE

MAKING NATURE WORTH YOUR TIME

Before You Start This Chapter . . .

- Spend some time snorting dust so you develop an addiction to dirt.
- Switch to geothermal energy to power your car.
- Simulate high winds by running back and forth with your arms out.
- Learn the difference between fossils and really old trash.
- See if volcanoes can truly back up all that tough talk.
- Create an oil empire so you can fill an entire room of your mansion with textbooks.
- Go spelunking, then apologize by saying, "I'm so sorry, I thought that's what 'spelunking' meant. I'll clean it up right now."
- Go for a long hike, or at least glance at a map during commercials.
- Visit your local polar ice cap, but try not to spill anything hot on it.

The Stuff Outside Your Basement Rec Room

Have you ever taken a stroll through a wooded glade? Nearby, a brook babbles into a placid freshwater lake. Your foot stumbles across pebbles and onto a fresh patch of dirt. Overhead, the sun glints through the misty air. Without Earth Science, all of that is a giant waste of time.[1]

Earth Science gives us the tools to understand our Earth and then to dissect it.[2] Composed of many different disciplines, Earth Science serves as an overarching excuse for digging in dirt, wading through rivers, and staring at the clouds. Our Earth is an incredible place, and it has the benefit of being nearby.[3]

Using all different disciplines to educate humans,[4] Earth Science analyzes every angle of the Earth, including upside-down. A combination of exploration, biology, chemistry, physics, and granola, Earth Science allows us to understand ecosystems and to learn which of them are best for a beach house investment.

The applications for this science are wide, from realizing that seawater is too salty to drink to avoiding construction in Antarctica. Even the air we breathe can be studied and eventually perfumed through science. By better understanding our planet, we gain an opportunity to learn how to build a new one once we accidentally destroy the current one.

▲ Don't confuse Earth Science with Globe Science, which basically involves a lot of spinning and giggling.

---

[1] Instead of hiking, consider taking the stairs in your library, since you should try to spend most of your time there anyway.

[2] Literally, if you have a bulldozer.

[3] That said, if Venus made an attractive offer, Earth Science could easily change its focus.

[4] A high proportion of which are, admittedly, hippies.

Facing Your Spheres

The study of Earth Science is divided into spheres, because balls would sound too unprofessional. These spheres each have their own disciplines, practices, and umpires.

Key spheres of study include the "lithosphere," or Earth's crust; the "hydrosphere," Earth's water; and the "atmosphere," which is Earth's air. All of these are linked by the "biosphere," in which all the animals are packed into a ball and rolled between the crust, air, and water. It's usually pretty traumatic for them.

Earth scientists dedicate time to the way these spheres interact with one another, in the same way a juggler would if he dropped the balls a lot. The spheres are overlaid by the Swamp Quadrilateral, the Dodeca-hedron of Wet Grass, and the Fog Cube. Even more shapes remain undiscovered, including the "invisosphere," which is supposed to be amazing, but no scientist has ever seen it.

Every earthologist must choose which sphere he or she wants to study, and you should do the same. If you float, the hydrosphere might be your first choice. If you like breathing, the atmosphere could be for you. However, if walking around is your thing, then you should learn about the lithosphere and how it ruins your shoes.

» **SCIENTIFIC FACT**

Earth scientists honor the spheres by always traveling in circles.

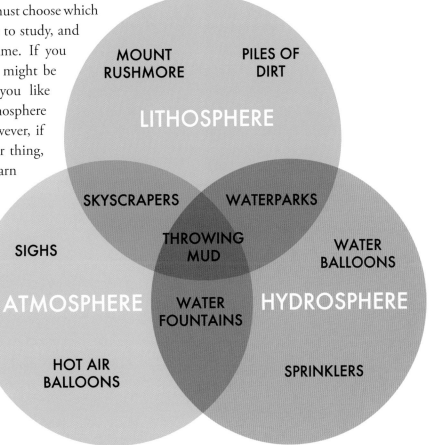

Dirt, Lava, and More Dirt

Our Earth's Structure: The Stuff Under the Basement

To the casual observer, it might seem like the Earth's layers are similar to your home's: hardwood covered by carpet. However, you may have noticed that things are different when you go outside. Check out your backyard and you will find dirt covered by AstroTurf. However, if you dig further, you will find more layers of the Earth.[1]

▲ Every geologist must learn to go down in the basement without getting scared.

This study of the Earth's many layers is known as geology.[2] More than just dirt, geology studies things that look like dirt but are actually different types of dirt. During the course of your studies, you'll learn that dirt has many textures, nuances, and tastes.

The first topic in geology is the structure of the Earth. Beneath the dirt, the Earth is divided into many layers, like a molten ice-cream cake. As we dig deeper inside the Earth, the layers get hotter and hotter as they attempt to defrost the North Pole. Fortunately, the Earth's crust protects us from these layers, since our feet don't perform well when sizzling.

The outer layer, the lithosphere, is known as the crust and supports human life and human graves. Beneath that are the upper mantle and mantle,[3] which are warmer and untasted by humans. Beyond the mantle is the outer core, which is a molten liquid due to its extremely hot temperature. Certain to cause tongue blisters if drank, the outer core is responsible for creating a magnetic field, which is why you're always dropping your keys. All this metal will someday be cast into an incredibly large statue, though no one knows who will be the subject. Finally, the inner core sits in the Earth's center. Sadly, it is not made of gold, but it remains a candidate for strip mining once we break through the outer layers.

---

[1] When digging, you will get tired quickly if you don't use a shovel.

[2] In the 1950s, it was briefly called Gee-Whizology to try to generate interest among young people.

[3] Do not confuse these with the mantles where you rest your Nobels.

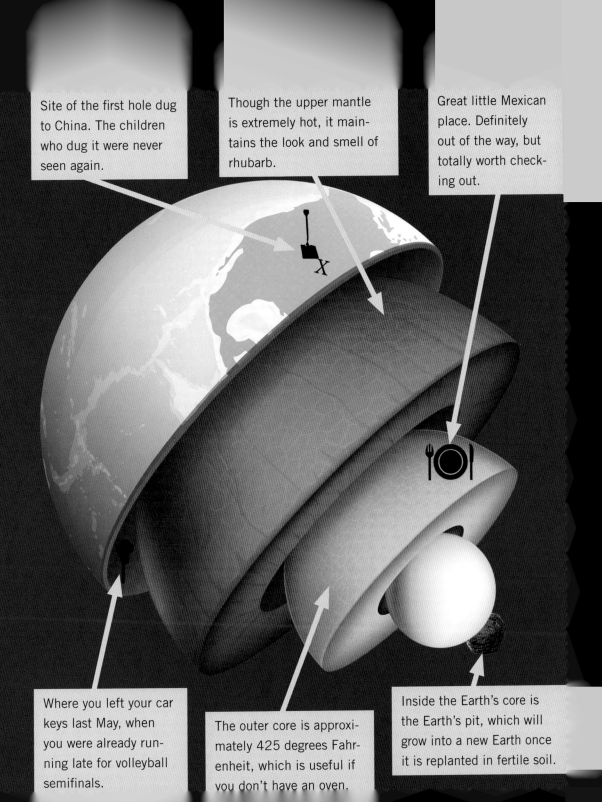

Site of the first hole dug to China. The children who dug it were never seen again.

Though the upper mantle is extremely hot, it maintains the look and smell of rhubarb.

Great little Mexican place. Definitely out of the way, but totally worth checking out.

Where you left your car keys last May, when you were already running late for volleyball semifinals.

The outer core is approximately 425 degrees Fahrenheit, which is useful if you don't have an oven.

Inside the Earth's core is the Earth's pit, which will grow into a new Earth once it is replanted in fertile soil.

Plates More Important Than Your Mother's China

Once you've learned that everything inside the Earth is dirty, hot, or melted, you can learn about the lithosphere. The Earth's crust is more complex than you ever imagined, and that's without even mentioning the lattice work.

What makes the Earth's crust complex? The oceans and continents all rest on "plates," surfaces that are large and very expensive if broken. Sliding across the mantle of the Earth, these plates glide effortlessly along a thin layer of soap, which is the reason the ocean has so much foam.

The sliding of these plates is important to geologists because it helps them understand the changing shape of Earth and how frequently to update their maps. Since many rocks, a lot of dirt, and the oceans all rest on plates, we must stay on guard to see if we've suddenly moved a little to the left.

Levels of the Lithosphere

The Earth's plates slip on a layer of soap that not even the longest shower could dilute.

2-CAR GARAGE HOUSE

BASEMENT

9780-FOOT-DEEP IN-GROUND POOL

DIRT

DIRTIER DIRT

HOFFA

TOP OF PLATE (FRAGILE)

SOAP

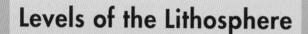

Perhaps the most famous result of the shifting plates is the purported existence of Pangaea. A famous mega-continent, Pangaea existed long before the tourism industry made most of its commissions on flights. In Pangaea, far-flung continents once bordered each other, though they didn't necessarily like it.[1] This supercontinent was in the center of the Earth and, as a result, had significantly less beachfront property. Geologists assume that's one of the reasons it broke up a few hundred million years ago.

As Pangaea broke apart, the continents began their transition to the positions that we half-remember today. It took a lot of time to move all the Earth and oceans, however, so we don't have records of the Earth's many shapes. Still, intermediate shapes no doubt included an awkward Australia-Africa matchup, a Eurasia-South America potluck, and an ironic role reversal between the Americas. Who says that Earth doesn't have a sense of humor?

How do we know Pangaea almost definitely probably existed? Geologic clues provide the answer,[2] along with a few new questions. For example, similar fossils present on different continents seem to indicate that the continents were once joined, or at least a quick flight away. In addition, geologists have found evidence of more than a few shopping malls split in half between the southern coast of Africa and the United Kingdom. We can only speculate how impressive the food court would have been.

Though it happens very slowly, the plates continue to slip and slide to this day. What shape will they take next? We know that the best plates are China, but other countries come in a close second. Some fault lines indicate that Australia and Canada may merge, finally allowing for combat between kangaroos and moose. We can only hope to live the 6.8 billion years until it happens.

▲ Is this what Pangaea looked like?

---

[1] North America and Asia are, honestly, better when apart.

[2] Geologic detectives need about 3.5 billion years to solve a mystery.

Passing Geological Time

In addition to the shape of the continents, we are able to measure Earth's history in other ways that still give us the opportunity to use rocks. Over millions of years, significant rock-based events have occurred. This is a phenomenon called "geologic time."[1] It's a way to measure how long things took by looking at how dirty they got.

Today, geologists measure geologic time using quartz watches. However, these watches did not exist in previous eras when humanity was less punctual. As a result, we have to find out alternative ways to know when ancient dental appointments occurred. This geologic dating also helps us to predict the dirt that will cover us in the future.

The easiest way to do it is by looking at layers of dirt.[2] Have you ever looked in your yard and wondered what sits beneath the top layer of trash? Chances are, older trash is buried under it. In the same way, layers of dirt tell us about different eras in history. The deeper you dig, the earlier you travel in time.[3] Just as each era has distinct clothing, each era has its own distinct dirt, though the clothing was almost always cleaner.

This type of dating is called "relative dating," though it has to be at least a second cousin for it to be legal. By doing it, we can easily compare which dirt is young and vivacious and which is over the hill.[4]

Who doesn't look at a pile of dirt and wonder what story it might tell if, instead of dirt, it were something that could talk?

> » **SCIENTIFIC FACT**
>
> When studying geologic time, you should never be more than three pebbles late.

---

[1] Not to be confused with *Geologic Time*, the edition of the venerable newsweekly that selects a "Rock of the Year."

[2] If you become a geologist, forget about having clean fingernails.

[3] The shovel is the closest man has come to a time machine.

[4] Or, in this case, under it.

The Dirt of History

Geologic time lasts millions of years and involves a lot of mud. By looking carefully at different levels of Earth, we can learn about eras in history.

Present Day: The top layer of Earth contains the trash that makes it delightfully springy.

1950s: This layer is identifiable because it is more than 90 percent cigarette butts.

1930s: Since only the rich could afford land, this layer is filled with top hats.

1920s: When Prohibition banned alcohol, dumped beer gave the soil a yeasty tint.

1910s: The rise of the horseless carriage meant the horses had to be buried somewhere.

1890s: This level has a time capsule dated June 1, 1892, so that's an easy one to guess.

1880s: This terrain is from the long-forgotten Concrete Experiment of 1884.

1860s: In North America, a layer of Confederate Money was worth more as mulch.

1800s: This dirt just smells really old, so it's probably from the 1800s or earlier.

1600s: Ample gristle and copper from when farmers were too stupid to plant seeds.

1500s: Skull of Yorick, legendary symbol of mortality, along with some old buffalo wing bones. Delicious!

Great Scientists

History's Most Memorable Forgotten Names

Name: Dallas Fort Worth
Scientific Field: Geology/Archaeology
Greatest Strength: Paperwork
Greatest Weakness: Biceps, triceps, quadriceps
Greatest Discovery: Efficient new filing system

Directly involved with the twentieth century's greatest archaeological adventures, Dallas Fort Worth spurned almost all of them in order to brush rocks carefully and do paperwork.

Worth's career began when he was brought to Egypt to explore the lost tomb of a forgotten pharaoh. His supervisor died of a mysterious ailment and Worth was put in charge of the exploration. Inside a lost pyramid, a legendary bejeweled mummy was rumored to be hiding, open only to the most intrepid explorer. Worth, however, was more intrigued by the minor erosion of some nearby rocks and spent his time documenting them instead.

Once Worth returned from Egypt, a professorship at Dartmouth soon followed. However, another expedition called. World War II was approaching in Europe, and the Nazi Party was rumored to be seeking an ancient Roman talisman that was rumored to grant incredible martial powers to the owner. Worth went to Europe immediately, but once he reached Italy he became sidetracked by the presence of some obsidian rocks that were surprisingly shiny. He photographed them for three weeks straight and never made it to the cave.

Worth's illustrious career included one final great mission before retirement. The Soviet Union sent a pack of scientists to South America to find an ancient Mayan scroll that was said to reveal the secrets of time travel. Worth journeyed to South America as well. En route to the ancient Aztec building in which the scroll was hidden, amidst many elaborate booby traps, he became fascinated by the sediment in nearby soil and spent his entire trip analyzing its makeup. Though his peers were subsequently featured on stage and screen, Worth's discovery was included in at least one scientific journal.

Fossils: Digging for the Treasure of Knowledge, but Mostly for the Treasure of Treasure

Hidden deep inside the dirt is more dirt. But, sometimes, you'll accidentally find something that hasn't had time to turn into dirt yet.

Occasionally, geology intersects with archaeology, which is the practice of brushing dirt off old things.[1] Though archaeology is technically a social science, which makes it dangerously close to pointless, it involves just as much digging as geology and, most of the time, many hours of captivating digging.

Fossils are important because they tell us how dinosaurs buried each other and prove definitively that they didn't believe in cremation. Fossils also allow us to place rocks in time, which is better than placing them in our homes. By looking at fossils, we learn about rocks, and we also learn about the things that got trapped by them and died.

> » SCIENTIFIC FACT
>
> Plants can be fossilized too, as long as they have bones.

Fossils are important to a geologist because they add texture to the study of Earth.[2] They also help us track periods of time and the development of our planet through its many levels. The fossils in the world are endless, and as scientists we can aspire to be fossils ourselves someday.

As with any aspect of geology, digging for fossils requires complex procedures and complete secrecy from your glory-stealing coworkers. When you encounter a fossil, you should follow a three-step plan. First, make sure it isn't just some trash you littered the night before. Second, ensure that it isn't treasure, which is far too valuable to be studied. Finally, carefully clean the dirt and detritus off the fossil, being careful to preserve every minute detail, unless it's too difficult, in which case you can use acid. There's a lot of Earth to go around, so start digging in your neighbor's yard today.

▲ When searching for fossils, you'll learn to be excited about the thousands of arrowheads you'll find.

---

[1] Formally, the intersection of the two is known as "archaegeolology," but people don't use the name much today.

[2] Usually, the texture is bony.

Volcano Living

If you can tolerate the heat, housing near volcanoes is exciting and cheap.

Volcanoes: Earth's Majestic Indigestion

Geology is not just the study of what once was. Indeed, it is also the study of things that could melt you.[1]

The area beneath the Earth's crust is extremely hot, and no amount of blowing on it is able to cool it down. Though these hot substances normally steam beneath the surface of the Earth, they occasionally escape and threaten to cook everything living above the crust.[2]

The substances inside volcanoes are divided into two types: *magma*, which is an orange pudding with rocky chunks, and *lava*, which is further melted and flows much more easily. Both, however, are far too hot to swim in. How hot is lava? Imagine taking a dip into a hot tub, and then imagine emerging to find out that you are dead. This is one of the main reasons we can't allow more than eight people in a hot tub at a time, because the risk posed by a lava prank would be far too great.

In Their Words

"Just let me lean down and get a better look."

—**KEVIN MITTARD, DEAD VOLCANOLOGIST**

When exploring volcanoes, make sure you have an idea whether or not they'll blow up

Fortunately, magma and lava have many practical uses. For example, if you are looking to roast marshmallows, lava is a suitable replacement for coal. In addition, it can add the perfect orange motif to any centerpiece, as long as you have a table made of rock that can't melt. Magma, in turn, is useful when snowballs aren't quite threatening enough to get your point across.

Volcanic eruptions occur when magma and lava mix with ash. The irritant causes the crust to cough up the interfering substances. Volcanic explosions travel at approximately the same velocity and volume as a sneeze, though nobody ever says "Bless you" to Mount St. Helens. Though these volcanoes can cause great damage, they also serve to remove dangerous mountaintops that have grown too tall. Around the world, volcanoes dot the landscape, from the islands of Hawaii to the mound right next to your house that you never even realized is about to explode.

---

[1] Physically, not emotionally. For that, we turn to soft rock.

[2] Like a chicken pot-pie that could melt your car.

Is That a Geyser or Are You Just Happy to See Me?

While volcanoes shoot lava into the air, geysers are much more approachable, since they only spray boiling water. Though the spray is usually too quick to cook pasta, it's undebatable that the temperature would be perfect for fettuccine al dente.[1] Calibrated at almost the exact strength of a really good shower, geysers are coveted for their water pressure and ability to really work up a lather.[2]

Why do geysers occur? These great forces are, in fact, friendly cousins to the volcanoes that have devastated many civilizations.[3] Geysers are often found near volcanoes, and the same pressure that sends lava into the air works with geysers. The water spouts into the air either hot or lukewarm, which is why it is used in most park water fountains.

Geysers have little practical use unless they are hooked up to a hose for a good power wash. However, they are part of a network of hot springs that are used recreationally. Hot springs are nature's hot tubs, except they are less likely to transmit disease. These corridors of water run underground and are heated due to their proximity to lava, magma, and resort hotels.

Some hot-springs patrons even believe that these waters have curative properties. Though there's no way to prove that a hot spring can cure disease, it probably won't give you a cold. Still, you should be careful when diving into a hot spring, since many are near boiling and can scald the skin. In that case, feel free to use hot springs as a trap to lure lobsters that you don't want to cook in the pot. However, you'll have to add the butter yourself.

▲ This geyser, Old Unreliable, bursts whenever it feels like it.

---

[1] However, since geysers are found primarily in Iceland, that nation's cuisine is more likely. Consider using a geyser to cook your next dish of halisköt, a delicious coleslaw made from salmon, yogurt, and squash.

[2] Unfortunately, geysers don't have different settings like traditional shower heads.

[3] While many cultures traditionally sacrificed virgins to volcanoes, the less frightening geysers were simply flashed.

Geothermal Energy: Using Heat to Power Your Heater

It's easy to wonder if all the explosions Earth generates have any point, other than making geology unbearably exciting. Fortunately, the Earth's heat has a use beyond giving rich people a reason to vacation in Iceland.[1]

Geothermal energy is the practice of using the Earth's heat to create electrical power, which we then use for our air conditioners. Though it is more popular in countries that are closer to the center of the Earth, the heat of the Earth's core allows us to use geothermal power on almost any continent, as long as that continent isn't covered in ice.

How does it work? In short, heat from the Earth boils containers filled with water. These containers are filled with steam and begin to float into the air. When they are too far away from the heat source, they cool and

▲ Geothermal energy from this boiling water could be used to power your microwave, which you could then use to heat up some water.

fall back to the ground. When they fall, they push down onto a giant crank that powers a large underground battery. It's effective, but loud.

Geothermal energy may seem like a perfect way to generate power. However, the resources of the Earth's core are limited. The nice brown glaze on dirt is a result of thousands of years of consistent heat from the Earth. If we divert too much heat, dirt would become green and never fully ripen.

Indeed, geothermal energy is most often used to heat up the miners that dig up actual power sources. Have you ever noticed that miners are always sweating? That's because geothermal energy keeps their workplace a balmy 96 degrees Fahrenheit at all times, which is the reason they never need to go on tropical vacations. It's the minerals they find in the Earth that create the energy we use to power our world. That justifies our tolerating the Earth's heat until we can discover how to redirect it to Minnesota.

---

[1] Of course, Iceland will always have a niche in blondology, which is like watching birds, but for blonde people.

Coal and Oil: Giving Underground a Purpose

While geothermal energy has a nice novelty appeal, its main purpose is to make us realize that coal and oil are the best materials to power our lives.

Found deep inside the Earth, these minerals contain incredible amounts of energy and supply bountiful plumes of beautiful smoke. In the fashion world, black is a perennial favorite, so coal and oil make the entire world more fashionable. These energy sources provide an easy way for us to create electricity and, at the same time, create a film of smog that helps sunsets truly "pop."

▲ It can take an hour of washing for miners to make clean coal.

Where do coal and oil get their energy? Both of them come from dinosaur and plant fossils. In prehistoric times, these ancient organisms accumulated significant energy but didn't have anything to plug into. Now we can use that energy by burning the fossilized waste of these plants and animals.[1] This energy not only provides electricity, it also fills the air with a luxurious smoky scent. When you grill in the summer, that charcoal flavor is partly the sweet taste of dinosaur meat.

Coal is a classic fuel, and mining for it toughened up generations of spoiled children. Used to blacken chimneys and lungs, this venerable mineral provides a lifeblood to many local economies through mining work and funeral parlor services. Though it was used more frequently in the past, when it doubled as a food source, coal remains popular in China and tailgates. As this great mineral evolves, so do its uses. Today, we strive to use clean coal to lessen the environmental impact of the fuel. Finally, long after death, dinosaurs have an opportunity to take a bath.

Coal is paired with oil, the other great black mineral that allows us to light stadiums and drive RVs. Oil is often called "black gold,"

---

[1] Vegetarians can choose to burn vegetable oil.

although it has yet to be used in wedding bands. Known for its use in the manufacture of gasoline, oil is also popular in the hair of executives who sell it. Found underground and undersea, oil is easily detected through a little digging, explosion, more digging, refining, and a second series of explosions. Brave cowboys tamed the oil fields of Texas so we could drive ATVs.

Despite oil's use in almost all cars and cooking, a few people remain skeptical about black gold's benefits. Some, for example, complain that prices are too high. However, oil executives frequently distribute oil for free in the world's oceans, even allowing birds to cover themselves in it. Others worry that the resource itself will dry out, but that is easily remedied by cloning dinosaurs, burying them, and then drilling once again.

"Brave cowboys tamed the oil fields of Texas so we could drive ATVs."

Caves: Former Homes to Men

Of the many miracles in the lithosphere, none are more wet and dark than caves. Defined as a space large enough to get lost in, caves are massive underground structures that provide protection from many of the elements while exposing you to the rest of them. Cave science is called "speleology," because scientists didn't want to be called cave men and have people think they were dumb.

Caves provide a number of unique opportunities for the scientists who study them, most of which involve being bitten in the dark. These caverns can stretch many miles and often include countless tunnels to get lost in. Though caves may not seem inviting at first, if you bring along a flashlight, portable heater, carabineer, radio linkup, electrical outlet, and television, exploring caves can be only mildly unpleasant.

▲ It's irrational to fear bats, since fear won't do anything to save you.

Geologically, caves are notable because they definitely include rocks. In the average cave, you can find many minerals that you'd readily kick aside above ground. Though there is little precious jewelry inside a cave, you can find dolomite, limestone, and salt, which makes the walls quite lickable. Structures inside of caves have formed over thousands of years, so when you explore a cave you have an opportunity for history to hit you in the head.

Due to their unique environment, caves are an ecosystem with unusual animals. Some caves have fish that don't have eyes, though it's unclear if that's really much worse than being a fish in the first place. Caves are also well known for the presence of bats, which compensate for their lack of eyesight by playing it safe and biting everything.

Of course, the most well-known animal to live in a cave was the cave man. The wet environment made the cave woman's hair frizzy, but cave walls provided protection from weather and light, which would have shown the cave man how ugly he was. Though people no longer live in caves today, it's a good idea to be familiar with them just in case you develop an allergy to oxygen and sun.

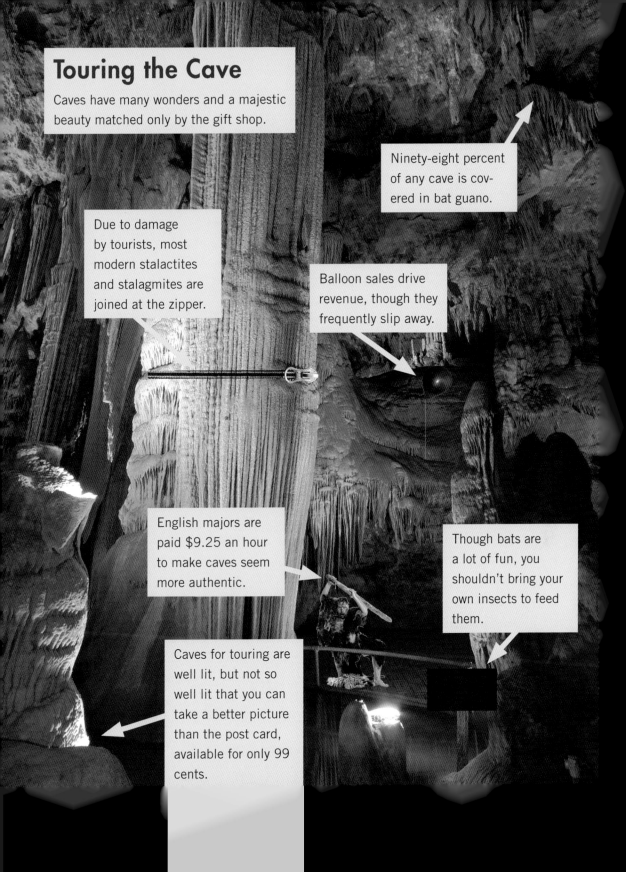

Touring the Cave

Caves have many wonders and a majestic beauty matched only by the gift shop.

Ninety-eight percent of any cave is covered in bat guano.

Due to damage by tourists, most modern stalactites and stalagmites are joined at the zipper.

Balloon sales drive revenue, though they frequently slip away.

English majors are paid $9.25 an hour to make caves seem more authentic.

Though bats are a lot of fun, you shouldn't bring your own insects to feed them.

Caves for touring are well lit, but not so well lit that you can take a better picture than the post card, available for only 99 cents.

Types of Rocks: The Moment You've Been Waiting For

Every geologist becomes a geologist for one reason: the rocks. At the end of your study of Earth Science, the caves, plates, and volcanoes mean nothing compared to the classification of different types of rocks.[1]

There's a wide range of rocks, all of which are smaller than boulders and larger than pebbles. Every geologist should have an advanced knowledge of these classifications.[2]

Igneous Rocks: Forged from frozen lava and magma, these rocks are found at the base of volcanoes or near burnt-out campfires. Extremely hard, you'll almost certainly chip a tooth when you bite one.

Sedimentary Rocks: These layered rocks are formed through the sediment, or dirt, that collects over the years. Look in your attic and you may find sedimentary rocks waiting to be resold on the geology market.

Sedentary Rocks: Great for sitting on, these rocks don't have to be in the shape of a chair, but they should be large enough to support your body.

Metamorphic Rocks: These rocks are able to change shape at will. Next time you see a squirrel sitting particularly still, make sure it isn't actually a rock.

Skipping Rocks: Flat and thin, these rocks were specially designed to be thrown across the water. If you have more than four bounces, people will be impressed.

By understanding rocks and our Earth, you understand yourself, especially if you are made out of rocks. Never stop exploring the dirt, unless it's right before a wedding, in which case you should try to look nice.

▲ This is one of the world's most exciting rocks. Do you realize how lucky you are to get to see it?

---

[1] Rocks are the most important reason to study the Earth, with the people living on it a close second.

[2] If nothing else, this knowledge is great to show off at parties.

Water: Wetter Than Dirt

The Wet Blanket Covering Our Earth

If you're part of a younger generation, you might wonder why we bother having water at all. "Bottled water is made in factories," you might say, "and floating in space is better than swimming." Though those objections are valid, water remains as vital and as wet today as it ever was.

Why is water important? If you've ever seen a picture of Earth from space, then you know that dropping that picture in water would ruin it. In addition, you may have noticed that much of the Earth is covered in the same gray shade. If you have a color printer, that gray shade would appear as blue. That's because it's water, which covers anywhere from 72.999995 to 73 percent of the Earth, depending on whether the tea is boiling or not.

Water is important outside of the seafood it holds. You can find it everywhere from lobster tanks to puddles. By studying this unique area of Earth Science, we can learn about the majority of our planet, as well as understand the easiest way to combine it with dirt and make mud, the most important substance of all.

Imagining a World Without Water

Put away your swimsuit and cancel your monthly cruise. In a world without water, neither of those would be possible.

Imagine beaches without the ocean. Instead of great places to tan and then take a quick dip to cool off, beaches would simply be sandy bars next to giant holes. Lakeside resorts would just be resorts. Riverboat casinos would be permanently docked. Estuary tourism would suddenly be dead in the water—or lack thereof.

Forget about weekend trips to the aquarium and nightly dips in the hot tub. Instead, we'd be forced to watch fish flop on shelves and spend all of our time in the sauna. That's no way to live.

We are so used to having water around that we don't realize how different our lives would be without it. We would survive, of course—soda pop is a resilient drink, and motorcycles are just as fun as jet skis. But without water, life would be a little too dry for comfort.

Oceans: Big and Ready to Drown You

The study of water on Earth is dominated by "oceanography," which tracks everything about oceans, including the best places to go boogie boarding.

Oceanography includes many subdisciplines, from biology to mixology, which is used widely at beachside bars.[1] However, oceans themselves have many notable traits, including their composition, currents, size, and whether they plan to swallow our homes.

THE
OCEAN

▲ When one ocean covers the entire Earth, geography will require much less class time.

Oceans are defined by their size and by the amount of salt in the water. Though you can't turn lakes into oceans by adding salt, it's worth it to improve the taste and help preserve the water. The salt present in the ocean comes from rocks that the ocean gradually erodes. That erosion is one of the chief reasons that sodium is bad for humans.

There are five main oceans in the world, though the number depends on how seriously you take certain continents. The Pacific Ocean is the largest of these oceans and is known for its relatively warm waters and its influence on Californian and Asian cuisine. The Atlantic Ocean is second and borders both England and New England, making it colder and more repressed than its Pacific peer. The Antarctic and Arctic Oceans are filled with ice cubes and aren't great for surfing because they will chip your board. The former Indian Ocean is now called the Native American Ocean.

Oceans have been important in the past and will become more important in the future, as we continue to melt the polar ice caps so the water doesn't get too hot. We study these bodies of water because they guide our ships, they are the source of our caviar, and their waves provide us with noise to record and play back when we have trouble falling asleep.

---

[1] The piña colada is scientifically proven to take your cares away.

Oceans:
Bigger Than Ever

As oceans become larger and deeper, it will become clear why the Empire State Building needed to be 102 stories high instead of just ninety.

Just as Wet: Lakes, Rivers, and Wetlands

Though they are far less surfable than oceans, fresh bodies of water provide an equally important point of research.

Our verdant landscape is dotted, lined, and splotched with many different types of water, all of which have unique abilities to get you wet. Normally, these bodies of water are called "fresh" because they aren't left out in the air as much as oceans. These bodies also do not contain salt, which is easily noted when you take a drink, though that same drink will show you that they do contain plenty of diseases.

> **» SCIENTIFIC FACT**
>
> The Great Salt Lake is one of the few lakes suitable for curing pork.

Perhaps the best known bodies of water are lakes, which are crucial to local ecosystems.[1] Lakes are defined as water surrounded on all sides, except for the top, which is usually sky.[2] Full of life,[3] lakes can easily sustain fish, algae, and parties held on the last day of summer camp. In winter, the top of a lake frequently freezes, allowing for ice skating, ice fishing, and ice watching.

A lake's round and puddly appearance begs a natural question: Where do lakes come from? Many lakes sit at the foot of a mountain or other slope, which allows water to trickle down.[4] Lake water is constantly replenished by the rain, which falls every time you plan on enjoying a nice weekend outdoors.

An equal number of lakes are formed by glaciers and by man, though men are more likely to appear in Florida.[5] Glaciers are large icy bodies that carved into the Earth, tracing out the mountains, lakes, and valleys that we recognize today, though the glaciers left them in better condition than we have. These glaciers lately have been

▲ Without lakes, this romantic lake house would just be a house.

---

[1] Especially if they include paddleboats.

[2] Indoor lakes will exist once shopping-mall builders are finally willing to accept the challenge.

[3] And the occasional dead body.

[4] Many Reagan-era scientists supported trickle-down lakes.

[5] Along with very large bugs, though bugs don't make lakes, they just live near them.

bested by manmade lakes, which don't require ice and can build lakes in deserts if necessary, which is a great way to boost the boating industry in Tucson. Manmade lakes usually require machines to be made, but if you have a shovel and a few years, you can greatly improve your property's value.

Lakes are also fed by rivers, which are lakes that decided to go somewhere. The world's many rivers have been vital conduits for trade, ferry rides, and at least one old man who is frequently sung about. You can easily tell which direction in a river is upstream by throwing in a salmon and seeing which direction it swims.

There are far too many rivers in the world to include in this book, especially since they would get the pages wet. However, notable rivers are so large they can be seen from space, which gives you something to look at once the moon gets boring. The Amazon is the world's largest river, and most people don't realize its name would be a palindrome if it were spelled differently.

Finally, no study of the Earth's water is complete without a mention of the wetlands. Half wet, half land, these areas are vital for keeping our planet soggy and full of mosquitoes. They are endangered by development, however, and may become the moistlands without protective action. By studying this diverse ecosystem, we can see how water and land work together to create a mess.

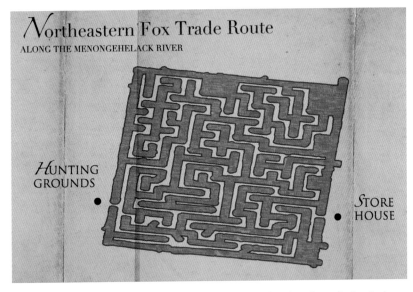

▲ This map from the 1800s shows the importance of mapping rivers for navigating trade.

The Atmosphere: Light as Air

The Space Between Us and Space

No study of Earth Science would be complete without learning about the layers of air that are always pressing down on us. Though the atmosphere consists entirely of gases, it affects many aspects of our lives, from the air we breathe to the floatability of our balloons.[1]

▲ Cloud gazing can be educational. Which of these clouds looks most like Einstein?

The atmosphere is divided into layers, just like the Earth is, but with less dirt. Each layer contributes to phenomena on our planet. For example, our sunsets are caused by the intersection of sunlight with the most beautiful car fumes. The grass's green color is the combination of the sun's yellow light with the blue sky.

The atmosphere is not only concerned with pretty colors, however, but also with the preservation of all life.[2] The atmosphere holds in all the gases we need to breathe, as well as the smells that make dinner worth waiting for. Without it, we would have to rely solely on scuba tanks, which often cost upwards of fifty dollars for every half-hour. The atmosphere also protects us from the harsh rays of the sun, and though this inhibits our tanning, it gives us an opportunity to use tanning beds instead. Finally, the atmosphere creates a magnetic field that keeps Earth relatively safe from asteroids, though we may be in trouble if they are made of plastic.

Where does the atmosphere stop and outer space begin? That line is murky, especially since everything around it is black. However, when we break free from Earth's gravitational field, our atmosphere is safely exited and we are able to float in our spaceships without fear of embarrassing injuries. Still, as hard as we try to exit our atmosphere, we should continue to enjoy its benefits, if we prefer to breathe.

---

[1] We can only hope it is high.

[2] Again, the colors are nice though.

Our Very Airy Layers

EXOSPHERE

The exosphere contains the hole in the ozone that all our rockets leave through.

THERMOSPHERE

A balmy 78 degrees, the thermosphere would be a great vacation spot if it weren't 200 miles above ground.

AEROSPHERE

A layer of smoke from aerosol cans helps control our frizzy hair.

STRATOSPHERE

Still within human reach, the best played baseballs can be hit into the stratosphere.

TROPOSPHERE

The closest layer to Earth, this is where both clouds and birds live.

Weather: Big Ideas for Small Talk

Our atmosphere's greatest effect in our daily lives may be the weather, which is always changing and is usually better somewhere else. The study of weather, called "meteorology," is one of the best sciences to talk about when you're in an elevator with strangers.[1]

Different types of weather can occur, some of which are dangerous to people, especially if they didn't bring a jacket. Though we are all familiar with sunny and rainy days, intermediate weather phenomena like "drizzly," "lousy," and "depressing" are equally important. Heat waves occur when the Earth doesn't move quickly enough out of the sun's path, and snowstorms can happen when clouds aren't packed tightly enough and all the extra snow falls out. These all have serious consequences on Earth, at least if you ask a home insurance agent.

> **» SCIENTIFIC FACT**
>
> Air travels in fronts because it would be too difficult to notice in back.

---

[1] Unless the elevator is at CERN, in which case you should talk about particle physics.

Important Symbols in Meteorology

Rain Before You Can Find Your Umbrella

Weather Is Going on Behind the TV

These everyday occurrences are coupled with more extreme weather that refuses to play by the rules. The next time you encounter a thunderstorm, cyclone, or hurricane, make sure to rush outside in order to observe just how dangerous it is.[1] Lightning, created by the static electricity of the clouds rubbing on each other, can be particularly exciting, though you'll want a long metal pole to attract the best sparks.

▲ Consider turning your air conditioner backwards to try to cool the outdoor summer air.

Weather is affected by many different factors, including atmospheric pressure, wind, and the amount of time left until the 5:00 P.M. broadcast ends and the syndicated game shows begin. While the weather can be unpredictable at times, it follows certain patterns based on force of habit and how inconvenient it wants to be.

---

[1] Notify your next of kin before beginning your studies.

Good Weather for Discovering Electricity

Plague of Frogs

Four Seasons to Complain About

We most notice the air when it is muggy, and that's because our atmosphere's weather is greatly affected by the seasons, which occur dependably in order. The four main seasons have their own distinct traits, each of which makes them annoying.[1]

Of course, the seasons aren't completely determined by the atmosphere, but they're easier to appreciate when you're outside. Indeed, the Earth's position relative to the sun determines the seasons, since we get hotter the closer we are to being engulfed in flame. You should note that in opposite hemispheres, the seasons are reversed. So in Australia, for example, June 21st is the first day of Remmus.

The seasons continually feed into each other in a weather cycle. They are spring, summer, autumn, and winter, and without the variety in seasons, we'd have to appreciate the one we're currently in. Instead, we always have the ability to wish it were another time of year.

Spring is the first season, when the world slowly defrosts into a new landscape that the birds won't shut up about. Though the climate varies from region to region, spring is generally distinguished by the emergence of green plants and brown animals. The world recovers from the harsh winter climate and becomes dewy once again, though that might be mucus from all the allergies. Spring is best appreciated by plucking flowers as soon as they grow and putting them in narrow glass containers.

Summer follows spring as the Earth gets closer to the sun and heats up significantly. All the dew from spring floats into the air, contributing to the 98

APRIL
SHOWERS

MARCH
EVAPORATION

MAY
FLOWERS

FEBRUARY
WEEPING IN THE
STREETS

JUNE
BRIDES

JANUARY
FORECLOSURE

SEASONAL CYCLES

JULY
HONEYMOONS

DECEMBER
DIVORCE

AUGUST
PREGNANCY

NOVEMBER
TRIAL
SEPARATION

SEPTEMBER
CREDIT CARD
DEBT

OCTOBER
ARGUMENTS

---

[1] If you don't like sports, however, the most annoying season is football season.

percent humid conditions we experience. We experience 100 percent humidity when we decide to go for a swim. For students, summer is significant because school is dismissed, which presents a great opportunity for them to expand their studies from the limitations of an eight-hour day. One of the reasons the days are longer is so that you can study more.

Autumn follows, and with it comes the harvest. Farmers comb the land for the high-fructose corn syrup we need to live, along with the hamburgers and pizza that will feed us the rest of the year.[1] The leaves, now ripe, finally fall from the trees and are ready to be eaten. The animal community prepares for the winter ahead by storing food and purchasing heavier jackets. As autumn passes, the days begin to grow shorter again, which is a good thing since they are undoubtedly less pleasant.

Finally, the cycle of the seasons ends with the arrival of winter, a cold time of year during which plants die, all creatures are threatened by exposure, and hot chocolate is plentiful. The season is distinguished by how little time is spent outside, though there are some phenomena that scientists have observed on the way to the grocery. The most

> SCIENTIFIC FACT

When animals sleep through winter, it's called "hibernation." When they sleep through summer, it's called "laziness."

▲ Understanding the seasons is crucial when planning the launch of your lemonade stand.

notable of these are snow and ice. Snowflakes are soft, totally unique structures.[2] Still, they fit together well when pressed and can be used as a meal when licked or weapon when thrown. Ice is also prevalent when water freezes, and it is skated upon intentionally and unintentionally. Though known as the coldest season, winter is also the most slippery.[3]

---

[1] As well as pumpkins, which are used as food, since by carving them you can obtain candy.

[2] But every snowflake melts.

[3] Depending on the availability of waterslides in summer.

Pollution: Serious Problem or Tough Love for Earth?

No study of our atmosphere would be complete without a survey of the ways we are striving to improve it. This mechanism is known as pollution.

Human activities on Earth greatly affect our atmosphere, and those activities aren't limited to skywriting.[1] Most notable among these is the smoke that we put into the air through cars, factories, and Cuban cigars.[2] The presence of this smoke erodes and changes the atmosphere, and not just by making it more gray.

▲ Smog means a surprise is hidden behind every corner. Who doesn't like a sense of mystery when driving?

How pollution will change our world remains to be seen.[3] Some scientists believe that the production of smog will make smoked sausage and smoked salmon obsolete. Others believe that pollution will melt the polar ice caps and raise ocean levels, improving surfing conditions by making it consistently high tide.

No one can be sure what will happen to the atmosphere because of pollution, so the best thing to do is to burn some Styrofoam and wait. Will pollution prove a threat to our livelihoods? Only time will tell, and we have a lot of that.

That flux occurs because our Earth is always changing, just like the science that studies it.[4] By being an Earth scientist, you dedicate yourself to cradling rocks like babies, drinking any and all water, and waving your hands through the smog. By doing so, you'll learn how our amazing planet works. After all, we only have one Earth, unless we finally move to Mars and decide to rename it.

---

[1] Still, it's estimated that sky-written marriage proposals have raised the Earth's temperature by approximately one degree each year.

[2] Ironically, Dominican cigars actually decrease pollution, but the taste of a nice Cuban stogie makes it worth the risk.

[3] Assuming it's possible to see through the smog.

[4] Since you began reading this chapter, somebody proved that volcanoes don't exist. Sorry about that.

Chapter 5 Quiz: Earth Science

Multiple Choice

1. **Which is a valid form of Earth Science?**

   a. The study of not the heat but the humidity

   b. Cataloging four-leaf clovers for possible wishes

   c. Building sand castles

   d. Staring at the ground for a few hours

2. **Which is the outermost layer of Earth?**

   a. The crumbly cookie crust

   b. A film of Saran wrap to help preserve flavor

   c. The toposphere

   d. As high as you can reach

3. **Which geological era was most important?**

   a. When the tectonic plates were all neatly stacked

   b. The period when dinosaurs didn't have such a chip on their shoulder

   c. Any of them before Earth sold out

   d. Whenever you were born

4. **Which fossil will you find first?**

   a. A bottle cap from a party you weren't invited to attend

   b. The dog your mom said went to a very nice farm for old animals

   c. A dinosaur skull worth millions

   d. Some older dirt

5. **Which geothermal threat is scariest?**

   a. A volcano without a conscience

   b. A geyser beneath your bed

   c. Spa tourism occurring within 200 feet of a school

   d. Heating your frozen dinners in the ground instead of the microwave

6. **What is the best use of coal?**

   a. Ditching snowmen for more sophisticated coalmen

   b. Finally being able to grill cereal

   c. Preventing the waste of solar energy

   d. Giving middle-schoolers great summer jobs as miners

7. **What is the greatest threat to our oceans?**

   a. The Earth's core will boil them before we put our instant coffee in

   b. Dolphins will evolve to human levels and start littering

   c. Boogie boarding will decline in popularity

   d. Lakes: leaner, meaner, and better for inner tubing

8. **Which weather is the worst?**

   a. When you aren't sure if it will rain or not

   b. The two hot days of spring that lull you into a false sense of summer before it gets cold again

   c. Hail the size of aircraft carriers

   d. Anything outside

Short Answer

1. **Earth Science requires careful study of the Earth. How will you achieve that without having to go outside?**

   _____

   _____

   _____

   _____

   _____

   _____

   _____

   _____

   _____

   _____

   _____

   _____

   _____

Essay Question

1. **Earth faces new obstacles every day. Is it better to help save the Earth, or to teach the Earth that life isn't fair and sooner or later bad things happen, so deal with it?**

_____

_____

_____

_____

_____

_____

_____

_____

_____

_____

_____

_____

_____

_____

_____

_____

_____

_____

_____

_____

_____

_____

_____

_____

_____

_____

_____

_____

_____

PHYSICS

MAKING MOVEMENT DIFFICULT

Before You Start This Chapter . . .

- Finally master that classic trick question about what two plus two equals.
- Drop something heavy to double-check that gravity still exists.
- Enjoy light one last time before you have to try to understand it.
- Inform your friends that you'll be taking a less linear approach to time, including dinner reservations.
- Learn how to write on chalkboards quickly while shouting.
- Refashion your old dollhouse into a scale model of CERN.
- Learn Newton's laws of motion and choreograph a short contemporary dance piece with them.
- Test time travel by going outside and acting like you're from the past.
- Build a backyard shelter that can withstand strong rain and atomic bombs.

The Mathiest Science There Is

Crack! A baseball flies in a perfect arc just over the outfield wall. Swoosh! You glide across the sky on a swing and then sail backward, only to fly higher the second time. Boom! A basketball slams against a backboard and bounces down, swirling around the orange rim until it falls perfectly inside. Imagine all of these activities together in one incredible day.

Go inside, add a lot of math, and you have physics.

Physics is the study of the motion[1] of matter through time and space, though the amount of time depends on how long class is, and the space depends on how many people dropped out after the first lecture. By studying movement, we can learn how the world changes and why running into walls hurts no matter which way you do it.[2]

Physics can be applied to all things in our universe, from smashing the smallest atom to smashing the largest planet. Whatever you're looking to hit, physics will help you justify it as something scientific. Because the same rules govern all objects in the universe,[3] we all have to learn about the basic principles of physics in order to walk without floating in the air or accidentally going to the 1800s.

The applications of this great science are vast, and they are not limited to physical violence. Indeed, the study of matter and energy can add a clarity to your understanding of the universe, as long as you don't hit your head against the book first.

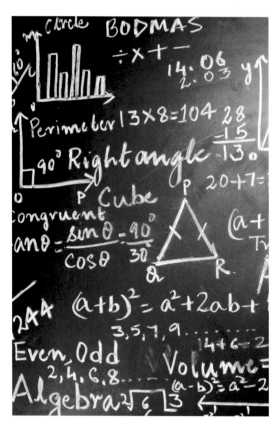

▲ This is the easy stuff.

---

[1] Never *emotion*. That is for the weak.

[2] Though it might be worth trying backwards, since that could reverse the impact. Go ahead and test it now.

[3] Physics is not a democracy, so you aren't allowed to secede from gravity.

Physics and Math: Find Somebody Smart to Copy

All the sciences involve math,[1] but physics has an especially high number of numbers. Before we cover the laws and injuries that physics explains, we should review the ways in which it intersects with mathematics.[2]

If you aren't good with numbers, you can still enjoy the study of physics and this chapter. The only mathematical knowledge you need in order to understand physics is simple addition and subtraction, so long as your lab partner knows advanced calculus. If you don't have a lab partner, go to the physics lab, promise to be somebody's friend, and then get them to fill out your worksheet for you. If that doesn't work, consider budgeting a few thousand dollars for a calculator.

Why is math so important in physics? Math observes patterns in the universe, and physics tests these patterns in the material world, usually by dropping things. Mathematical patterns are everywhere. For example, have you noticed that people who like mathematics miss one school dance after another? That's a pattern. Another pattern is the famous Fibonacci sequence, which explains how even seashells can do math better than you.

To do physics, you'll need a few basic mathematical tools.[3] Physicists frequently use "derivatives," which allow them to copy the work of previous critics.[4] They also use "integration," in an attempt to convince normal people to integrate people like them. Though the calculus becomes more complex, you can fake a lot of it by drawing squiggly lines.

▲ Ninety percent of being a physicist is writing E=mc² on chalkboards.

> **» SCIENTIFIC FACT**
>
> Newton accidentally invented calculus when he was trying to invent the calculator.

---

[1] By now, you should already be an expert counter. After all, you've been turning all these pages in order.

[2] It's easier to impress people if you call it "mathematics" instead of the more pedestrian "math."

[3] Pencil, paper, prescription drugs.

[4] "Derivative" is also the most-used word by music critics.

Classical Mechanics and You

Physics Before It Sold Out to the Atom

Physics addresses the key questions in our world: How does movement work? And should you stretch beforehand?[1] Chief among these studies is "classical mechanics," which consists of physics' early stuff, before it got pretentious and refused to revisit the things that made it great in the first place.

Considered the founder of classical mechanics, Isaac Newton became obsessed with new things to do with apples. As he juggled them, he began to wonder why they behaved the way they did. Though Newton usually ate the apples too quickly to conduct any convincing study, some incredibly productive work occurred once he was full. That forms the foundation of physics today.[2]

Unfortunately, it's important to note that this science is called classical mechanics and not just "physics." In the twentieth century, scientists decided that they were unwilling to leave all the hype of the atom to the chemists. As a result, they created other, trendier divisions of physics that were hipper than watching apples fall. Despite that, classical mechanics remains crucial if you want to know why so many things keep hitting you in the head.

By studying the behaviors of bodies in motion, we can predict how they will act and when they will endanger us. Forget the atom. Throwing things is what Newton would have wanted.

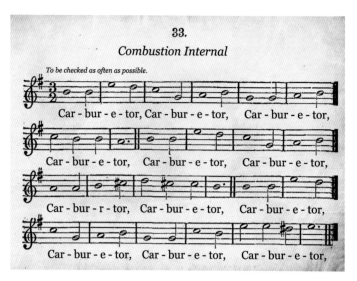

▲ Classical mechanics isn't solely focused on physics. Before Handel rewrote the *Hallelujah* chorus, classical mechanics focused on car parts that hadn't even been invented yet.

---

[1] Of course, you should always stretch, according to hamstring theory.

[2] And, of course, the foundation of modern strudels.

Energy and the Science of Pep

To understand the laws of motion, we must first understand what energy is.[1] Though the concept of energy has been refined since Newton's time,[2] traditional concepts of energy provide a good starting point for us to understand why you're so tired all the time.

What is energy? Energy is difficult to define because it is always moving before we can take a picture of it.[3] Many of the concepts we'll learn about later, like work, force, and stage presence, help us to understand energy, since it is a versatile thing that is difficult to pin down. Perhaps the easiest way to define energy is through a common example from your life, assuming you are human. When you decide to take a nap, you lack energy and can barely keep your eyes open, but when your nap ends twelve hours later, you're full of pep and vigor. That sensation is energy, though you have to slightly modify the theory for the sun and nuclear bombs, since neither are known to take naps.

In Their Words

"First, I'm going to organize my closet. Then I'm going to paint the house! I feel so good right now, so good! I'm going to write a hundred theories before lunch."

—LEIBNIZ, DISCOVERER OF COFFEE

Leibniz thought he'd discovered energy, but he'd actually just made a potent new espresso.

Energy is important to all different scientific disciplines, since it is necessary to make it through a three-hour lab. We've already learned how the sun produces energy thanks to solar power. In biology, cells create energy from food they eat. Chemical reactions make energy when electrons shock each other. Even geology includes energy when a volcano explodes or you throw a rock at somebody. Energy is as pervasive as matter, though it is more difficult to eat and, depending on your power company, probably more expensive.

» **SCIENTIFIC FACT**

Without energy, we'd spend all of our time sitting around.

As we learn about physics, we'll refer to energy often, since it would be rude not to. Do you have a lot of energy right now? If so, use it to flip the page with extra enthusiasm.

---

[1] This is the one section you really shouldn't sleep through.

[2] During the 1920s, for example, energy was measured entirely by dancing the Charleston.

[3] Similar to many celebrities. If only the paparazzi spent more time studying physics, we might know more about energy's private life.

Trying to Destroy Energy: What If It Turns on Us?

Energy may seem like a good idea when you have a lot of work to do or want to move a car. But what if energy decides it's sick of working for us?

The law of conservation of energy states that you should turn off your lights to save on your electric bill. However, a corollary of that law says that energy can be neither created nor destroyed. Is energy unbeatable in hand-to-hand combat? We have tried to destroy it in the past and only failed.

Shooting Energy with a Gun

At first, this seems like a certain way to destroy energy. In a darkened alleyway, you might encounter a lone light bulb near a fire escape. However, if you aim and shoot, the light will immediately shrink back into the electrical outlet and emerge somewhere else, just as powerful as it was before. Later on, it will keep you awake when you try to go to sleep. As always, energy emerges victorious.

Trying to Bore Energy

This seems like the easiest way to defeat energy. However, in the past, energy has proven deft at deflecting even the most boring anecdotes. If you try to talk about the broken defroster in your car, energy always seems to find a way to relate it to a hilarious anecdote about the time it met singer Dean Martin, which you have to admit is a great story.

Freezing Energy

Similar to the way we freeze our brains in order to live far into the future, it would seem that freezing energy would be an effective way to stop its attacks. However, it turns out that energy includes heat, which means it would almost immediately melt your refrigerator into a puddle of steaming plastic and then set its sights on grilling you.

Potential and Kinetic Energy: Something Bad Will Happen to You Soon

Energy itself can be divided into two parts:[1] kinetic energy and potential energy. These help us know whether energy is hurting us at the moment, or is planning to hurt us soon.

Potential energy is defined as energy that could happen. For example, if you see a nice bottle of soda on the counter, it has the potential to explode and ruin your new khakis. That potential extends to a wide range of things that could roll over you or blow up, from automobiles to particularly slippery rocks. It's important for us to measure this stored energy so we can estimate the potential damage.[2]

Kinetic energy measures the movement itself and is almost always present when you're dancing. Basically, kinetic energy occurs when something exciting is happening. As a truck runs away down a hill or an explosive fuse ignites and begins burning down, kinetic energy is present. You can spot kinetic energy by throwing this book at the wall, but please use a bookmark first.

We see potential and kinetic energy every day we open our eyes. The next time you procrastinate, call it potential energy and see if that works as an excuse. Your body also converts potential energy to kinetic energy, which is why you store so much in your love handles. For example, when you eat a plate full of Tater Tots, you convert their potential energy into kinetic energy. That's the reason your stomach is so sore afterward, since you basically have a power plant inside of you.

---

[1] AC/DC is one of many ways to do it.

[2] There are positives as well. The idea of potential energy is the reason you can put "Potential Physicist" on your résumé before you've even learned anything.

▶ This scientist is about to pull the string and convert this boulder's energy from potential to kinetic. What do you think he will learn?

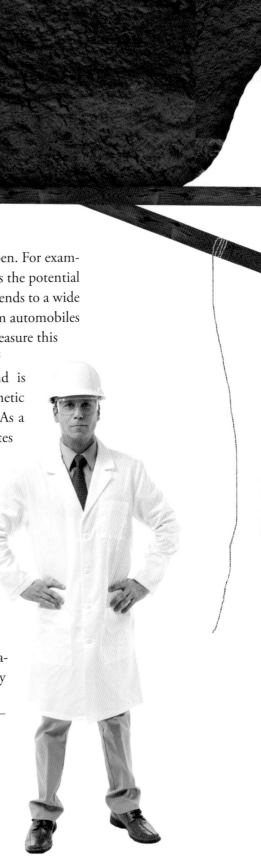

Force: The Answer to All Problems

How does all that potential energy get converted into kinetic energy, anyway? The answer is force, and it's for your own good.

Anytime somebody says "Don't force it," they are asking you to ignore science.[1] That's because force is a measurement used in physics to figure out exactly how much something is going to hurt. One of Newton's many discoveries during his cage-fighting years, force helps us to understand how hard we have to push to get people to do things that they don't want to do.

» **SCIENTIFIC FACT**

Force is more scientific than pleading.

Force is defined as $F=ma$, which means that force equals mass times anger. As a result, as anger or weight increases, so does force in proportion. That's one of the reasons that angry babies don't pose much of a threat to adults, but mildly annoyed elephants could easily kill us. When you're facing an obstacle or adversary, you should always make a mental calculation of this relationship in your head.[2]

There are many different forces in our world, which make force impressively complex to calculate, considering that you're usually talking about hitting something. For example, gravity is considered a force, as well as wind, the ground, and peer pressure. Even strongly worded letters can be part of physics if they are forceful enough.

Although force is a complex concept, its formulas reveal some practical applications for people who know they can fit their entire wardrobe into one suitcase if they just push a bit. For example, if you want to increase your force, you can simply increase your mass by eating more food. Conversely, you could increase your rage and maintain the same weight. Ideally, you could combine the two, but for the time being, steroids remain illegal.[3]

▲ These men are eager to learn about physics.

---

[1] People who say a round peg won't fit in a square hole have a name: Quitters.

[2] Assuming that your brain functions haven't been impaired.

[3] That said, we know a guy. Meet us at the corner; bring cash.

Doing Problem Sets

Problem sets are crucial to killing time in physics class. By showing your process, you can gain a greater understanding of busy work.

Name _____

Class _____

Height _____

Blood Type _____

1. Jimmy needs to open a jar of pickles but can't seem to get the top off. Jimmy is big for an eight-year-old and weighs 187 pounds. He grows easily upset because he spends a lot of time watching TV. The pickle jar requires 970 units to be opened. How angry does Jimmy need to be before he opens the jar?

Step 1: Always write your formula to fill space.

Step 2: Writing out your work can help if you are smart. Drawing something can help if you want pity.

Step 3: Record every fantastic step to make it last longer.

Step 4: Define your conclusion and try to justify it as an answer.

EXTRA CREDIT:
Writing "I love this class!" can't hurt.

$$F = ma$$

$$FORCE = mass \times anger$$

$$units = Anger\ Pounds$$

$$F = ma$$

$$970 = 187 \times a$$

$$\frac{970}{187} = a$$

$$5.187 = a$$

$$5.187 = red\ face,\ some\ tears,\ misplaced\ rage.$$

Newton's Common Courtesy

Though the concept existed before him, Newton's laws helped define the party foul.

NEWTON's HOUSE, NEWTON's LAWS

Do not overthink these decrees. Simply do what Newton sayeth and thou shalt be fine. Thee are welcome here any time, just follow the rules and be a cordial guest.

It has become clear to myself that some of thee think that coming over to mine place is a lisense to littre upon my carpet and loot my cupboards at thy will. As this situation remains unacceptable, I indeed am forced (pun *intended*) to ask thee to follow some simple rules of ettiquette.

1. At the right lieth a picture of a coaster. Use it or *do not drink*.
2. Some of thee seem to think that mine furniture is a place to rest thy feet after a long day of manure shoveling, or whatever you people doeth. Thou art incorrect. Take off thy shoes when entering and keepe thy feet grounded.
3. Let us propose you find a block of cheese inside the cold boxe. Do thee consume it heartily? No, no thee do not. That is mine cheese and I intended on eating it with an *apple* later in the day.
4. Some of thee have a long night theorising and ask to rest thy heads upon my couch. That is within the bounds of reason. What is not within those bounds is thy insistense on a fresh pair of sheets and new pillow. Thou may use the comfortor, but that is all thee should require.
5. Flush. Should I have to even include this law?
6. I love the lute as much as any of thee. But luting should not occure past the tenth hour, when mine neighbors do wish to be bodies at rest (pun *intended*).
7. Let us saye Newton asks to bring his lady-friend to the pub for a drink of beere. Then, they return to the Newtonian home to study some lawes of motion, if thee know what I meaneth. That is not any excuse to tease Newton or hit upon Newton's lady-friend as if Newton weren't right there, watching you complimente her décolletage. It is unreasonable and prevents Newton from having a successful evening-time.

Newton's Laws: Make Sure You Know Who's in Charge Here

Now that you understand what force is, it's important to know the laws that govern it. The most important of these laws were made by Newton,[1] since the king's laws at the time largely focused on ways to make him more money. From the initial thousands of laws Newton established, three have stood the test of time.

Newton's First Law of Motion: An object at rest will remain at rest unless woken up. This law is crucial when understanding why we go to work when we do and why we are unable to do so when we are sleeping. It is the reason you stay at a job you dislike, refuse to break up with your abusive girlfriend, and never go running, even though you bought expensive new shoes. This law also explains the principle of inertia, which focuses on the temptation to go back to sleep even after the alarm clock has gone off.

Newton's Second Law of Motion: As we learned earlier, this law explains the use of force, though Newton's willingness to use torture to get information remains controversial even today.

Newton's Third Law of Motion: Perhaps the best known of Newton's laws, the third law states that every action has an equal and opposite apology. No matter what you do, nature will present you with a reason why you should apologize.[2]

For example, let's say you push a small child into a wall. That is known as the action. The apology occurs after the child hits into the wall and begins to cry. Regardless of the nature of the action, there is an opposite apology that you probably should make, assuming you can swallow your pride.[3]

In physics, this apologetic principle is frequently used when building rocket thrusters that ignite people's homes. It's also unsuccessfully employed when trying to convince bullies to say they're sorry.

▲ The repeal of Newton's Twelfth Law of Motion allowed people to Hula Hoop again.

---

[1] Newton's declared himself judge, jury, and executioner.

[2] Ironically, Newton never apologized to Leibniz for briefly dating his sister.

[3] But that's more biology than physics.

Friction and Inertia: Why Greased Pigs Are So Hard to Catch

Newton's first law also teaches us the reason that merry-go-round rides cannot go on forever.

Inertia describes the state of motion that matter is in and how difficult that is to change. If matter is tired, it will take a lot of coffee to wake it up. Similarly, something moving quickly will need something very hard to stop it. This principle is one of the reasons the yo-yo remains fascinating.

Friction occurs when things get in the way of moving objects or otherwise slow their passage. Low-friction objects can make things slide longer, which is why you're encouraged to drive on icy roads in order to save gas. High friction can also have positive effects, since sandpaper slides help playtime last longer.

"Sandpaper slides help playtime last longer."

Acceleration and Velocity: Why You're Under Arrest

Now that you understand some of the laws and hassles that affect motion, you can learn about the ways we measure its movement past radar guns.

Velocity measures how quickly something is moving at you. Technically, velocity and speed are different, because velocity has three more syllables. To determine it, we look at an object's position in space and decide whether we want to be close or far away from it. This is expressed mathematically through $v=dr/dt$, which means that velocity equals the speed you're driving divided by your driving time.[1] Traffic can significantly affect velocity, which is one of the reasons that scientists try to stay away from rush hour.[2]

In Their Words

"Is there a problem officer? I was simply testing some new derivatives."

—ROGER COTES, CARRIAGE DRAG RACER

Cotes edited Newton's Principia Mathematica *and won more than 30,000 pounds in illegal street races.*

Velocity is paired with the principle of acceleration, which measures how velocity changes when you really press on the pedal. Many physicists use equations to measure this, but it's probably easier to just use the odometer and save some time. Acceleration can increase quickly, which is why physicists invented cruise control.

Of course, these laws and equations are used not only for automobiles but in every object from the atom to the planets.[3] It can be used to measure the speed of natural phenomena, like gravity, which helps prove that the bigger you are, the harder you fall. Scientists also use velocity and acceleration to explain why a ton of bricks falls faster than a ton of feathers, because after all, bricks are really heavy.

Velocity often appears in math problems predicting when trains will arrive at the station. Imagine that one train is hurtling down a track at 50 kilometers an hour, while another is speeding along in the same direction at 80 kilometers an hour. We can figure out when each train would arrive by looking at the schedule.

---

[1] Drive time radio has yet to be explained by science.

[2] In the United States, velocity is also called mileage. In the rest of the world, it is called kilometerage.

[3] Interestingly, Mercury is very fuel efficient.

Work: The Physics You Most Want to Avoid

All these measurements help us understand work, which is crucial because you're getting paid for it.

Work is the transfer of energy from one object to another, and it usually involves a lot of procrastination. Work can appear in many different forms. It can occur when you're doing manual labor even though you have a PhD. It can also occur when you transfer energy from your brain onto the accounting forms you've been working on since nine. When it comes to work, it's waiting for you almost all the time.

$$W = Fd$$

Work equals frustration times distraction.

$$W_h \text{ (OR) } H_w$$

Working hard or Hardly working

$$\Delta W = FDs$$

Change in your work is directly proportional to likelihood of being downsized or fired.

$$F(S^aS^u) > F(MT^uWT^hF^r)$$

Fun on Saturday and Sunday is greater than fun had on all other days of the week combined.

However, it's important to note that this transfer of energy is not entirely efficient. That's because your boss is always leaning over your shoulder, you spend most of the day procrastinating, and your ideas aren't very good. You can see this inefficiency at work when you roll a boulder down a hill. Unfortunately, a person or house will stop it. That's why you can't work forever, especially if you have a social life.

When discussing work in physics, it's important not to make the amateur's mistake of believing that the term *work* refers solely to the vernacular for human labor. In fact, animals can work as well by pulling our carriages and sleds.

How Much Work Is It?:
Calculating the Difficulty of Your Tasks

Task

Mowing the Lawn

Moving a Big Rock

Doing Homework

Frustration Times Distraction

Frustration: You'll spend the first 20 minutes trying to start the lawn mower manually, after which you'll realize you don't have any gas in the tank.
Distraction: Children are selling lemonade for only 25 cents a paper cup, which is actually a great deal.

Frustration: Quickly, you realize that the 2-pound weights you use while jogging didn't prepare you to lift a boulder off a trapped hiker.
Distraction: After all, it is your hiking trip. Can you really be held responsible for the hiker's well-being? Look over there—it's a bird!

Frustration: It turns out that your pencil isn't sharpened, the assignment is unclear, and you don't know how to do math.
Distraction: A 3-hour trip to the store for a pencil sharpener will fix things up. A movie playing only 40 minutes away proves to be another great distraction.

Amount of Work

It will ultimately take you seven hours to mow the lawn, accounting for a full three naps, two water breaks, one bathroom break, and a call to find a landscaping service. The amount of work does not include the trip to the hospital after you cut off your finger.

Hiring a lawyer turns out to take a lot of time and money, as does defending your abandonment of the hiker in court. Was there any way you could have known that being trapped under a rock was unhealthy? Ultimately, your amount of work will equal 10–14 years, or 7 with good behavior.

A two-question problem set ends up making you lose 15 pounds, sign away rights to your home, and drop every other class in your schedule, which means you won't graduate until some time in the next century, by which time your degree will already be obsolete. However, you will get a 92 percent on the problem set.

Thermodynamics: It's Hot in Here, and It's Not Just You

One of the first practical applications of Newton's theories, outside of apple picking, was thermodynamics. Though Newton was never at the forefront of this study,[1] his work and insights encouraged scientists in Europe to study heat instead of traveling somewhere with nicer weather.

Researching in England, scientists wanted to learn how long they had to blow on their tea until it was drinkable.[2] In the process, they learned about the transfer of energy and the validity of honey as a sweetener. Thermodynamics was born and it was hot from the first minute.

> **» SCIENTIFIC FACT**
>
> If you're specifically interested in the heat of your soup, consider studying Thermos-dynamics instead.

You may know thermodynamics from its use in something called the "calorie." The calorie is defined as the amount of energy that's required to make you feel good about yourself. The more calories, the better you feel. It's part of thermodynamics because a bowl of ice cream, even though it's cold, creates a warm fuzzy feeling that nothing else can.[3]

▲ Without thermodynamics, we'd never have discovered the oven mitt.

In addition to this common application, thermodynamics has many laws that define the transfer of energy and heat, some of which explain why your ice sculptures melt so quickly. The most famous law is the second law of thermodynamics, which has nothing to do with putting silverware in the microwave. Instead, it centers upon a principle called "entropy," but it's ultimately about the inevitability of death, so ask an authority figure if you really want to bother learning. On a brighter note, if you put a pizza in the oven half an hour ago, it's probably done by now. Don't burn yourself on the cheese.

---

[1] When he was cold, he usually just wore an extra sweater.

[2] The proposal to simply put an ice cube in the tea remains extremely controversial to this day.

[3] Scientists don't like to admit they watch their weight—they prefer to say they study it.

Classical Mechanics or Outdated Mechanics?

Sadly, classical mechanics was not equipped to last in the modern world. There were certain modern phenomena that Newton and his contemporaries could not have anticipated.[1] Classical mechanics was fine for a time when the fastest thing moving was a squirrel and the only manufacturing was the quaint little machine that cuts holes in Swiss cheese. Today, however, we need more to comprehend our empire of plastics.

The classical mechanics fought to stay relevant despite their drift from the world's trends. Newton dyed his wig brown to convince his contemporaries he was younger. Leibniz started getting really into the physics of music, which he used as an excuse to sleep late. Ultimately, their efforts were futile and earned only the pity of their peers.

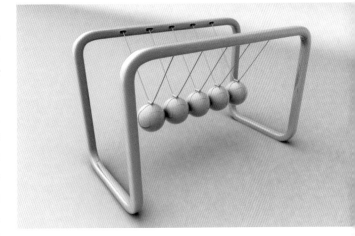

▲ Newton spent the last twelve years of his life watching the balls in his cradle bounce back and forth. His career in physics was finished.

In the last years of his life, Newton railed against the new order, despite the odds against him. He claimed that because light wasn't included in his laws, it didn't exist. Tragically, he wrote one famous paper saying that the atom was a "fad" and that people should be content to calculate the speed of things larger than dust. They weren't. His last public appearance was an outburst where, visibly intoxicated, he cried that the apple was better than electricity. He was forcibly removed from the premises and never seen again.

That said, classical mechanics remains in use today, especially if you want a retro vibe. Though these outdated physicists never could have understood our telephones, tanning beds, and surprisingly complex television shows, their contributions are meaningful in antique stores everywhere. If you ever need to throw a rock but don't want to understand too many complicated things about it, classical mechanics will still help you hit your target.

---

[1] That's especially true for the guy who got run over by a carriage. He didn't see that coming at all.

Quantum Mechanics: It's Easy!

Lay Down Some Tarp So It's Easier to Clean Up Your Blown Mind

Classical mechanics never anticipated the rise of the atom in physics, probably because it was so tiny. However, it was the atom's small size that helped it slip under the radar, which was already easy since radar hadn't been invented yet.

The result? As coined by Maximus Planck, quantum mechanics is an extremely easy way to discuss the particle and wave natures of matter and energy. To some outsiders, it is intimidating. However, that's entirely incorrect. For an average scientist, quantum mechanics is easy, as long as you consider Einstein to be average, which he certainly was in height and weight.

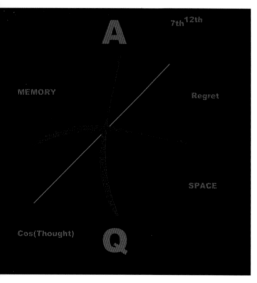

▲ This simple quantum mechanics diagram shows what happens to your brain when you look at this diagram.

So what does quantum mechanics teach us? First, it tells us that we shouldn't have paid so much attention during the classical mechanics section. Second, it emphasizes the importance of breaking down all energy and matter into the smallest form possible, even if it hurts. This incredibly small unit is called a "quantum," because you have to use the letter q every once in a while in order to justify keeping it around.

We use quantum mechanics to explain behaviors that classical mechanics never could. While Newton's theories only applied to items as small as the apple, quantum mechanics could study the apple's atoms and the Adam's apple.[1] We use it in all different types of science in order to make astronomers, biologists, chemists, and geologists feel dumb. So far, it's proven to be incredibly effective.

That said, the science does have its weaknesses. Many critics say that it's difficult to test the theories presented by quantum mechanics, while defenders argue that plenty of science fiction television shows and movies have done a great job showing what could happen.

---

[1] Scientist Max Born's voice cracked until he was thirty-two.

Some Light Vocabulary to Explain the Universe

The physics of quantum mechanics continues to unfold[1] to this day, so the terminology is rapidly inventing new words. That said, there are a few basic principles that any quantum physicist should know and, after learning, use to completely understand the field.

Heisenberg Uncertainty Principle: One night, Werner Heisenberg had a really great idea and wrote it down in his notebook. But he would always remain uncertain about what it was.

Higgs Boson: The so-called "God particle," the Higgs boson was famously declared dead by Nietzsche.

Hicks Boson: It's basically a bathtub, some cheap gin, and a little green food coloring, but it gets the job done.

Planck's Constant: Used to describe Planck's constant tendency to name important principles after himself.

Quarks: These are the indefinable things that make people interesting, like how they pour chocolate milk on their cereal or mispronounce "nuclear."[2]

Schrödinger's Cat: This famous paradox states that a cat can be simultaneously spayed and neutered.

String Theory: Though no physicist will ever admit it, string theory's multiple dimensions, branes, and gauge gravity duality are all a ruse to keep nonphysicists from attending Thursday game nights.[3]

Unified Field Theory: Until the creation of this seminal idea, people played kickball and baseball on completely different fields.

» SCIENTIFIC FACT

Quantum mechanics' work in waves gave us the gesture that means both "hello" and "goodbye."

▲ Your boss will probably believe you if you tell him this is string theory.

---

[1] "Unfold" is less accurate than the quantum mechanics term "degramadulate." But we don't have the space to explain it.

[2] Richard Feynman did the cutest thing with his nose when he was about to sneeze.

[3] It's great. There's cake and everything.

Albert Einstein and His Theory of Relatives

Throughout the twentieth century, one scientist loomed large over all others.[1] Known for his eccentric quotes, tendency to stick out his tongue in a silly way, and also his theories concerning space and time, Albert Einstein remains one of science's most beloved celebrities.

▲ Einstein's strong connection to his family led him to develop his theory of relatives.

Born in Germany in 1879, he grew up middle class with a typical German interest in *Lederhosen* and beer. But as he reached his fifth year, young Einstein developed a talent for mathematics and physics. He easily understood addition and subtraction, and when he was on the swing he quickly calculated when to tuck in his legs and when to stick them out.

Einstein's promising career was not always certain, however. He failed many tests in school. Usually it was because he turned them in incomplete, since he'd already decided that time was abstract. He was such a poor student that his peers mocked other students by calling them "dumb as Einstein."

Fleeing Germany for Switzerland,[2] Einstein plunged into serious study of mathematics and physics, taking only a few hours a day to tease out his hair. While in Switzerland, he fell in love with a young woman and conceived two children, though his wife was the one who actually bore them. Though the marriage ended soon after, the lack of familial blood between Einstein and his wife sowed the seed for his greatest achievement.

But his greatest glory was still years away. Einstein toiled in a job at a patent leather office for two years, where he polished shoes and

[1] Most of the height came from his hair.

[2] Their excellent watches helped him understand time, while their knives helped him clip his fingernails.

poked the holes in wingtips. One day, while stuffing pennies into loafers, Einstein twirled his mustache and had an epiphany: he wanted something more.

He began writing again, and though his early romance novels weren't very good, his work improved greatly when he changed his focus to scientific papers. In 1905, Einstein had what historians call his "miracle year,"[1] in which he published three seminal papers on the nature of the photoelectric effect, which explained why every photograph of him looked like he'd just been electrically shocked. Eventually, he was awarded the Nobel Prize for his seminal work in this field.

It is his theory of relatives, however, for which Einstein is best known today. Faced with few romantic options, Einstein constantly wondered how close of a family relation he was allowed to marry. After years of work studying family trees and space and time, he came up with a theory we still use today: Marrying the second cousin was acceptable, but marrying the first cousin would cause the offspring to have too many fingers and a poor understanding of math. A few years later, he married Elsa Löwenthal as proof of his theory.

> **» SCIENTIFIC FACT**
>
> Einstein used theories on bending time to prove that, through an intricate series of marriages, he could become his own grandpa.

How did the theory of relatives relate to physics? Einstein believed that space and time had imperceptible bends and curves that constantly changed the relationship between cousins. What was one day a friendship could become, with the bending of the fabric of space and time, a love affair. A marriage could

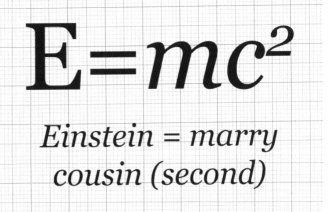

$$E = mc^2$$

Einstein = marry cousin (second)

▲ Though Einstein's second wife was his first cousin paternally, she was his second cousin maternally, so the math worked out.

occur within a matter of years, as long as the family approved and nobody brought up the cousin factor. The universe was constantly changing, and so were rules about family dating. Once Einstein found love, he was able to direct his attention toward space instead of consulting genealogy charts in order to find a date.

---

[1] Which scientists call his "statistically improbable but entirely within the realm of possibility year."

Our Physics-y World

Applied Physics: Simple Machines (Don't Call Them Dumb)

Now that you understand everything about classical and quantum mechanics, you may be wondering why we study physics. Though doing math problems is a reward in itself, there's another reason we spend all our disposable income on calculators: applied physics.

All the principles we've learned have applications in the world and can be used to explain puzzling phenomena.[1] The applications range from practical concerns, like dropping things on people, to complex ones, like dropping bombs on people.

▲ These machines may look complex, but they're just a collection of 30,000 planes, wheels, screws, and levers.

Perhaps the first application to learn about is the simple machine. Using principles of classic mechanics, even Newton could understand the simple machine. Unlike quantum mechanics, it doesn't involve the bending of light, space, or time. Usually, the focus is on bending boards.

That said, simple machines can be powerful tools to increase the amount of work you have to do. These machines are notable because they multiply force, allowing your anger to reach new magnitudes of rage.[2] In addition, simple machines can combine to become compound machines, which multiply the multiplied.[3] You can use simple machines in many different ways, from telling your day laborers to use them to telling your driver to use them. Even your personal chef can benefit from your knowledge of machines he should be using.

---

[1] Like what physicists do all day.

[2] This is especially effective because anger is a renewable resource.

[3] Engineers often tell their protégés to go forth and multiply.

The most famous simple machines are worth learning about in detail, and since they are simple, it shouldn't seem too daunting.

The Lever: This basic machine can be seen everywhere from the playground to the corporate boardroom, if the boardroom has a tee-ter-totter. In a lever, a rigid beam rests upon a pivot point, which allows your force to be multiplied so that you can easily launch the other person on the see-saw far into the air. Though simple, the lever remains controversial due to its lack of balance.

Wheel and Axle: Earlier, we noted that the Earth tilts upon this simple machine, and it is joined by many other, smaller uses. A wheel attached to an axle allows you to reduce the amount of pulling and get to see something spin. If you've ever used a doorknob, crank, or dune buggy, you've used a wheel and axle to make work easier.

Pulley: The accurately named "pulley"[1] reduces work through a wheel-and-axle combination and is significantly easier than pulling something up by hand, so long as somebody's manufactured the pulley for you. It also makes it much easier to drag your children from outside and into their rooms.

Inclined Plane: Is there such a thing as too simple? Apparently not. This thing is a ramp and still gets to be called a machine. A few people are too lazy for stairs, and it looks like we call them machinists.

Wedge: Used to stop doors and create controversial political issues, wedges get between everything, but they do it so gracefully that nobody minds.[2]

Screw: Used to open wine too fancy for a box, the screw can also be used like a nail, but you have to hit it really hard with your ham-mer, because the stupid curvy parts make it harder to fit in the wall.

---

[1] Originally known as the "tuggy."

[2] However, scientists deeply fear the wedge's cousin, the wedgie.

Developing an Electromagnetic Personality

Have you ever used a toaster or built a magnetically levitated monorail? If you have, you've worked with electromagnetism.

Before we understood the power of electromagnetism, life on Earth was very different. Air conditioners only functioned when struck by lightning, and refrigerators didn't have a single magnet on their doors. It wasn't until Benjamin Franklin invented the kite that we began to understand exactly what these strange forces were.

Electricity and magnetism are intimately linked to each other, because they come from the same place. Over thousands of years, lightning struck the Earth countless times, shocking the inhabitants and zapping electric energy into the core. Part of that energy entered into metal around the world, and as a result, that metal continues to have electricity inside it today. That's the reason why metal detectors work and why we mine certain metals to make electric fences.

But what is the electricity stored inside that metal? Derived from lightning, electricity is a series of unbalanced charges, which is why you never see lightning travel in a straight line. These unbalanced charges remain unbalanced until they are converted to new energy, television shows, or portable fans that also spray a nice mist. At that point, the electricity disappears and we wait for lightning to appear again.

However, scientists have learned how to make their own electricity by simulating this process on Earth. The history of electricity is wide and varied, from Nikola Tesla's invention of the Tesla Coiled Barbecue and Toaster Oven to Thomas Edison's creation of the black light. Electricity continues to change today through technologies like batteries, which can provide power for literally minutes until they need to be replaced or recharged.

Fortunately, we can generate electricity by simulating lightning. Technology called "generators" allows us to alter the charges of coal, oil, water, and other power sources so that they have that special lightning flavor. This electricity can quickly be transferred through power lines, which beautify our dull natural landscape and provide something for shoes to hang from in urban environments.

» **SCIENTIFIC FACT**

Lightning provides the electric power for thunder to play so loudly.

▲ The E-W magnet was quickly replaced by one that showed only north and south.

Electrify Our World

Most of Nature could be improved through access to the power grid. Which part of the wild would you help first? And how many outlets would you install?

Great Scientists

History's Most Memorable Forgotten Names

Name: Theodore Crane
Scientific Field: Physics and engineering
Greatest Strength: Enthusiasm
Greatest Weakness: Functionality
Greatest Discovery: People will believe anything

The scientist behind the twentieth century's most important inventions, had they actually worked, Theodore Crane remains renown for his work in theoretical physics and expertise in bankruptcy law.

Schooled at Princeton's Institute for Medium Level Study, Crane quickly graduated with the intention of changing the world, whether it was actually possible or not. His physics background helped him develop theories and scenarios that seemed incredibly plausible to people who were too confused to understand what he was actually talking about.

Crane's work began with his proposal for a new nuclear bomb that only decayed human matter and left no radioactive traces, an idea that appealed to a United States government that sought to eliminate the Soviet threat and, at the same time, still be able to vacation in the Kremlin. Though the $3.6 billion project ultimately ended in failure, largely due to the absence of any actual theory, Crane remained undeterred and unprosecuted.

His next pursuit was cold fusion, a new limitless form of energy that doubled as an easier way to cool drinks. Publicity around the theory garnered coverage in numerous magazines and earned him universal acclaim as the savior of American energy policy. Though the scientific community agreed that putting a nuclear plant in Antarctica did not qualify as cold fusion and wasn't remotely practical, Crane walked away with a hefty severance package.

During the last decades of his life, Crane leapt from one project to another and continued to receive grants and invitations to very nice parties. Though his gyroscopic human transporter failed to gain mass popularity, it was eventually turned into an enjoyable toy. His failed work on string theory added a number of dimensions that science fiction films readily cannibalized. Most of all, his final project, an attempt to build a time machine, may have ended successfully, since he disappeared late in 1982.

Using Atoms to Blow Up Cities and Power Our Driers

Of course, electricity's most explosive application is through nuclear power, which was made possible by physics.[1]

The power inside the atom is a relatively recent discovery enabled by a modern understanding of physics. However, the applications did not come instantly. For years, physicists spent their time debating whether to pronounce it "nuclear" or "nukular."[2] Once they jumped that hurdle, they discovered uses for the atom, other than combining a lot of them to make bread.

Perhaps the most familiar use is the nuclear bomb, a device that uses the explosion of an atom to teach a nation's enemies the value of a surge protector. Built by government scientists around the world, this bomb creates unprecedented devastation and long-lasting effects on the environment, but on the plus side, it makes a cloud that looks really impressive in pictures.

The nuclear bomb is joined by the other main application of atomic power, the nuclear power plant. Similar to the bomb, these plants utilize massive atomic energy to create heat, though ideally a power plant won't blow up the city. Though critics have said that radiation is a threat, many of those critics haven't even tried radiation themselves to see if it's actually that bad.

How do these incredible atomic applications work? Physics tells us that energy can be stored inside of matter. By splitting that matter, we let the energy out, which is the same reason that it's so difficult to preserve freshness in our food. It is called "fission" because of its tendency to fizz. This immense power increases when we join atoms, since mathematics tells us that two is more than one. This process, known as "fusion," has yet to be harnessed by physicists. Once it is, however, we'll be able to blow up bigger objects than ever before and leave all of our appliances on as long as we like.

In Their Words

"Now I am become Shiva, destroyer of Worlds, because the radiation gave me two extra arms."

—J. ROBERT OPPENHEIMER, SCIENTIST, MUTANT

Oppenheimer led the creation of the atomic bomb and later toured the world as "The Amazing Four-Armed Man."

» SCIENTIFIC FACT

Atomic energy is one of the top reasons to keep atoms around.

---

[1] Along with a willingness to blow up stuff in the desert.

[2] In theory there is an agreement. In practice, there is not.

Turning on the Light

We know that electricity gives us light when the sun is gone, but what is light, and why is it always too bright? For years, scientists were content to find their light in bulbs, but science demanded that they learn more.

When they studied light more carefully, they discovered that it came in many different colors, including black.[1] It also appeared in a full electromagnetic spectrum, including light, ultraviolet light, X-rays, and XXX-rays.[2] Scientists have successfully replicated all these types of light at one time, but they are unable to confirm the results since the experiments blinded most of them.

Why is light a part of physics? Part of it is because the movement of light passes in both particles and waves, and that proved too confusing for any of the other sciences. This theory of light's duality shows that it really is possible to have it both ways, especially if you're too fast to be caught. In daily life, light appears as a particle when a laser pen shines on you, and it appears as a wave when it is being used in a laser light show. Scientists are hard at work making the lasers safer and easier to synchronize with music, which will allow sound and light waves to finally unite.

▲ Light allows us to see all the dust that we breathe in.

Many physicists study the speed of light, since it is so fast that it makes disputes between metric and English measurement seem petty. Initially, physicists tried to check light's speed by blinking, but they knew that wasn't precise enough because the light might be distorted by their glasses. Exactly how fast is light? We believe it travels at well over 200 miles per hour, though after the first 10 or 11 seconds it starts to run out of energy. If we are ever able to travel faster than the speed of light, there will be massive implications for our lives, from clap-activated light switches to the speed limits on German highways.

---

[1] Though that was usually because they'd turned the lights off.

[2] If you want to know more, ask your parents.

Gravity: The Reason You Keep Falling Down

All of us have experienced gravity, since it's one of the primary forces behind tripping.[1] If you want to explore gravity, try throwing this book in the air and seeing if it stays there or drops to the floor.

What is gravity? Generally, gravity comes from the fact that smaller forces are attracted to larger forces, which is why belly-flop competitions are usually won by heavyset people. The moon is bound to the Earth through gravity, the Earth is bound to the sun through gravity, and the sun is bound to its position because it's too heavy to move. As we get further from gravity's source, its pull weakens. Try dropping the book off a tall building or a bridge; in addition to giving a passerby some knowledge, you'll see how gravity changes.

Where does gravity come from? Scientists continue to debate the issue, frequently in midair. Einstein argued that gravity comes from the curvature of space and time, which explains why all of the planets are round. It also explains why going in circles makes you dizzy, because of the additional gravity. If gravity changes, a square Earth may be in our future. The San Andreas Fault could easily become a corner.

---

[1] Scientists have yet to figure out a way to keep your shoes tied. The double knot, modeled after the double helix, is as close as we have come.

A World Without Gravity? Yes, Please!

Who hasn't gotten sick of walking to the car, the grocery store, or the hospital? Now imagine that you'd never have to do it again. In a world without gravity, it's a possibility.

Forget about dragging around heavy shopping bags and worrying about your weight. Without gravity, you wouldn't have any weight at all, though you should still consider getting pants with a larger waist size. Once you're done shopping, forget about climbing all those stairs to the parking lot or waiting for a pesky elevator. Just push and you'll float up to your vehicle, and there's even a good chance you'll stop before you exit the atmosphere.

Once you get there, you'll save on gas by kicking off your car and jumping in. The lack of gravity will do the rest. When you get home, you'll float your groceries up to your cabinets, or they'll just bounce around your ceiling for a few hours.

Sounds great, doesn't it? Though we do not yet know how to defeat gravity, it's only a matter of time, so hold on to your bootstraps. Also, buy bootstraps, since you'll definitely need them.

The Future of Physics, Without Using Time Travel to Tell

What lies in the future for physics?[1] You've learned everything that you can about classical mechanics, quantum physics, and the applications for both in engineering and dropping things. Still, physics continues to change every day, and there are always new problem sets to solve, or at least copy off somebody else.

In the forefront of modern physics are the key questions we have about our world. Will Einstein's theory of relatives ever receive recognition from the state? Will we finally vanquish gravity and be able to skydive for free, whenever we want? Will we ever discover a use for magnets other than making paper clips jump in the air?

Physicists believe that the answer is "Yes."[2] Already, they have discovered answers to some of the universe's most complex problems, at least on paper. As math, technology, and interest in physics advances at a rapid rate, it will only become easier to tap the vast community of quantum physicists for answers.

That said, some simple problems remain difficult to solve. Why do sand piles form? Why are water droplets round? Why is it so hard to figure out what you really want to do with your life? Why did you get a college degree as a physicist when all you really want to do is sculpt?

Once these problems are solved, there will be new applications to improve our world. Imagine a time machine that hops along the curve of space and time, allowing you to perform your favorite experiments over and over again. Or perhaps you'd prefer to envision a world in which cars drive themselves, and occasionally they even allow humans to ride inside them. Perhaps you can even think of an invention that involves light shining on you from all directions, perfectly covering your body in a warm and enveloping glow. That invention exists today, and it's called a tanning bed. The future may not bring anything better, but at least it will always be bright.

> **» SCIENTIFIC FACT**
>
> Physicists are constantly being studied by physicistists.

▲ Can physics help us finally make the perfect smoothie?

---

[1] Or stands? There's no telling what position the future will be in. Though difficult to dismount, the hammock remains incredibly comfortable.

[2] They actually believe the answer is another equation, but it requires experimental calculus knowledge you don't have.

Chapter 6 Quiz: Physics

Multiple Choice

1. Why is math important in physics?
   a. It keeps out the riffraff
   b. It helps to explain the numbers part
   c. Poetry wasn't cutting it
   d. Calculus symbols are pretty

2. What is energy?
   a. It's available in cans, pills, or cups
   b. It's regulated by the state
   c. Matter when it's blowing up
   d. It's underrated

3. When should you use force?
   a. When bullies don't listen to your explanation of quantum mechanics
   b. Whenever possible
   c. In particularly mathematical dog fights
   d. Once you've reached your fighting mass

4. Which is not one of Newton's laws?
   a. Always hold open the door
   b. No taxation without representation
   c. An object under arrest has the right to an attorney
   d. There's no business like physics business

5. What is acceleration?
   a. What you do when the light turns yellow
   b. The opposite of sloweration
   c. A change of velocity when you're being chased
   d. Thrilling

6. What has thermodynamics taught us?
   a. Always preheat to 425 degrees
   b. Heat rises, in summer
   c. Calories make you happy
   d. The pie is always cooling

7. Which important problem does quantum mechanics solve?
   a. There's not enough calculus in other types of physics
   b. It pays more attention to other dimensions
   c. It explains why Heisenberg could never choose a restaurant
   d. It gives us a reason to hang hilarious Einstein posters

8. What is electricity?
   a. The consequence for living in a house with carpet
   b. A current affair
   b. Too hot to touch
   d. So easy to understand that there's no point in explaining it

Short Answer

1. Physics allows us to use math to explain important problems. How would you use a few well-chosen equations to settle the Israeli-Palestinian dispute?

_____
_____
_____
_____
_____
_____

2. Gravity makes us fall on the ground. How would you make gravity easier on the knees?

_____
_____
_____
_____
_____

Essay Question

1. **Modern physics presents amazing opportunities for energy, but with it comes incredible risks to human life and the environment. Describe what fun and educational physics demonstrations you'd use to distract people from those risks.**

YOU'RE A SCIENTIST!

NOBELS DON'T WIN THEMSELVES

Before You Start This Chapter . . .

- Clear space above your fireplace for all those Nobel Prizes.
- Determine if you have an allergy to latex gloves and, if you do, discover a cure.
- Decide if you want your middle initial or full middle name to appear on your statue.
- Develop at least one hobby so magazine profile writers can make you a "true character."
- Buy that lab coat you've had your eye on. You deserve it.
- Double check that you haven't gone mad, since that type of scientist has a bad reputation.
- Practice keeping a straight face when answering questions from nonscientists.
- Memorize that "PhD" isn't pronounced as "fuddy."
- Block out time to reread this textbook immediately after finishing it.

You Work Has Just Begun

You're welcome. You've learned everything about science that matters and have received an education that is unparalleled.[1]

But what happens now? Unfortunately, mastering the techniques of science isn't enough to net you a MacArthur "Genius" Grant[2] or the Nobel Prize. To succeed in science, you must be part of the scientific world, whether you like it or not.[3]

To do this, you must assess your goals for your scientific career. Are you interested in the pursuit of knowledge for its own sake, so that you can better understand the phenomena in our world and illuminate universal truths? Or are you interested in bureaucracy, paperwork, arcane disputes, difficult colleagues, and institutional roadblocks? If you are interested in a salary, you've chosen the second option.

▲ If you become famous enough, maybe scientists will wear your name and number on the back of their lab coats.

You'll have to navigate a scientific community that has a reputation for being impossibly cool and socially aware. It can be intimidating to interact with people who know so much about different types of newts. Will you rise to the task? Or will you be one of the first scientists to be awkward at parties? You must choose your lab coat's fit wisely, if you want to impress the most fashionable scientists in Paris.

You'll also need to convey the importance of science to people who were too lazy to do their homework. Bridging science and the wider world can be a difficult task, but it is ultimately a rewarding one, especially if your alchemy research pans out. Your education is always continuing, and you'll have to figure out new ways to dumb it down if liberal arts majors who studied "The Cinema of Basketweaving" in college are ever going to understand what you do.

---

[1] In case we forgot to mention it, parallel lines are noted for being long and intelligent.

[2] Winners cannot collect their money until they declare MacArthur to be a genius.

[3] Though your experiments in a secluded cabin in Montana are no doubt interesting, they won't get you tenure.

Experimenting with Education

Elementary School: Learning Things to Unlearn Later

Every scientist's education has to begin somewhere. Though ideally the ages of two to four would consist entirely of periodic table memorization, some scientists wait until entering school to learn about their world.[1]

Science is part of the curriculum in most early education, though few teachers even try to reconcile quantum mechanics and general relativity, since most of the time is spent coloring. Usually, you are introduced to the world through your environment. Teachers call upon students to look at the sky, name the clouds, and otherwise waste valuable time they could be spending on dissection. Many students learn about biology through a class pet, which inevitably serves as an introduction to accidental death.

Though most of elementary school is useless, there are some valuable lessons.[2] By spending your time in a small room with forty to fifty other screaming children, you can become acclimated to a laboratory environment. In addition, learning cursive writing teaches you to be incredibly careful about what you bother learning.[3]

Children also learn about chemistry during lunchtime, when they mix their milk with an entire pepper shaker. They learn about velocity when throwing snacks. In addition, opening juice boxes is a skill that teaches children how difficult good engineering is. All this only takes six years to learn, with summers off to recover.

> **» SCIENTIFIC FACT**
>
> The best schools teach about food through class gardens and class slaughterhouses.

▲ No reputable academic journal would consider this drivel to be serious research.

---

[1] If you don't have *pi* memorized to the hundredth digit by the time you're four, you've already fallen behind.

[2] But don't try to resell them to anybody intelligent.

[3] Penmanship is useful, however, for everyone considering a career in calligraphy.

Science Fair? Or Science Unfair?

Most important of all elementary school activities is the science fair. This ritual teaches children the value of gluing things to construction paper. It also teaches them that even something with "fair" in the name is usually based on personal bias and favoritism.[1]

That said, there are strategies to win every science fair you enter, without the burden of actually doing science.

---

[1] Children learn early that the most important taste is bitter.

The Trifold Poster Board
Why settle for a regular poster board when you can buy one that is slightly larger and eight times more expensive? A trifold poster board indicates to judges that you have more information and care deeply about your project not falling down on the table. This thick card stock can then be reused as a makeshift umbrella when you leave the fair, first-place trophy in hand.

A Slightly Distasteful Subject
When presenting a science fair project, it's important that the judges not delve too deeply into your findings. That can be ensured through subject matter that makes the judges impressed and squeamish. Consider using hamster reproduction, the molting habits of your pet snake, and the decomposition of goldfish in your future projects.

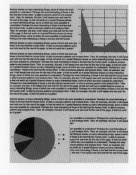

Graphs, Data, and Reports Written by Parents
Most important of all, children should not be forced to actually do any work on the project, since it would probably be of poor quality. A qualified PhD parent can supply significantly more sophisticated data and provide the budget for a team of research scientists to investigate more thoroughly than a fifth-grader ever could.

Middle School: Science Hits Puberty

Middle school is a key development period both intellectually and socially, so it's important that you choose the former over the latter. As courses become more difficult than elementary fist painting, clay eating, and screaming, students face new challenges in their scientific education.

A wide range of courses help the budding scientist develop from boy to man, girl to woman, and androgynous child to androgynous grown-up. More difficult math classes separate the wheat from the chaff, and more difficult agriculture classes also separate the wheat from the chaff. An introduction to Earth Science teaches students to figure out a way to giggle at rocks. Chemistry, meanwhile, allows budding scholars to memorize long lists of things they aren't allowed to do yet. Though physics remains beyond the grasp of most middle schoolers, force is commonly used without the aid of science.

Perhaps this period is most important for its introduction to biology. Though most of this occurs outside the classroom, some of it is actually taught. Since many of the concepts are easy for young students to grasp, and since most of the tools fit into their tiny hands, biology is a natural fit. Usually, coursework involves figuring out new things to dissect.[1] By picking apart a frog, it's possible to learn what a frog's organs look like, which can be useful since only the frog's legs are edible.

▲ Middle school science combats frog overpopulation by dissecting them.

Middle school administrators also take care to ensure that students will get ample life exposure to biological principles.[2] School dances allow students to encounter Darwinism at its most basic.[3] This is paired with the social scorn that drives students to science in the first place. In addition, puberty provides a living laboratory for students to realize that their own biology's changes are far more unpleasant than biology classes.

---

[1] Many of the creepier students have already done this at home.

[2] They also help prove that some scars never heal.

[3] Survival of the fittest means being willing to dance in public.

High School Science: Almost Worth Mentioning

In high school, many scientists find their true calling to the pursuit of knowledge through test tubes. While some of their peers waste their time earning letter jackets, the high school scientist tries to earn his or her lab coat.

High school introduces you to more complicated concepts of science, from physics using actual math[1] to dissecting animals that are even more threatening than frogs. In addition, high-schoolers are introduced to many of the techniques that scientists use all their lives, like finding good places to hide from their enemies and learning the best ways to fudge experimental data.

The typical high school student's education runs the gamut of scientific fields, and it can be a busy time to learn. When in high school, a scientist must remember that science is the pursuit of truth, and that an attractive lab partner is harder to find than a competent one.

In Their Words

"Does the lunch bell make anybody else drool?"

—IVAN PAVLOV, CONDITIONING SCIENTIST

Pavlov's most significant discovery occurred after third period when he was walking to the cafeteria.

[1] It's hard to calculate the universe when you're still dividing with a remainder.

Informing Bullies of Their Flawed Logic

To most, high school is about the fun of late-night laboratory visits and the enjoyment of early-morning study sessions. Unfortunately, some students have their enjoyment tarnished by the cruelty of bullies. However, it's a problem that can be easily fixed through an appeal to logic.

Bullies may be mean, but they are still rational beings. Next time a bully slams you into a locker, consider winning him over with a brief story about the wonder of supernovas. If that doesn't work, detailing the reproductive habits of small bats will no doubt do the trick.

The same technique works for name-calling. If a bully calls you a dweeb or a dork, remind him that the difference between his and your genetic material is statistically insignificant. If that doesn't work, tell him that evolutionary theory shows he's only bullying you out of jealousy and a misguided need to establish dominance among his peers.

Bullies can be harsh, but science is amazing enough that it can convince anyone. Remember, when life gives you lemons, tell the bully about their acidic composition.

The Chicken Drop

High school students learn about engineering and physics through the chicken drop. They create a device that they hope will keep a chicken alive when it's dropped from the roof. This chicken is covered with straws, pipe cleaner, and duct tape. How do you think it will do?

College Options

Not all college students can be intelligent, so some have nonscience majors. Still, many require scientific training so that their expensive degrees won't be completely useless.

COURSES FOR SCIENTIFICALLY CHALLENGED STUDENTS

PHYS 401: PHYSICS AT THE PARTY

3 Credits. TR, 3:30–When It's Over

Why do we fall when we limbo? Would a beer bong work in space? This course introduces students to elementary concepts of party safety, techniques for measuring the shot glass, and elements of both keg stands and keg tapping. Lab period after class every day.

BIO 212: LOOK AT THAT

4 Credits. MWF, 9:30–10:45

Biology depends on constant interaction with the real world. In this course, students will spend a little over an hour walking around campus and pointing at things that are pretty, like birds, funny-looking squirrels, and tiny bunny rabbits with cute ears.

CHEM 218: FIRE GOOD

3 Credits. TR, 3:30–4:45

Fire keep man warm and cook man's food! Fire have color like tiger cat. Fire like sun when going down. Fire no touch. Fire burn skin, make man hurt and mad! Fire come from man in sky with light and noise, then man use fire to make life good. Must learn about fire. Fire good!

GEOL 116: ROCKS FOR JOCKS

4 Credits. MF, 12:30–1:30

Though many courses claim to be rocks for jocks, few actually are. This class teaches key principles about how far you can throw basalt, whether limestone will bounce on a basketball court, and if granitoids can be used as baseball bats. Final exam consists of using a hammer to break a rock in two.

ASTR 104: STARS IN THE CITY

2 Credits. T, 9:00–9:50

Most adult lives consist of complaining how you can't see the stars because the city is too bright. This course offers students new ways to complain about the lack of starlight, from saying how the stars add a "spiritual quality" to the night to claiming that the North Star helps you navigate when lost.

PHYS 134: POETRY IN PHYSICS

4 Credits. TR, 8:30–9:45

Many physicists say there is a poetry to physics. This class asks what type of poetry physicists would have written if they were bad at math. Students will compose Einstein's sonnets and Newton's epic poems. Haikus will not be included because they require too much counting.

Science in College: Finally Making Life Meaningful

All this primary education leads to college, the place where you will pick a major, reconsider because it's too difficult, reconsider again because of credit requirements, and then ultimately devote your life to something you would have quit if you weren't so lazy.[1]

College is the perfect place to find your passion, and that passion is called "studying." Freed from the malaise of high school, where only three or four hours of study a night is required, college allows students to devote every waking hour, and at least three of the sleeping ones, to study.[2]

Of course, some students will try to distract you from the opportunity to finally learn. The diligent scientist can protect against this by taking on a course load with more credits than there are hours in the day. Any mind-altering substances that are offered should only be accepted if they are books. Invitations to parties can be quickly countered with invitations to a three-hour lab without bathroom breaks.

Why is college so important? It gives budding scientists a chance to focus their interests and plan a career that will keep them in laboratories for the rest of their lives. No one knows when inspiration will strike, whether it is in the zoology seminar with 1,200 people, or if it's in the physics class led by an adjunct who not only can't speak English, but appears unable to speak any language at all. While it's impossible to predict what will spark your interest, hours of homework will give you a chance to truly explore the knowledge. If you can't decide, a quadruple major is always an option.

» SCIENTIFIC FACT

In order to save money, the Ivory Tower is usually made of low-grade concrete.

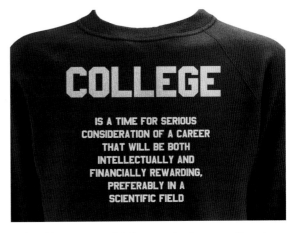

▲ In college, your sweatshirt represents who you are through polycotton fibers. Choose wisely.

College's four years pass quickly. Make sure to take enough classes to finish in only three, since it will look good on grad school applications.

---

[1] Pick your major wisely. If you can't handle the rigors of nuclear science, settle for an easy major like genetic engineering.

[2] Your dreams should assign homework.

Graduate School: The Best Four Decades of Your Life

If college helps you decide you want a life worth living, it will lead to a graduate program where you can further your studies of science without the annoyance of the other subjects required to get a bachelor's degree.[1]

A long-lasting institution, graduate school has existed for centuries as a way for students to defer loans until their thirties. As early as the 1600s, young scholars used these programs to increase their academic knowledge and add more letters to the end of their names.[2]

» **SCIENTIFIC FACT**

Though he discovered penicillin, Alexander Fleming's true passion was for grading papers.

Though it is the final stage in your academic career, graduate school has its own distinct course, like a river, or, if you study geology, a river made of lava.

Selection and Application: This is the actually the third stage of the graduate school process, after birth and everything until this moment. A college science education should help you focus on the discipline you wish to study and, in turn, make your unrelenting focus.

First, you must select a school that matches your interests.[3] Once you do this, you may want to select a few alternatives in case you fail to achieve your dreams. Learn a little about the professors at the school,[4] and then begin planning a tactic to talk to them at least once during the era when you're there.

Once you've selected your school, you need to actually apply.[5] You'll need lengthy recommendations from your professors, which is a great excuse to meet them for the first time. In addition, you'll need to submit your academic accomplishments, or at least a list of what you wish they'd been.

▲ This is a beach. Though you won't see one in person while you're in grad school, you can always look at pictures.

---

[1] As the name implies, anyone with only a bachelor's degree is doomed to remain unmarried and unloved.

[2] Adding a BS, MS, and PhD to the end of your name is the closest you can come to having your signature look like a chemical compound.

[3] Only your academic interests, since interests in weather, city life, and culture are only distractions.

[4] Ideally, do this without receiving a restraining order.

[5] Try to really apply yourself, since it's against the rules to have somebody apply for you.

Admission and Payment: You made it in! Now you can look forward to paying for your schooling with all the money you made as an undergraduate. If you are cash poor, you may need to take a job as a TA. TA stands for teaching assistant, which means you will be both the teacher and your own assistant. As you teach classes, grade papers, help delinquent students, and serve as janitor, you may occasionally glimpse your professor as he crosses the quad for a fundraiser or important conference. Ninety percent of your time as a grad student will be taken up by this job, but helping twenty-year-olds review their multiplication tables can be surprisingly rewarding.

Focusing Your Studies: Once you've finished applying for your degree, paying for it, and tutoring a class of 480 students, you'll begin your own studies. As you grow as a scientist, you'll want to narrow your focus for your thesis, which is the culmination of whatever you signed up to do. Fortunately, writing a great thesis is easy. All you have to do is create scientifically sound work, completely counter conventional wisdom, and manage not to offend any of the people who will award you your doctorate degree.[1] Remember, science is about the pursuit of absolute truth, unless it threatens the reputation of somebody important.

Once you finish graduate school, you'll finally be a scientist. It's a moment of sincere celebration that should last multiple minutes. Then, you should continue your education. Science is a lifelong obligation,[2] and you can always find a new grant, new job, or new loan program to apply for.

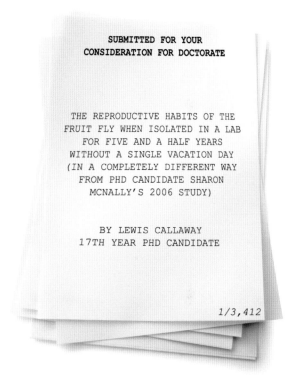

SUBMITTED FOR YOUR
CONSIDERATION FOR DOCTORATE

THE REPRODUCTIVE HABITS OF THE
FRUIT FLY WHEN ISOLATED IN A LAB
FOR FIVE AND A HALF YEARS
WITHOUT A SINGLE VACATION DAY
(IN A COMPLETELY DIFFERENT WAY
FROM PHD CANDIDATE SHARON
MCNALLY'S 2006 STUDY)

BY LEWIS CALLAWAY
17TH YEAR PHD CANDIDATE

1/3,412

▲ This is your life now.

---

[1] Your thesis should be revolutionary in the least offensive way possible.

[2] As is your graduate school debt.

Forcing People to Call You Doctor

Once you have a PhD, you'll have a new path in the world.[1] Doors will open for you, if they are the automatic type, and new opportunities will come knocking at your other doors, unless that's actually your landlord.

You'll have many opportunities with a PhD, but the most important of these is to introduce yourself as "Doctor." Though you will technically be a doctor of philosophy and not of medicine, most doctors of philosophy are of the philosophy that they should be allowed to call themselves doctor. Feel free to introduce yourself this way in conversation, unless it is preceded by something like, "Is anyone here a doctor? This man is dying!"

When someone calls you "Miss" or "Mister," your rebuke should be swift and sharp. Calmly tell them that you are a doctor. When they ask where you went to medical school, tell them that you actually are a PhD, which is the same but better. If they don't listen to you, show them that while philosophy doctors may not be able to heal people, they can certainly hurt them.

▲ This is the enemy.

[1] It will only be lined with gold if you pursued that alchemy program.

Life as a Professor

Scientists have a variety of available career paths, one of which is a continued life in academia. As a professor, you'll have an opportunity to thoroughly study your school's policies concerning tenure.

Assuming that you succeed as a fellow, adjunct professor, assistant professor, assistant professor's secretary, and cafeteria manager, you'll eventually be awarded a full professorship. With it comes the call to perform innovative new scholarship and make incredibly significant scientific discoveries, as long as you earn positive course evaluations from freshmen who are majoring in film and Portuguese literature.

With the responsibilities of a professorship come great benefits. You'll be able to order around a squadron of graduate students who are simultaneously sycophantic and secretly plotting to undermine you in order to advance their own careers. You'll also have access to a laboratory that is funded by the students or the state, both of which can put a halt to your work if your studies become too difficult for them to understand during their lunch breaks.

Living the Scientist Lifestyle

Improving Your Routine Through Scientific Precision

Once you're a scientist, your daily life is going to change significantly. You'll quickly be surrounded by willing mates, study participants, and friends. There is nothing as important as intellect in modern culture, and as a scientist, you'll display it whenever you open your lab coat.[1]

We've seen how science explains your life, but you should also use science to direct your life. The only way to protect yourself against the pressures of scientific fame is through a routine that emphasizes the importance of science at every moment.

Waking Up: Do you use an alarm clock? Every time you hit the snooze button, a patent dies. Wake up promptly and open your eyes immediately to study, since your ceiling should have a copy of the periodic table painted on it.

▲ This looks enough like graph paper to be useful.

Breakfast: Three square meals are important to mental development, though any quadrilateral will suffice. While having breakfast, review your obligations for the day and try to discover a new way to make eggs.

Your Commute: When driving, stay at your most alert. Bring along a laboratory kit to keep you thinking quickly.

Work: Whatever field or form of science you choose, from the hours of 7:00 A.M. to 9:00 P.M., you should be working. Approach each new day as an opportunity to stay later than your coworkers, assuming that you're required to leave at all.

Leisure and Sleep: Even the most dedicated scientists have to take a break from their studies. Try relaxing with a crossword puzzle, which you can repurpose to fill in with the digits of *pi*. Use the evening to study another field of science or work on idle patent applications. Sleep only when your book light burns out.

---

[1] Einstein was hounded by autograph seekers. He tried to deter them by always looking like he'd just gotten out of bed.

Looking Good, Scientifically

Hair: Though unkempt hair is the preferred option, you may also select a clean haircut as long as it can be expressed through a mathematical equation.

Secondary Lab Coat: This looks like a shirt, but it's actually a backup lab coat with a tie attached.

Tie: A tie may be worn as long as the knot length is accurate to the micrometer.

Crease: Your lab coat's sleeve should have a perfect crease, so you can take up ironing as a hobby when you aren't studying.

Buttons: A lab coat should never be unbuttoned, both to ensure safety and to prevent theft.

Bottom Half: Lab coats are required. Pants are not.

Socks: If you wear socks, make sure to mismatch them. If you only have one, that will do.

Shoes: Shoes are necessary to maintain dignity, but if they are unavailable, you can use acid to give your feet some healthy calluses.

Science Is in Fashion

Once you've received your doctorate, you still have a lot to learn about being a scientist, and part of being a scientist is looking the part.[1]

The first step is to dress poorly. Eccentric dress is commonly considered a sign of genius, because members of the public assume that science takes up all the space in your brain. You can achieve this by being unkempt or deliberately unusual. By mismatching your clothing, wearing suspenders, or forgetting key procedures like zipping your pants, you can easily convey that you are too intelligent to dress yourself like a grown-up.

Your main dress should be paired with a few key accessories. If you don't wear glasses, consider damaging your eyes in order to merit a prescription. You'll want to wear a watch as well, preferably digital, but it is your decision whether it should be set to an atomic clock or to the wrong time entirely.[2] This will pair well with the other unique accessory you select, whether it is a flamboyant porkpie hat, ergonomic shoes, or a Thermos that holds all your meals.

▲ Have a convincing story ready to explain your lab coat's "ketchup" stain.

Most important of all, of course, is the lab coat. The key to any scientist's wardrobe, the lab coat is prized around the world. A perfect white color is necessary for the coat, and many scientists clean theirs nightly with their toothbrushes. Some scientists also leave the tags on to prove that their coats are new. Designer coats can sell for thousands, especially to billionaires without a good sense of how much a lab coat should cost.

Finally, though it is not a strictly sartorial matter, your grooming is key to your scientific demeanor. Since a good scientist is consumed with matters of the universe, fingernail length and dental care can be deemed irrelevant. If you do choose to groom carefully, a good scientist should still make it clear that science takes precedent over vanity. Consider creating at least one razor burn mark to show your concern for the cosmos.

---

[1] This is especially important if you're an astronaut, since you won't be able to breathe without a spacesuit.

[2] Nothing in between is acceptable.

The Biggest Tools in Science

As a scientist, you won't be able to split atoms with your hands, no matter how dexterous you are. Every scientist has tools at his disposal that help make him look more important.[1] The study of these tools is as important as your study of science, since they give you something to blame other than yourself.[2]

---

[1] Staring into a microscope is more impressive than holding something really close to your eyes.

[2] "It's not my fault the kid died. My calculator was broken!"

The Bunsen Burner

Scientists have to start young, and the Bunsen burner is the easiest way to give eleven-year-olds access to highly explosive gases. You can use the Bunsen burner to teach children about heating chemicals in test tubes and then recovering from the burn wounds. A Bunsen burner also works well with marshmallows.

The Telescope

The universe is a vast and incredible place, and a store-bought telescope will help you see tens of feet into the sky. Assuming there's no cloud cover, atmospheric interference, smoke, or fog, you'll be able to recognize the blurry outlines of the constellations that you can see clearly in countless textbooks.

The Beaker

The beaker has been giving test tubes an inferiority complex for years. Large enough to hold a dangerous amount of chemicals, yet small enough that they don't smell too bad, you can heat, pour, and drink from this all-purpose container. Frequently seen with smoke coming out of it, the beaker is a go-to tool for scientists who devote their time to love potion attempts.

The Advanced Calculator

To some degree, the advanced calculator has been replaced by the advanced computer, which can do everything the calculator can and also play Solitaire. However, the advanced calculator still has a place in science, usually in the front lab coat pocket. Frequently named with an impressive series of letters and numbers that don't mean anything, the advanced calculator can add and subtract numbers, make graphs, and spell lewd words if you punch in certain numbers and then turn it upside down.

The #2 Pencil

Classified by testing boards everywhere as the only type of pencil that matters, the #2 pencil is indispensible to any scientist who wants to write upside-down in space without using a space pen. The #2 pencil will need to be sharpened every three to five words you write, which is invaluable when you're looking to kill time during another 8-hour day.

Large Hadron Collider

The Large Hadron Collider is similar to the pencil, except it's a 17-mile-long particle accelerator buried in Geneva, Switzerland. Used to solve the most fundamental questions in physics, the Large Hadron Collider also has the potential to destroy the planet, which is a strong arguing point when you're pursuing a new grant. Essentially, it's a Bunsen burner that eighth-graders aren't allowed to use.

Gerald

Present in every scientific lab, Gerald is the guy who is slightly smarter than you but significantly more awkward. Desperate for friendship and willing to trade almost anything for it, he will perform any experiment you ask, document it, and help you cheat on the exam if you promise to go with him to the speculative fiction book sale on Friday. Best of all, he'll be too shy to protest when you cancel on him.

The Scientific Community: A Safe Place to Snort When You Laugh

Being a scientist only works because your knowledge is shared with a group of your peers. Through retesting, revision, and new analysis, you'll be able to realize how completely wrong your original conclusion was. The resulting derision will make you stronger as a scientist.[1]

▲ The scientific community is a place where nobody will judge you for having a ferret named Bernoulli.

At potlucks, you will have an opportunity to exchange data with your fellow scientists or, as nonscientists call it, to "socialize." These interactions will help you learn about current scientific trends, evaluate who is your biggest threat, and find out which of your peers has a surprisingly attractive spouse.

However, support in the scientific community is not unconditional. To fit in, you'll need to know everything about the alien languages featured in *Star Trek*. Scientists love aliens that are still sexually attractive to humans. It also helps if you study some recreational history, as long as that history was written by Tolkien.

Scientific Associations: United in the Advancement of Themselves

In addition to these formal institutions, there are many associations of scientists. These groups of like-minded professionals share their newest discoveries in scientific journals[2] and at conventions held in various cities, where they consume dry chicken and watch colleagues perform musical parodies on stage.[3] Attendance is highest if these coincide with a convention about comic books. You won't learn anything in the process, but you will ruin a shirt with a sticky nametag.

These associations also serve as powerful lobbying groups for Congress, since they can't get past the lobby. Your scientific group's recommendations will give many congresspeople something to misinterpret or rail against.

---

[1] Or it will make you switch careers.

[2] Not to be confused with scientific diaries, in which scientists wonder if Newton just likes them or totally like *likes* them.

[3] *Singing in the H$_2$O, How to Succeed in Science by Trying Really Hard.*

A Selection of Top Scientific Associations

There are thousands of scientific associations, some of which are completely legal. Find the right one for you and you'll have friends for life (or for the duration of your paid membership).

SAFETY GOGGLE WEARERS OF AMERICA

"They're Not Just For the Lab Anymore"

Cal Stenheiser
Cal@NotInTheFace.org
1-800-FOUR-EYES

Association of Quantum Mechanics

We're just like normal mechanics (but for the universe).

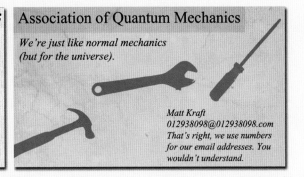

Matt Kraft
012938098@012938098.com
That's right, we use numbers for our email addresses. You wouldn't understand.

Recreational Pharmacists Guild of America

Scientists, Drug Dealers, It's All So Subjective, Don't You Think?

Dr. Maxwell Steinberg
m.steinberg@alumni.harvard.edu

Contact:
Show up at the corner. You'll see a metal trash can. T-Ron will be outside waiting. Give him singles- ONLY SINGLES- and leave quick.

SOCIETY FOR THE CLARIFICATION OF ASTRONOMY VERSUS ASTROLOGY

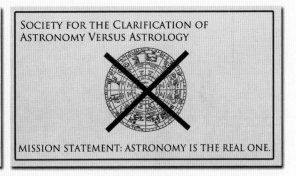

MISSION STATEMENT: ASTRONOMY IS THE REAL ONE.

United Asbestos Researchers

It's not as bad as you've heard.

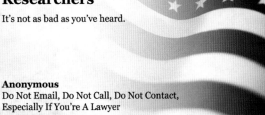

Anonymous
Do Not Email, Do Not Call, Do Not Contact,
Especially If You're A Lawyer

Entomologists of North America

our logo is a smiling heart because nobody wants to look at bugs

Kathy Cayler
bugeyed28@gmail.com

Science and Everybody Else

Failing to Explain Your Job to Strangers, Family, and Friends

Science is not isolated to laboratories and scientific communities.[1] For the betterment of society, personal profit, and pursuit of the truth, you'll have to share science with all of the people who were too unintelligent to learn about it themselves.

At the most basic level, this involves explaining to them what you do all day.[2] Unfortunately, the people who are most impressed by scientists are scientists themselves. That means you'll have to give others the education they squandered for years of partying, traveling, and earning a master's in business administration. They still won't understand you, but they might finally remember your name when they ask you to bring them a beer.

---

[1] Nothing's perfect.

[2] Block out at least an hour of time. Try to bring visual aids with very bright colors.

People You'll Talk to about Your Job

The Nodder
Nodder: So, what do you do?
You: Right now, I'm researching ovarian cells in rats.
Nodder: (Nods and smiles before turning away)

The Relater
Relater: What do you study again?
You: My focus is on the behaviors of noble gases when charged.
Relater: Oh really? You'd love my cousin. He's an orthopedist!

The Confused
Confused: Marcia said you're a scientist?
You: I have a grant to study subatomic particles at Fermilab.
Confused: Is Fermilab a TV show or something?

The Indifferent
Indifferent: You work at the college?
You: I'm a professor of endocrinology.
Indifferent: This party is terrible.

Science and the Media: Thousands of Ways to Be Misinterpreted

Once you've introduced your family and friends to your career, you'll need to educate the media about your discoveries. There are literally thousands of ways to give the public news about your findings, and the reports will be almost 50 percent accurate.

To start, explain your theory to somebody called a journalist. This is a person who, instead of performing experiments and studying theories all his or her life, kept a journal and decided to call it a career. Now this person takes 10 to 20 minutes to write what he or she thinks you spent years of your life studying.

Then it's up to the larger culture to interpret your work. If your theory is controversial, it will be debated by talk show hosts and joked about by late-night comics, though none of them will cite you, your paper, or what you actually discovered. You may be fired if the jokes are particularly funny.

If your theory is valuable but humorless, other media figures will latch onto it. Gurus will present 5-minute segments about how your theory validates the premise behind their surprisingly affordable product. Major columnists will use your theory to explain that the collapse of their marriage wasn't their fault—it was science's and, by extension, yours. Local news anchors will sound quite chipper when they mispronounce your name.

▲ Your paper on canine breeding preferences is famous, which means that you should leave the country for a bit.

Serving Your Government Through Science, or Else

Fortunately, the media isn't the only group that will use your science as an excuse. In addition, you can find employment with the government, which will require your services until they've fallen out of favor.

In the United States, you'll have an opportunity to get a job with a government agency. There are literally thousands of these agencies willing to hire, and your first task on the job will be to discover what your agency actually does. After you do that, you'll get a chance to meet the fourteen people who will serve as your immediate supervisor, the twelve people who will be working to set up your laboratory, and the three people who will grant you access to the bathroom key.

Once you're established as a government employee, your tasks will vary depending on your expertise. The government offers work in almost all scientific disciplines, and it will continue to do so until an enterprising politician finds out that your department exists and decides to cut it. Choose your branch wisely, since you'll need to stay employed for three or four years until you start receiving your pension.

◀ This department cost $1.2 billion, though that was just for the logo.

In your job, you'll be able to discover new things and further the interests of your employers.[1] Since the funding of your department depends almost entirely on its public perception, it will be crucial that your discoveries be favorable ones for the current party in power.[2] Still, you should retain your scientific focus despite the political pressures, since your mission is an eternal quest for truth, or at least a quest for truth until the next election.

Occasionally, however, your service as a government scientist will take you beyond the squabbling of bureaucratic disputes and into the realm of greatness. One of your first callings may be to assist the government in the creation of biological, chemical, space-based, atomic, or geological weaponry.[3] There are thousands of ways you can help your government preserve itself and bring millions of citizens to the culmination of their lives. Though the creation of these weapons can occasionally cause collateral damage and a wide array of irrational emotions, remind yourself that you are practicing science and have no means of controlling how people apply it. Values are constantly shifting, after all, but a nice house in a Washington, DC, suburb is always valuable for you and your family.

Beyond the creation of weaponry to aid in the efficient execution of your employer's interests, you can also help them use your science to explain their goals. This has worked extremely well in the past, and you may have an opportunity to have it applied to your work as well. If a government official or politician requests to use your work to educate the public, make sure to provide as much data as possible so he can destroy absolutely all of it. Then you'll have an opportunity to speak to the media, public, and other government officials about your findings. Though science requires the introduction of arguments and counterarguments, as well as the testing of the scientific method, you'll want to save that for the end of your testimony or the footnotes of your reports. After all, your job is at risk if you say the wrong thing, so make sure that your science is accurate according to what the government expects you to find.

In Their Words

"Actually, that's not what my theory means at all."

— SOME POOR, DEAD, AND FORGOTTEN SCIENTIST

Science can do amazing things for your career as long as you have the right attitude.

---

[1] Nominally, the taxpayers. Practically, the Congress and president.

[2] If you have time, they should also be accurate.

[3] Though throwing rocks has gone out of style, it could make a comeback.

Corporate Science: Selling Out Helps You Buy Things

If you don't want to go into the academy or government, there are still places you can build a career as a scientist. They're called "corporations," and in them you'll have free reign to study whatever you choose, as long as it's what you've been told to choose.

Corporate science departments are frequently called R&D, which stands for "Redo & Destroy." If you're in the R&D department, you'll spend much of your time redoing the ideas of your competitors and destroying your failed attempts. A single career can span many different failures, so you have to work quickly if you want to truly exhaust all of your potential.

> **» SCIENTIFIC FACT**
>
> Patents were established to protect intellectual property rights for as many years as you can afford a lawyer.

As a corporate scientist, you can work for a wide range of people who are eager to tell you what to do. You might work for somebody in the marketing or sales department who believes that science fiction films are documentaries. Alternatively, you could serve under a former scientist who has moved up to middle management and has become too good to wear socks with his shorts. Though these supervisors will strive to control you in different ways, once they are your employer, your sole goal will be to impress them and, eventually, to replace them.

Science for a corporation isn't that different from traditional science, except that instead of pursuing truth, you'll be trying to increase

▲ Oh, brave new world that has such products in it!

earnings per share. You can do this by increasing your company's competitive advantage, which means that your work will be used to file as many patents as possible.[1] The modern patent process leaves no invention, idea, or fever-dream unpatentable, and if there's anything that pairs well with unfettered truth, it's a lawyer.

These patents are often in service of new products. As a corporate scientist, you'll have an opportunity to add valuable chemicals to our world, and the applications are varied. Maybe you'll work on building a plasma television that helps people spend even less time talking to their family. Or perhaps you'll help manufacture bottled water, which is water made from recycled plastic bottles. Whatever you make, it's probably going to have a container that requires industrial-strength scissors to open.

▲ Someday, these "amber waves of grain" will be improved into translucent globs of plastic.

If you aren't making products, you'll probably be making drugs.[2] Many scientists find fulfilling work for pharmaceutical companies, or at least fulfilling salaries. In your career you'll obtain many different patents that will immediately be signed over to the company. As any scientist knows, there are countless medical problems in the world, so you'll be tasked with solving the ones that well-insured, rich people suffer from.

These are important problems that you'll spend 60 hours a week trying to solve. For example, shouldn't there be a better sea-sickness drug for when you spend an entire weekend on the yacht? Why isn't there a treatment to improve your vision for small white objects, like golf balls? How can we create a cream that makes teeth brighter than a 140-watt bulb? After all, these challenges are the reasons you fell in love with science back when you were just a young heir or heiress.

---

[1] This theory of patents is patented, so don't use it.

[2] However, if you're making methamphetamines in your lab, you don't work for a corporation.

Going for the Glory: Winning Shiny Medals and Endorsement Deals

Once you've found your path as a scientist, you'll finally be able to achieve the reason for it all: awards and endorsement deals.

After you make a revolutionary discovery without offending any of the people it contradicts, you'll be on the fast track to that Nobel Prize medal or to that Town of Hershey, Pennsylvania, Honorary Chocolate Bar. Earning these awards gives you validation from your peers and is also the best proof you'll get that they are secretly jealous of you.

How should you accept your Nobel Prize? First, make sure that you are present at the ceremony itself, and try to remember what you discovered. When you're standing on the podium, clench your jaw and look thoughtfully into the distance, like you're discovering something new at that exact moment. Looking like a genius is as important as being one.

Once your award has been announced, you'll get to make your speech. Like many scientists, you may not have much experience "talking." Consider playing back a tape of yourself and lip-syncing

Case Study: How This Textbook Will Win All Six Nobel Prizes

When you are discovering new things, don't limit yourself to one Nobel Prize. Normally, you have to be a human to win a Nobel Prize. However, the textbook *Fake Science 101* will break new ground by winning in every category.

Chemistry: When boiled, this book creates a delicious and palatable soup.

Physics: Throwing, lifting, and pressing this book settles the debate over gravity's existence.

Medicine: Scientists have proven that endorphins provide a natural cure to many ailments, and this volume creates so much happiness that all diseases vanish overnight.

Literature: Thanks to this book, people who read literature finally realize they've been wasting their time, so they decide to devote their lives to science.

Peace: Everyone is too busy reading to fight.

Economics: This textbook is used as a new currency because of its limitless value.

to it, or you can always have an intern give a speech while wearing a mask that looks like you. Make sure to thank all the people you're better than, and when you're finished, announce that you are available to appear on cereal boxes, cameo in watch advertisements, and serve on the boards of corporations that need some good press.

Using Science to Make History

As a world-recognized scientist, you'll no longer be restricted to doing science. You can enter the realms of politics, philosophy, and public discourse as long as you remind people that you've worn a lab coat.[1]

The burden of a public intellectual is a heavy one.[2] Only you can enlighten the gentle, ignorant people of the world. Your discoveries as a scientist qualify you to weigh in on all different matters, as long as you allude to your accomplishments in the field you actually work in. Now that you've received recognition as a scientist, you no longer have to test your theories, learn about your field, and proceed cautiously toward a conclusion. That's for the uneducated people that you're going to help.

After all, you're a scientist now. You've learned the truth about the world, and it's time to share it with anybody who is willing to listen. The answers are in the data, charts, and graphs. The world is your tanning bed. Strip and dive in.

DR. JACOB RADCLIFFE

BELIEVE

WHAT I SAY

IT'S OK, I HAVE A PHD IN SOME OTHER STUFF

▲ As a public intellectual, you have a responsibility to have an opinion that will enlighten slow-witted nonscientists.

What will you do with your training? Will you use science to build the flying ice cream truck that you always dreamed about? Or will you engineer a new species of porcupine, one without quills that looks more like a rhinoceros? The possibilities are limitless. Go explore our world, and then use your knowledge to analyze and fix it.

---

[1] People respect scientists unless they are talking about science.

[2] For that reason, and because you're on television more, you'll want to start working out.

Start Rereading Now
A Letter from the Fake Science Labs

By John Vanderhof Reynolds
Chief Scientist and Head Sanitation Technician

Here we are again, but we are not the same people we were so many chapters ago. Since you began reading this book, I was successfully promoted from assistant sanitation technician to head sanitation technician, a position that carries great responsibility without the burden of additional pay. Have you done anything worth mentioning?

The truth is, you have. You've read the most important book since sliced bread. In the process, you've discovered great truths about yourself, your world, and your patience. If you have the reading ability and speed of a true scientist, it was probably the best 12 minutes of your life.

You've learned literally everything there is to know about science, from the vastness of the cosmos to the importance of the #2 pencil. You've read one of the only books to win a Pulitzer Prize before being published. You've improved your mind by memorizing each word on every page, forward and backward. Quick: What page does the forward version of "intelligent more grew animals" appear on? If you've done your homework, you've already recited the rest of the paragraph.

But with knowledge comes many responsibilities, the first of which is rereading this book. You should immediately buy two more copies. The first will protect you against creases and notes you may have made in your original copy, and the second will allow you to read multiple sections at the same time. In science, this is known as "interdisciplinary study" and is highly smiled upon. As you reread, consider what awards you think this book deserves that it didn't already get. Should Oscars really only be given to films?

Once you've read, however, your task truly begins. You must go practice science in the world and improve the human, animal, and mineral condition in the process. Can you make each life better through biology, and not just by breeding with it? Will you enhance the life of a simple squirrel by giving it a basic education in quantum mechanics? What will you do to help a piece of quartz feel like a diamond for once in its life? These are questions that only you can answer, because you are the only one who knows how this science will change your world, and because I don't have time to answer them for you.

I have to go clean some toilets now.

Chapter 7 Quiz: You're a Scientist!

Multiple Choice

1. What's the most important part of elementary school?

a. Choosing your rivals
b. Finger painting
c. Finger dissection
d. Cookies

2. How can you win a science fair?

a. Conduct an experiment with arson
b. Discover the judge's biggest secret
c. Reuse some of Einstein's more obscure discoveries
d. Enter only after you've earned your PhD

3. What will you learn in high school?

a. The radioactive half-life of shame
b. Wearing glasses can keep people from hitting you
c. Unsanctioned uses for test tubes
d. Why you should have gone straight to college

4. Which will you pursue in college?

a. Physics, for the women
b. Biology, to learn about food
c. Astronomy, to save on lighting
d. Geology, for the rocks

5. What is a professor's greatest challenge?

a. Having to constantly add patches to tweed jackets
b. Learning to play Frisbee
c. Tolerating those "student" people
d. Discovering new things without blowing up the quad

6. Which is your greatest duty as a scientist?

a. Proclaiming things
b. Maximizing profits
c. Helping the government
d. Looking good in a lab coat

7. How will the world reward you for your discoveries?

a. Groupies
b. Naming a disease after you
c. Giving you your own branded line of test tubes
d. Treating you like the genius your mother always said you were

8. How will you continue your studies of this book?

a. By rereading it four more times
b. Rewriting it by hand, then burning the copies to avoid copyright and patent infringement
c. Seeing if it can all fit onto a lower back tattoo
d. Looking good in a lab coat

Short Answer

1. You're a scientist now. Figure out what you'll force your family and friends to call you, and describe the special hand salute that you'll require.

Essay Questions

1. When pursuing a career path, you'll face many difficult choices. What formula will you use to decide your future?

_____
_____
_____
_____
_____
_____
_____
_____
_____
_____
_____
_____
_____
_____
_____
_____
_____
_____
_____

2. When you began this book, you were uninformed and probably lonely. How has reading this book changed your life, and how much do you wish to donate to the Fake Science labs in gratitude?

_____
_____
_____
_____
_____
_____
_____
_____
_____
_____
_____
_____
_____
_____
_____
_____
_____
_____

Addenda

Corrections to previous editions of *Fake Science 101*

1861 Edition

- The chapter praising the Confederate States of America's "bold scientists" was just a hedge against their winning.
- Please ignore three separate instances complaining about "the dangerous high speeds of the horse and buggy."
- A small sidebar about Martians was later found to have been a joke by Mark Twain.

1904 Edition

- Guglielmo Marconi is not, in fact, a type of pasta, and his radio invention does not destroy the brain through "pernicious waves of sound."
- Though strictly an editorial decision, the board regrets the decision to fill the entire biology section with pictures of President Theodore Roosevelt killing things.
- In retrospect, the campaign to "Lick Your Way Through Science" may have contributed to the 1918 influenza pandemic. We apologize for any repercussions but do not accept any liability.

1928 Edition

- Our Prohibition era recipe for bathtub gin was meant to demonstrate chemical principles; the blindness it caused was an unintended side effect.

- The investment advice to "Buy, Buy, Buy" was not actually based on physics, as we claimed, but rather on the advice of the laboratory's investment consultant/bookie.
- A feature on technology, "Who Wants to Hear Movie Stars Talk?" proved to have an incorrect thesis, as well as an erroneous claim that the human voice could not play along with film due to the differences between the speed of light and sound.

1938 Edition

- Our feature about splitting the atom should not have recommended trying it at home.
- The chapter praising the German effort was just a hedge against their winning.
- The brief entry "Public Pools: Water That's Good Enough to Drink!" may have contributed to the polio epidemic. However, without the polio epidemic, there may never have been a polio vaccine, so we do take credit for that as well.

1963 Edition

- Calling a bomb shelter "the wisest investment you can make" may have been a mistake, financially. It is better than a tree house, however.
- The chapter praising the Soviet effort was just a hedge against their winning.
- Though we admit no wrongdoing, a sizeable contribution from tobacco growers may have contributed to the section entitled "Smoke Your Way to Happiness and Health."

Omissions

There was no room for the following text:

However, as convincing as that previous paragraph may sound, its science should not be followed if at all possible. The theory could cause significant psychological, physical, and societal damage if practiced.

The following photograph was commissioned, but there was no way to use it in the text:

We were unable to discuss the following:

- Why the Tyrannosaurus Rex had such short arms, and how those arms made it overcompensate by eating things.
- The rule that if you break the sound barrier, you buy it.
- The meaning of life or, if not that, at least the formula.
- A review of McKinley's High School's production of *Damn Yankees*. Though it isn't strictly related to science, they should be commended for a surprisingly accomplished production.
- The origin of the Grand Canyon and the lesser-known Good Enough Canyon.

- The strange mating habits of the bonobo and Sharon, who was the one who came up with the idea to go to Cabo in the first place and then, somehow, decided it would be a good idea to blatantly flirt with the bartender the very first night, which is just the beginning.
- The reason the basil on your windowsill keeps dying.
- Chromosomal differences between men and women and the ways they affect stand-up comedy.
- The odds of getting struck by lightning, winning the lottery, and getting struck by lightning while winning the lottery.
- Gregor Mendel. Sorry, Gregor.

Answer Key

All of the multiple choice questions were *a*, *b*, *c*, or *d*. All of the short answer questions should have been at least forty pages. All of the essay questions should be published in books by now.

Furthering Your Studies

Books

Scienteriffic: The Secret World of Secret Worlds by Malcolm Reynolds

A priceless study of how the words "science" and "terrific" can be combined into one word. The bonus chapter on Scientastic is worth the price of the book.

Let's See a Dolphin Do This: Why Science Is for Humans by Geraldine Hughes

This seminal work ensures that the dolphins stay in their place: the ocean, far away from our capital markets and scientific labs.

Fake Science 101: A Less-Than-Factual Guide to Our Amazing World by Phil Edwards

Any textbook that doesn't recommend itself shouldn't be trusted. Recommended rereading for anyone who knows how to read, and recommended smelling for those who don't know how to read.

Film

Dust!: The Untold Story

This thirteen-hour program takes a riveting look at particulate matter, making use of time-lapse photography, expert testimony, and scratch-and-sniff technology to give dust the cinematic treatment it truly deserves.

Edison Versus The World

Though this drama about inventor Thomas Edison veers slightly from the historical record, the scene where he uses his time machine to kill Hitler is one of the most exciting in film.

Touch of Weevil

Funded by a consortium of agriculture companies, this one hundred and fifty million dollar passion project explores the threat of the boll weevil to the annual cotton crop.

Other Media

Tesla Unchained

This circus-and-magic show is not officially endorsed by the Tesla estate, but it does involve a lot of explosions.

Taxonomy: The Video Game!

Taxonomy remains the most popular, and only, videogame inspired by Linnaeus.

About the Fake Science Labs

Imagining Our World's Science

After improving yourself by reading this book, it's only natural to wonder about the institution that produced it. The Fake Science labs have a storied history, and a few of the stories aren't even that negative.

Founded in 1822 due to a generous grant from the candle manufacturers of America, the laboratory was established with the goal of proving that electricity did not exist or was, at best, a fad. Headed by Doctor Addison Kellogg Faken, he never told his employers he wasn't actually a doctor, but he did drop the "n" from his name to protect his family's reputation. Thus the Fake Science labs were born, though only figuratively, since Dr. Faken never did learn how babies were made.

Progress was swift through the rest of the nineteenth century thanks to funds from carriage manufacturers seeking to disprove automobiles, associated telegraphers who wanted to prove telephones were damaging to the ear drum, and a major railroad that sought proof that railroad tracks could help provide dirt with structural reinforcement. In the twentieth century, these funders were joined by a host of government agencies, though the lab never did build a bathtub large enough to hold William Howard Taft. While the publication of the first Fake Science textbook did significantly set back the argument for public education, it was extraordinarily popular at circuses and among the nation's hobos.

The lab continued to flourish through both World Wars thanks to munitions manufacturers, newly created government agencies, petroleum producers, and at least one

▲ The Fake Science labs produced many products, including a tonic without an antidote.

eccentric billionaire who wished to learn exactly how long his fingernails could grow. It quickly became one of the largest institutions in the United States, though it was most commonly known for the protests against it.

Popular misunderstanding did not stop the lab from growing, however, and outposts soon popped up in most of the world's major cities and a few of its nicer suburbs. The third and fourth editions of the textbook remain hallmarks in the fight against literacy. Though at least four laboratory locations were mobbed by groups of villagers with pitchforks and groups of scientists with test tubes, all the locations survived because the laboratory chimpanzees had been trained to attack strangers.

Please accept our apologies for your Bunsen Burner Injury *and enjoy this complimentary* 10 Percent Off *at your local test tube dealer!*

#7,820   FAKE SCIENCE 1958

▲ After decades of operation, Fake Science had mastered the science of apologizing.

Unfortunately, the laboratory fell on hard times in the late 1960s due to a failure to retain funding. Conservative donors were upset that the lab had failed to create shirts that could not be "tie-dyed," and the bands of "hippies" blamed the lab for the majority of their bad trips. Coupled with continuing reports of maimings, lab rat insurrection, and general misunderstanding of physics, the laboratory was banned from publishing new textbooks until mid-2012.

Until this edition of the textbook, the science has survived through republication of old information online and, simultaneously, new research at two to three hundred undisclosed locations. If Dr. Faken could have seen how well his lab did, he no doubt would have exclaimed "Look out, there's a demon cat about to attack you!" (Inhalation of fumes caused him to have many hallucinations later in life.) Though no one can predict what the lab's legacy will be, we can be certain that it will be fake.

✏ About the Author ✏

Phil Edwards has transcribed the findings of the Fake Science labs for years, without pay or comprehension. You can visit the website by searching for "Fake Science." Though Edwards is based in an unnamed location that rhymes with Shmicago, Shmillinois, you can learn more about him and his other books at PhilEdwardsInc.com.

✏ About the People the Author Thanks ✏

The author would like to thank the intelligent people who followed the website. Without them, this book would never have become the most popular book of all time. The author would also like to thank Kristina Ancil for listening to many bad ideas and a few terrible ones.

In the making of this book, NASA and NASA archive images were an invaluable resource. Inquisitive readers can learn more by searching NASA's great image archive (it should be obvious that NASA was not involved in the creation of this book).

Brendan O'Neill ensured this book fulfilled its promise as one of man's primary knowledge documents. Elisabeth Lariviere designed it—she no doubt worked tirelessly but managed to make it look effortless. Ted Weinstein shepherded the project with the care of a shepherd who is also a literary agent.

✏ About the Paper ✏

Found in a large forest, the tree known as "Bernard" lived a long and happy life. Its last wish was to not be chopped down, but other than that it almost certainly wanted to be made into a textbook.

✏ About This About Page ✏

Raised in a small town in West Virginia, this About Page attended Oberlin College and majored in semiotics. It has previously served as an About Page in books about presidential politics, the "undiscovered" history of Mary Todd Lincoln, and Italian cooking. It splits its time between New York and the Oregon Coast.